Writings from Life

Third Edition

Tom Tyner

Breadan Publishing

Breadan Publishing

Writings from Life
Third Edition
Tom Tyner

Publisher, English	Pat Nishimura
Editor, Writing	Susan Wiesick
Marketing	Lori Jones

Address for Domestic and International Orders

Breadan Publishing, 4706 N. Quail Lake Dr., Clovis, CA 93619

Website: www.breadanpublishing.com

Telephone: 559-291-2152

Fax: 559-291-1978

Printed in the United States of America   ISBN: 978-0-615-57044-0

Breadan Publishing

Preface

Writings from Life is a process-oriented writing textbook that helps students continue to grow and improve as writers. Students learn by writing, and the textbook provides a variety of writing assignments that require students to develop and apply different writing and thinking skills as they progress through the book.

Writing Process

In each unit, students use the writing process in the text to develop their paper. The basic process of prewriting, drafting, revision, and editing is repeated in each unit, with new instructional elements introduced in each section that apply to the type of writing the students are doing. The process is repeated in each unit so that students become familiar and comfortable with the approach to use for any writing they may do.

The text also recognizes the individual differences among writers. For some writers, prewriting may involve detailed planning while for others, it may involve coming up with an idea to get started. The text acknowledges such differences and allows for individual flexibility within the writing process rather than a one-size-fits-all model. The textbook also recognizes that some students come to the course with considerable writing experience, and they are encouraged to meld what they learn from the text with their previous experiences to create the most effective personalized writing process.

Writing Assignments

The title *Writings from Life* indicates the kind of writing students will do: writings based on their personal experiences, interests, observations, knowledge, beliefs, and opinions. They write about aspects of their lives, and the world around them, that they find most important, significant, and interesting. They use the writing process in the textbook, along with the instructional guides, to develop and express their ideas most effectively.

Writing as Communication

Writings from Life also emphasizes writing as a form of communication. To that end, students write for different reading audiences, such as their classmates, and for a particular purpose: to inform, entertain, influence, educate, or move readers to action. The writing assignments in the text are real in that they are written for others and for a purpose, which is more meaningful than writing as a textbook exercise.

Importance of Revision

Writings from Life also strongly emphasizes the role of revision in the writing process. Throughout the text, students work on revising and improving their writing in a number of areas: wording, organization, content development, paragraphing, openings and conclusions, transitional wording, and so on. The text provides specific revision guidelines for the type of writing students do in each unit.

Commonality of Writers

The text also emphasizes to students the commonality of writers and the writing experience. It is assuring to students to discover that all writers share similar challenges: struggling to come up with a topic; figuring out how to begin a paper; rereading previous sentences to decide what to write next; working to stay on topic; considering the best way to end a particular paper. Once students understand that writing is a messy, non-linear process, they understand that the head scratching, the long pauses, the failure to find the right word, or the constant rereading of sentences is a part of the writing experience for all writers. Such assurance leads to greater confidence and better writing.

Writing Correctness

As the last step in the writing process in each unit, students proofread and edit their papers to eliminate errors. Correct writing is emphasized as the best way to showcase a writer's ideas, as a courtesy to readers, as a goal that all writer share.

Within each unit, the text provides instruction in the areas of punctuation, grammar usage, and spelling where writers have the most problems: run-on sentences and comma splices, sentence fragments, comma usage, subject-verb agreement, and so on. Students are also taught to proofread a paper several times, looking for a different kind of error each time. In addition, the text provides an editing checklist in each unit for students to apply to the paper they are working on.

Writing Samples

Throughout the text are writing samples that students use in number of ways: to get ideas for their writing, to see how writers develop, organize, and paragraph their papers, to read and evaluate different openings and conclusions, to see how writers develop a thesis statement, to see how writers work dialogue into their writing effectively, and so on. The sample writings provide models for the type of writing that students are doing and material for class or group discussion.

Contents

Readings

Unit One
Experiences

Our lives are made up of thousands of experiences, most of which we forget over time. However, some experiences remain etched in our minds, forever memorable due to the impact they made on our lives.

Such experiences are a valuable part of our backgrounds, often shaping the way that we think and feel about life. For writers, life experiences are a rich source for writing, one that you will tap for your writing assignment in this unit.

Experiences can have a powerful effect on us for different reasons. They may be painful, thrilling, disappointing, fulfilling, frightening, or amusing, or trigger a range of different emotions. They may affect us in ways that we are very aware of and in other more subtle ways. Analyzing the impact of a particular experience is a valuable part of the writing process.

Writing about a personal experience, called *narrative* writing, is your first writing assignment for several reasons. First, since you have a number of experiences to draw from, finding a topic should not be too difficult. Second, since you will select an experience that you remember well, you can draw on your recall of the experience to write the paper. Third, you will write about the experience chronologically, in the time order that it occurred, one of the most natural organizations for a paper. Fourth, writing about a personal experience allows you to tell, or narrate, a "true" story in a vivid, interesting way, and to analyze the impact that it had on you. Finally, narrative writing provides readers with an interesting story, a glimpse into the life of the writer, and an experience that they may relate to or learn from.

The papers that you write during the course will be for a reading audience, frequently your own classmates, along with your instructor. One writing consideration will be the impact that your writing may have on others: what they may find interesting, what they may learn, how they may react or respond, or how they may relate. As a writer, you share your thoughts with readers in ways that may affect their own lives.

Why Write?

Writing texts often launch into writing activities without answering a question that is on some students' minds: why write? While the value of effective writing may be evident to some students, it isn't to all, and some may say, "I'm not going to write much beyond school, so why should I waste my time now? Writing has little to do with my future." Such concerns certainly deserve a response, and there are good reasons for all students, and for people in general, to develop their writing skills. Here are a few you may or may not have considered:

1.   Being able to write well is one mark of an educated person. All students should leave college with the writing skills to communicate effectively. If students don't develop these skills in college, they may always struggle with their writing.

2.   For better or worse, other people judge us by the way that we write. Employers, for example, make critical judgments about job candidates based on their writing ability, often selecting the person with the best-written resume over all others.

3.   Writing can be a rewarding activity. Whether people write journals, fiction, letters to the editor, or e-mails to friends, they often derive enjoyment and a sense of accomplishment from their writing.

4.   There are not many jobs today that don't require some writing, particularly those that require at the least a four-year college degree or a two-year degree or certification. Report writing, self-evaluations, memos, e-mail communications, work-site improvement suggestions, questionnaires, inventory assessments, research write-ups, grant requests, letters to customers, suppliers, or clients, in-house studies, analysis of competitors, and marketing studies are commonplace writing tasks across the job market.

5.   The age of electronic mail has put an added emphasis and value on writing. With the ease of e-mailing, more written communication is occurring today than ever, both personal and business. Never in recent times has the ability to write effectively been more useful or important.

6.   Writing is often the most effective mode of communication, and in many instances, the best means to an end. People use writing for many purposes: to inquire into a health insurance billing; to request copies of college transcripts; to rally supporters for a peace demonstration; to convince trustees not to raise tuition; to provide experiences and work attributes to a potential employer. The written word is a powerful tool for which people find many uses.

7.   Writing well builds self-confidence. Writers who are confident in their ability welcome educational and professional situations where writing is required. They are more apt to take courses that involve writing and to consider professions where writing skills are an asset. As writers improve their skills, they find more and more doors that open to them.

8.   Writing well leads to college success. Good writers are at a great advantage in the classroom, often performing well in the many courses across the curriculum that require writing.

9. Good writing and sound thinking go together. Though some people can get by verbally with more style than substance, writers have only the quality of their thoughts and their ability to express them to rely upon. When an illogical thought sits on the page, no stylish flourishes can hide it from discerning readers. With writing, weak thinking is most easily exposed and sound thinking most highly valued. Writing also helps to develop sound thinking as writers learn to support their ideas convincingly, dissect an unsound argument, and organize and express their thoughts effectively.

Writing Process

As you write your first paper, you will be using a writing process that is similar for most writers and that involves *prewriting*, *drafting*, *revising*, and *editing* steps. While all writers don't follow the same process, and may combine and configure parts of the process in individual ways, there are enough similarities about how people write to conclude that writing, at its best, is a process-oriented task.

The writing assignment for each unit will be divided into different parts beginning with pre-writing activities and followed by writing a first draft, revising and improving the draft, proofreading and editing the draft to eliminate errors, and writing the final paper. In each unit, you will be introduced to new writing considerations based on the writing task at hand, but the process itself will be duplicated and become a natural part of how you write.

The text also assumes that you have had other writing experiences both in school and out. The process approach in the text may be similar to your current writing practices, or it may extend or alter what you are doing. In the end, you may take what is most useful from the process approach in the text, combine it with what already works for you, and create a most effective writing process. If you have done little writing in the past, or have not used a process approach, the text will provide you with a writing process that will serve you well for most writing that you may do.

Prewriting

In each prewriting section, you prepare to write the first draft of your paper by selecting a topic to write on and giving some thought to what you may want to include in your paper. In the prewriting sections of the text, you will use a variety of prewriting strategies that you will find useful for different writing tasks.

Writing Assignment 1

The title of this text, Writings from Life, indicates the kind of writing you will do for the course: papers that are based on your experiences, interests, beliefs, and opinions. You are writing about aspects of your life, and the world around you, that you find important and significant. This first writing assignment begins your exploration.

   You will select a particular experience that you remember well and that has had an impact on you. As you recall memorable experiences, consider those that you remember best and that have most affected you. Through such experiences, you may have experienced a variety of emotions: excitement, joy, shock, anger, sadness, disappointment, regret, satisfaction, relief, shame, or a mixture of feelings. You will write about one particular experience that stands out and analyze its impact on you.

Free Writing

Free writing is a prewriting activity that helps writers decide what experience to write about, what they may want to write about the experience, and how much they may remember about it. When you free write, you write whatever comes to your mind without concern for order, logic, or correctness. Free writing allows you to put your thoughts on paper without being judged on your writing, and you take from your free writing whatever might help you write your paper.

Prewriting Activity 1.1

Write freely for ten minutes or so on three or four different experiences that you remember well and that made an impact on your life. You may write about experiences from any time in your life. Write without hesitation or concern for what you are putting on paper. From your free writing, you may decide on a topic for your first paper and create some material that you will use in your first draft.

Sample free writing:

#1
When I was in grade school, my mom came home one afternoon and said my sister was in the hospital. She had had some seizures which had hurt her brain. I didn't

know what a seizure was or what to expect when Emily came home. I was shocked when I finally saw her. This wasn't the sister I had known. My fun-loving, talkative sister had been replaced by someone who couldn't talk or even walk. She had to have therapy to regain her normal abilities, and I kept waiting for my real sister to come back to life. Unfortunately, that never happened, and I went through a terrible time of being lonely, angry, and frightened. Eventually I grew to realize that the sister in front of me was the only sister I would ever have. As a young child, all I could do was selfishly think of the effects of Emily's condition on me. Later I came to realize that the real tragedy had befallen Em.

#2

I was on a relay in high school and our team won so I jumped in the pool to celebrate. Trouble was, one other team on an outside lane wasn't finished swimming yet, so because I jumped in, our team was disqualified. The referee came over and disqualified us because of my jumping in, and I swore at him, including the f word. The words just came out before I could think. He wasn't just the referee, he was also the principal of the high school that was hosting the meet. There were other consequences. I was kicked out of the rest of the meet. I was also suspended from the team after the referee called our principal and told him what had happened. One big slip of the tongue got me in a lot of trouble.

#3

When I was a senior in high school I got pregnant and had a hard decision to make. I didn't want to get married and neither did the father, and I wanted to go to college. I didn't feel I was ready to raise a baby. I thought about an abortion or adoption. My parents weren't against an abortion, and that seemed like the easiest way out. However, the thought of killing my unborn baby was too strong and I couldn't do it. As the months went by and I felt my baby growing inside and then felt it kicking, I began to realize that I wanted this baby, that it was a part of me. I made the decision to keep the baby, and it didn't ruin my life. It was the best decision I could make.

#4

When I was a young child, my cousin had a little electric car that he rode on top of. It was a little car, but it would go almost five miles an hour. Riding up and down in front of his house, he made it look easy, so I wanted to try. My uncle showed me how to use the hand throttle and break and warned me not to turn the hand throttle hard because the car would jump forward and go up on its back tires. I got on and slowly moved forward. I went down the street a ways, turned around, and then went back by my uncle the other way. I started to turn around again to come back, and somehow I turned the throttle handle hard. The car jumped forward and I slid off the back. Trouble was, I held onto the handle bars, so I was dragging on the street behind the moving car. It stopped when it hit the curb, and my uncle ran over. I was in shock and crying, and my legs and stomach were burning. I ended up with some good road burns and more pain than I'd ever experienced. To this day I remember that accident clearly and the days that followed in the doctor's office and the long nights

when I couldn't sleep. I learned a painful lesson.

Prewriting Activity 1.2

Take some time to reflect on your free writing and also on other experiences that you may have not included. In the end, select an experience to write about following these suggestions.

1. Choose an experience that you want to write about and that you remember clearly.

2. Choose an experience that readers - your classmates - may find interesting or get something out of.

3. Choose an experience that had a powerful effect on your life, or that may still affect you.

Prewriting Activity 1.3

After you have decided upon a particular experience to write about, spend some time thinking about the impact of that experience on your life. Consider what you may have learned from it, how it may have changed you or your life circumstances, what you may have learned about yourself or other people, or how it may have changed your way of thinking about someone or something. Then write freely for a few minutes about the impact the experience has had on you, and include anything that comes to your mind.

Sample Freewriting

From #1
Emily's sickness changed my life forever. I had lost the sister I had always known, my talkative, fun-loving best friend. A loneliness remains with me today for that lost sister. But I came to understand that what happened to Em wasn't her fault and that she had suffered the greatest tragedy, not me. Because of Em, I grew less self-centered, I learned to love more deeply, and I discovered that helping others had its own rewards. I'm a better person because of my sister, and I treasure the time that we have together. I hope that she is in my life for a long time.

From #2
I realized that I really have to watch my mouth, that bad language comes out of it really easy when I get mad or upset and that I don't even think about it. I think that's because that's the way I've often acted around my brothers, just cussed them out

when I get mad, and then I did it to the principal without thinking at all - it just happened. But more than that, I realized that when I mess up like I did, it affects more people than just me, and that made me feel ashamed of myself. I was ashamed at how my coach felt about what I did and our principal and of course my mom and dad and even my grandma found out about it. It was like a bad chain reaction and I felt like I let everyone down. I wanted everyone to know I wasn't a bad person but something like what I did can mark you for awhile, except there were always some kids at school who thought it was really a cool thing but I know it wasn't. Since that experience I've really watched myself and haven't cussed so badly when I get mad or frustrated. Really it's just a bad habit I need to break.

From #3

I learned some things about myself, like I'm a stronger person than I thought I was. Going through pregnancy and staying in school was tough, but I finished up in continuation school the last semester and graduated. I also knew that the baby's father and I didn't have a future together and that I'd be raising the baby on my own, with my mom's help. That's something I've been able to do, and I love my daughter and try to be the best mom I can. You also find out who your real friends are when you get in a tough situation. I had some friends who never judged me and were there for me whenever I needed them. They really helped me get through my pregnancy. Finally, I realized what a great mom I have, although I already knew that but the way she's helped me is more than I could ask for. Thanks to her I'm able to attend college while she takes care of my baby. She also said I always have a place to stay with them as long as I need to, which may be quite a while. She's been a second mom to my baby, and I know she will always be a big part of my daughter's life.

From #4

The pain I think is what I remember the most. I knew as a young child that I didn't want to experience that kind of pain again. I was afraid to ride any kind of a motorized car or bike or scooter after that, and I still am. I realized as I got a little older that it only takes one bad fall to really mess you up, and you never know when that's going to happen. So I've been pretty cautious because of that experience, and I still am today. It took me longer than most kids to learn to ride a bike, and I never got good on a skateboard or a scooter, probably because I was so cautious and anxious about falling. I realized that an accident like that, even at an early age, can stay with you for a long time, maybe a lifetime. I know it will also affect how I raise my own children if I have any. I know I'm not going to let them do anything like I did with that car. I also know that when they do ride a bike or something, they're going to wear helmets and pads and long pants, all the things I didn't have on when I took my spill. I can still remember the feeling of getting dragged along the street behind that car and it was like I wasn't able to let go of the handles. That was one scary experience for a six year old.

First Drafts

After you have completed your prewriting work, you are ready to write the first draft of your paper. This draft is the first version of your paper, the first time you put the complete experience into words. It will be followed by a second revised draft, and other subsequent drafts may follow until you are satisfied with the finished product. Writing drafts is a part of the writing process for most writers, and the writing usually improves with each draft.

Why do writers write drafts of a paper? Writing is a complex task, and seldom can any writer create a final, polished paper in one writing. The complexities of writing include choosing the best words to express your thoughts, organizing your thoughts in the most effective manner, including the best details and examples to develop your thoughts, adding new ideas as you write that you hadn't previously considered, assessing the impact of your writing on readers, and making sure that your paper is free of spelling, punctuation, or grammar errors.

Even the most experienced writers can't accomplish everything they want in a single writing. The drafting process is the natural way that many people improve their writing. Writers create drafts because that is how they write best. We have learned that through years of research that analyzed how people write, including effective student writers.

Of course, writing drafts without understanding how to improve them from one draft to the next is rather a waste of time. During this course, you will be provided specific revision guidelines to help you change and improve your drafts. Revision is a critical part of the writing process, and it leads ultimately to the best paper you can write.

First Draft Guidelines

As you begin writing the first draft of your paper, keep the following in mind.

1. The purpose of your first draft is to get the experience on paper as clearly as you recall it. Don't worry about how you word your sentences or whether you make an occasional error.

   Writing is a *recursive* activity, where writers continually go back and reread what they have written in a previous sentence or sentences to help them decide what to write next. Rereading sentences is not a waste of time; it provides you the momentum to continue writing and to make sure your next sentence follows logically from the previous ones.

2. Providing some background information is helpful to prepare readers for the experience lying ahead. You might include your age at the time and describe where the experience took place and what occurred leading up to it.

3. As you write, you are leading to the heart of the experience: whatever happened that made the impact on your life. Try to bring the experience to life for readers by describing it in detail.

4. The experience no doubt was an emotional one. Include your feelings and thoughts during the experience as you recall them so that readers can sense what you went through.

5. You might include some dialogue in your draft if what you said, or what others said, is an important part of the experience. If you or someone else is speaking in your draft, insert quotation marks (" ") before and after the spoken words, and identify the speaker: "I'll never trust you again to borrow my car," I told my brother. (See how the writer uses and punctuates dialogue in the sample draft "The Accident" in Drafting Activity 1.4.)

6. Conclude the draft with what happened as a result of the experience, and your analysis of why the experience was so memorable: the impact it had on your life.

7. Write your draft in paragraphs, changing paragraphs as you move to something new in your paper: a different time, a different place, a different aspect of the experience.

8. Your reading audience for this paper is your classmates, and of course, your instructor. Keep them in mind as you write.

9. Title your draft in a simple manner that indicates what it is about.

Drafting Activity 1.4

Write the first draft of your paper following the guidelines presented. You may first want to read the following sample draft.

Sample First Draft

When I returned home from 3rd grade one afternoon, I was greeted with the news that my younger sister was sick and in the hospital. I could tell by my mother's looks that she was concerned, and she said I would be staying with granda some evenings while she was at the hospital. I asked if I could go and see Emily at the hospital, and mom said, "Not right now, honey. But you can see her in a few days."

For the next days it was very lonely in the house without my sister, who was my best friend and playmate. My mom was somber most of the time, and I would hear her talking with grandma in low voices. In bits and pieces I learned that my sister had had a high fever and had a seizure, in fact several of them. Mom said that the doctors were helping Emily and controlling the seizures, but that her brain had been hurt. I didn't really understand what any of it meant except that it seemed serious and I became very worried. "Emily may not seem like her old self for awhile," mom warned me. "It will take her time to recover."

I learned much later, when I was old enough to understand, that Emily was a victim of status epilepticus, a relatively rare condition resulting in multiple seizures which can severely impair the brain. She would have seizures on and off for the rest of her life, the frequency and severity controlled by medication, but it was that initial series of seizures that she had as a six-year old that caused the damage. Apparently no one knows what causes the condition or why one child in thirty thousand is afflicted. We will never know why it happened to Emily.

When Emily finally came home from the hospital, I was shocked by her condition although mom had tried to prepare me. Em just lay in bed, a blank stare on her face that I had never seen. She couldn't talk or walk, and she didn't even seem to recognize me. Mom said because of Emily's illness, she would have to relearn much of what her brain sickness had erased: being able to talk, walk, and recognize people. A therapist from the hospital started coming to the house three days a week to help Emily with her recovery.

Very slowly, Em began to recover some motor skills, first sitting up, then standing, then taking a few halting steps. She also began making noises although they didn't form into words. Her eyes began to focus better and when she looked at me, I could see some recognition in her eyes. She also began to smile sometimes and with mom or me helping her, walk slowly around her room. Mom was encouraged by the progress she was making, hoping that every day would bring more improvement.

I however was hoping for a miracle. Every day I woke up I would hope that I'd walk into Em's room and my real sister would be there, the fun, active, loving sister I knew. I missed that sister so much and sometimes I would become angry at that "imposter" who had taken my real sister from me. I also resented that mom's life now seemed to revolve around Emily and that I was never the center of her attention. As a self-absorbed child, all I could think of was how Em's illness had affected my life and how lonely I was without Em to play with and talk to. I was also fearful that what happened to Emily could happen to me, and I was sometimes afraid to go to sleep at night, worried that I might wake up like Emily.

After months and then years, it became apparent that Emily was never going to be the person she had been. My mom, the doctors, the therapists, and the special needs teachers did everything possible to bring Em to her highest developmental level, but there was just too much permanent brain damage for her to recover greatly. She could walk in her shuffling gate and seemed to enjoy walking from room to room around the house. She never talked but made noises which made it clear when she was happy and when she wasn't, but she had a good temperament. She had a good appetite and enjoyed eating. She also grew to know her family again, and was always happy to see me when I came home from school. Thankfully, my mom said that Em knew nothing of her previous life or what she had been like before her illness. The only life she knew was the one she now lived, so thankfully, her great loss was much more painful to our family than to her.

As I grew older, I learned to accept my sister as she was. I always carried a sadness for the sister that I had lost and for the normal life that was taken away from her. It was truly a great tragedy, and at some point I knew that it was important to help make Em's life as happy as it could be. Sometimes I would feel guilty at relative gatherings when I was having fun playing with the cousins and Em would be curled up on the sofa staring out the window, but mom assured me that Em's situation didn't mean that I shouldn't enjoy my life and have fun. "I don't want you to live your life for Emily, honey," she said. "Emily would want you to have the best life possible, and so do I."

My life with Emily grew into a routine. I would come home from school and she would be happy to see me. She'd often take my hand and we would walk around the house for a while. Then we would sit on the sofa, and often she would put her head on my shoulder and stroke my hand. With all of the abilities that her illness had taken away from her, she had not lost perhaps the greatest: the ability to love. "I love you Em," I would tell her every day, and the words came from my heart. She never had to say a word to show her love.

Our family's life changed dramatically eleven years ago when Em became sick. It's been hard at times on everyone as we've all changed our routines and given up something of our more active lives to care for my sister. And the fact that Emily will never have a normal life weighs on all of us at times. Seeing her sitting on the sofa cuddling her baby doll can bring tears to my eyes, thinking what her life might have been like. But I've learned that dwelling on such thoughts doesn't help anything.

We don't know how long we will have Emily with us, as someone in her condition may not live long into adulthood. There was a time when I spent time with Em more out of a sort of free-floating guilt, a feeling that I somehow bore some blame for Em's condition. I also had moments when I wondered, "Why her and not me," and felt the guilt of being the "normal" person that my sister couldn't be. Today, however, I spend time with Em out of love, a love that has grown more deeply as I have gotten older and want to appreciate every moment that I have with her.

While there is little that I do for Em but spend time with her, there is a lot that she has done for me. I am no longer the self-absorbed person who was mainly concerned with how anything that happened affected me and my happiness. Through my relationship with my sister, I have grown more patient, more caring, and more loving. I don't always have to be doing for myself to find happiness or contentment. I may also have found my professional calling in life: working with people with disabilities, perhaps as a therapist or speech pathologist. Because of Em, I'd like to think that I've become a better person.

Revision

Now that you have written your first draft, you are ready to take a look at it to see what you might improve. In each unit, you are given some specific guidelines for revising your drafts, based on the type of writing you are doing and the revision emphases for that unit. As you work through the text, you will develop a mental checklist that will help you revise any writing you may do.

The purpose of revision is simple: to make a paper better. Improving a draft seldom means a major overhaul of what you've written. Instead, it might include adding a detail here or an example there to develop a thought, rewording some sentences to make them clearer or smoother, dividing an overly long paragraph into two, moving a particular sentence to a more effective location, or strengthening the opening or conclusion of the paper to make a greater impact on readers.

In this first "Revision" section, you will concentrate on three particular areas: providing description, improving your wording, and paragraphing your paper. These considerations are common to all writers, and you will focus on them throughout the course.

Providing Description

In a paper relating an experience, writers often describe the sights, action, people, and feelings involved to heighten the readers' interest and understanding. This does not mean bogging the paper down in a minutia of details but rather using vivid description to capture the essence of the experience and help the reader visualize what happened.

The following suggestions will help you provide effective description as you revise your paper.

1.   Use details to describe the setting for readers and help them see and hear what is happening during the experience.

From a sample first draft:

We gathered at my house to decide how to handle the situation. We made a lot of noise and caught my dad's attention.

Revised first draft:
My four high school friends and I gathered in my small bedroom to decide whether to tell the coach about our drinking before he found out himself. We yelled a lot because we were all scared and couldn't agree, and soon my dad stood in the doorway shouting, "What's going on in here?"

2.   Use details to describe your thoughts and feelings as the experience occurred.

From sample first draft:

In a ceremony at city hall, I was given a medal by the chief of police for helping pull a child out of a canal. I put the medal in a drawer.

Revised first draft:

In a ceremony on the steps of city hall, I was given a medal by the chief of police for helping pull a child out of a shallow, dirt-banked canal. I didn't feel like a hero because I just jumped in the water without thinking, and I knew I wasn't risking my life. I was embarrassed when anyone called me a hero, and I put the medal in a drawer and never looked at it again.

3.   Use details to describe something or someone when that description is important to understanding the experience.

From sample first draft:

I had never been in a fight in my life, but as I sized up Maria, I felt she knew how to fight.

Revised first draft:

I had never been in a fight in my life, but as I sized up Maria, her face contorted in an angry mask, her muscled legs taut and ready to spring, I knew I was in for trouble.

4.   In general, use details to describe anything that will help bring your experience to life for readers.

From sample first draft:

Henry was too busy to notice that his son had climbed onto the roof and was making motions with his arms.

Revised first draft:

His head stuck under the hood of his '68 Chevy, Henry was too occupied to notice that his eight-year old son had climbed atop the tin shed roof and was flapping his arms like he was going to fly off.

Revision Activity 1.5

Read the following first draft paragraph. With a classmate, note places in the draft where you would recommend that the writer add a particular detail to improve the paragraph. Be prepared to discuss your suggestions with the class.

I'll never forget my quinceanera party. My court of friends looked wonderful, and I wore a white gown that made me feel like a princess. Our back yard was turned into a wonderland, and lanterns flickered in the trees like fireflies. For one night, I was the center of attention, which embarrassed me but also made me feel special. I'll never forget dancing with my father, the changing of the shoes, or the delicious food. It was all like a dream, and the look on my mother's face said everything.

Revision Activity 1.6

Read your first draft looking for places where you might include some detail to help readers see, hear, and feel what you went through. If you are revising on a computer, add the details into the draft. If you are revising a written draft, write in the details above the lines where you want to add them.

When you finish, share drafts with a classmate, or a small group of classmates, and make suggestions if there are places in your classmate's draft where some added description would help you visualize or better understand the experience.

Improving Sentence Wording

In a first draft, you word your thoughts as they come to you the first time. As with most writers, your thoughts don't always translate into written words as smoothly or clearly as you would like. Among your first draft sentences, you will usually find some that are wordy - overly long to make your point - and others that are a little awkward, not quite sounding the way you want. Sentence revision is a task shared by all writers, and the first draft of a sentence is often a beginning point for crafting a really good sentence.

For example, let's say a writer wants to express her feelings about global warming and our government's lack of action in addressing the situation. As an example, she starts out with a sentence like this:

The effects of global warming throughout the world can be disastrous, including the flooding of cities and millions of people displaced and homeless, and our government is doing nothing to solve the problem but in fact is adding to the problem by ignoring it.

The sentence contains a lot of good information, but it is also rather long and unwieldy. A revision of the sentence might read something like this:

Global warming can have disastrous effects throughout the world, such as flooded cities and millions of people losing their homes, and our government just adds to the problem by ignoring it.

The revised sentence is clearly more readable and less wordy, and no meaning has been lost. This final revision may improve the sentence further:

Flooded cities and millions of homeless people are just two of the disastrous effects that global warming can wreak on the world, and our government makes matter worse by doing nothing.

Whether you favor the last sentence or the previous one is a matter of choice, with each about the same length and providing similar information with a different emphasis. Clearly, there is more than one way to revise and improve any sentence, and it is not uncommon for a writer to tinker with a particular sentence for some time before being satisfied with it.

Sentence Wording Guidelines

The following suggestions will help you revise and improve your first draft sentences.

1. First draft sentences often contain more words than necessary. Ideally, every word in a sentence is needed to complete the thought. Look for sentences that appear overly wordy or that repeat the same words or phrases, and see what can be eliminated or reworded without changing the sentence's meaning.

   Example:

   The current below the ocean's surface, which is called an undertow, is flowing outward, and it is dangerous because it makes it difficult for a swimmer to get back to the shore.

   Revised:

   An undertow, a current flowing outward below the ocean's surface, is dangerous because a swimmer must struggle against it to get back to shore.

2. Sentences that seem awkward to you will probably have the same effect on readers. Revising an awkward sentence often requires moving words or phrases around, eliminating unnecessary words, and replacing questionable words with better choices.

   Example:

   The mother cat behind the washing machine hid her kittens, which was in the garage.

Revised:

The mother cat hid her kittens behind the washing machine in the garage.

3. Finding the best word to express a particular idea, action, thought, or feeling is a challenging part of effective writing. If a particular word or group of words doesn't capture a thought or feeling quite the way you want, revision is in order.

    Example:

    Gretchen felt downtrodden by the bad behavior of her best friend.

    Revised:

    Gretchen was badly hurt by the cruel behavior of her best friend.

4. Some first draft sentences are rather vague, leaving readers in doubt as to what the writer meant. Such sentences need to be revised, sometimes dramatically, to clarify their meaning.

    Example:

    For positive reinforcement to work, you must factor in the child's positive reinforcement history and any over-reliance thereon.

    Revised:

    If a child is constantly praised for even the smallest accomplishment, positive reinforcement becomes meaningless.

5. Some first draft sentences may contain slang - informal words that are more suitable for conversation than writing. Replace slang words and phrases such as *cool*, *neat*, *hang out*, *hassle*, or *dude* with more appropriate ones.

    Example:

    I give that dude his props for always sticking by his friends.

    Revised:

    I respect Frank for being loyal to his friends.

Revision Activity 1.7

Revise the following first draft sentences to make them clearer, smoother, and more concise by eliminating unnecessary words, replacing awkward wording, moving words or phrases around, and improving word choice. Try out different wording options until you are satisfied with the wording of each sentence.

Example:

First draft: The moon was rounder and brighter and bigger last night than I had ever seen it.

Revised: Last night's moon was round, bigger, and brighter than ever.

1.   Seats at a Los Angeles Lakers basketball game are very hard to come by and also are very expensive, especially on the lower level.

2.   The crowd at a Lakers game is usually late arriving, and it seems like there will be a lot of empty seats, but by half way through the first quarter, all of a sudden all the seats are taken.

3.   The atmosphere in the arena, which used to be somewhat boring, is more electric now because the team is much better than it was in the past years.

4.   Many famous people like Jack Nicholson, who is one of the most famous, can be seen in the arena, always sitting in the front row with his sunglasses on.

5.   The crowd at Lakers games is still pretty laid back compared to crowds in arenas like San Antonio and Chicago, where the crowds are louder and more activist.

6.   Some people come to the Lakers games just to check out the celebrities and socialize, and they don't spend a lot of time watching the actual game of basketball or anything else like that.

7.   The atmosphere changes in the fourth quarter near the end if the game is close and the Lakers have a chance to win the game, and people start yelling and standing up.

8.   The only people that maintain their high enthusiasm for the entire game are the Lakers cheerleaders, who dance during every time out and during halftime often perform.

9.   If the game is not close in the fourth quarter, people begin filing out of the arena early at the game, sometimes with ten minutes or more left for the

players to play.

10.   It must be frustrating for the players to look up near the end of a losing game in the stands and see mostly empty seats, with only the most loyal Lakers fans remaining until the end.

Revision Activity 1.8

Read your first draft, looking for sentences whose wording can be improved. Eliminate unnecessary words, reword awkward phrases, replace questionable word choices, and clarify vague sentences. Read the sample draft in Revision Activity 1.11 to see how the writer revised her sentences.

Paragraphing

As you probably know, most writing is divided into paragraphs to make it easier for readers to follow the writer's thoughts. As writers move from one idea, example, place, or time to another, they frequently change paragraphs to indicate to readers that something has concluded and something new is beginning.

   Paragraphing is not an exact science, and there is no absolute right or wrong way to paragraph a paper. Paragraphing is effective when it moves readers smoothly through a writer's thoughts, and the best paragraphing is so natural that it is hardly noticeable.

Paragraphing Guidelines

The following guidelines will help you paragraph your papers effectively.

1.   As a general definition, a paragraph is a group of related sentences focusing on one idea, point, example, or thought.

2.   You change paragraphs as you move to something new in your paper: a different idea, a new example, a different part of an experience, a different time or place.

3.   You change paragraphs to avoid overly long paragraphs that readers can get bogged down in, ending a paragraph at a natural break in your thoughts.

4.   If you find yourself writing series of short paragraphs - two or three sentences each - you need either to combine the paragraphs or to develop them further.

5. Effective paragraphing is not that difficult. When you read a draft and concentrate on its paragraphing, you can often see where a long paragraph can be divided into two or where some short, related paragraphs can be combined. If you remind yourself to change paragraphs as you conclude one thought and move to another, you will paragraph your papers effectively.

Revision Activity 1.9

With a partner, analyze the paragraphing of the following paper. Discuss the content of each paragraph, and decide why the writer changes paragraphs when she does. Then paragraph the next two papers by marking off the beginning of each new paragraph.

Almost Like Flying

There was one special day in the 8th grade when I almost felt like I could fly. It was the best day of high jumping I ever experienced, and to this day I still remember the feeling.

I had been high jumping since grade school, and I was always pretty good at it. I never had any coaching, so I just learned how to jump by doing it. I was so involved in high jumping that the summer after my 6th grade year my dad bought a big foam pad and built a high jump pit in our back yard. I practiced a lot at home the next couple years.

In the 8th grade we had a regular track team that competed against other schools. I was not the best high jumper in the area but usually got around 3rd place in the district track meets. I would jump close to 5 feet and occasionally cleared 5 feet or 5 feet 1 inch. There were a couple of girls from other schools that could regularly jump over 5 feet, and sometimes up to 5 feet 2 or 5 feet 3, and that motivated me to want to jump higher.

One afternoon I was at school practicing in the high jump pit, which was located in a large dirt area north of the school's track. I was doing my regular routine, starting at the lower heights and working my way up. I wasn't having any trouble with the lower heights and I felt a good spring in my legs that day, so I was hopeful I'd have some good jumps.

I kept raising the bar higher and continued to leap over it without a problem. A couple of my teammates had come over to the high jump area to watch me and raise the bar as I'd clear a new height. Soon the bar was raised to 5 feet, which was always a great challenge for me. However, on this day it wasn't a problem. I leaped over the bar with room to spare, and it had never felt so easy. It was a great feeling.

Soon the coach had wandered over and a few more teammates as they saw me jumping. The bar had been raised to 5 feet 2 inches, and the coach measured it with his tape measure just to make sure that it was correct. I'd never jumped 5 feet 2 inches in my life, but as I stood about 40 feet from the bar, ready to make my approach, my confidence had never been higher. I took my normal run, pushed off my right leg, and sailed over the bar without touching it. My teammates let out a whoop and my coach was all smiles. It was the best feeling I had ever had in sports.

Amazing to me, I still wasn't finished that day, and ended up clearing 5 feet 4 inches, which was a new school record. It didn't count as a record, however, because you had to do it at a track meet. I couldn't wait for next Saturday's track meet and a chance to break the record and maybe win my first gold medal in the high jump. I felt I had an extra good chance because the meet was at our school and I'd be jumping in the same pit that I just jumped 5 feet 4 inches.

All the regular high jumpers from the other schools were at the meet, and as I warmed up, I felt like I had a secret that they were soon going to find out about. As I warmed up, however, I just felt like my normal self and didn't detect any of that extra spring I'd felt in my legs earlier in the week. I didn't let that bother me, however, and started my jumps. When I got to 4 feet 10 inches, I had my first miss, but cleared the bar on my second attempt. At 5 feet, I missed twice and barely cleared the bar on my last attempt. I knew I didn't have the same magic I'd had a few days earlier.

I disappointed myself, and probably my coach, by not going any higher. I went out on three misses at 5 feet 2 inches and got my usual 3rd place. Coach tried to cheer me up and said, "You know you've got better jumps in you, and there are a lot of meets ahead." Sadly, it never happened, and I returned to my usual self, working hard to clear 5 feet and never getting close to that 5 feet 4 inch jump I made that one special day.

I worked harder than ever in the next weeks to try and recapture that magic, and I figured if I could do it once, I could surely do it again. I'd try to picture exactly how I jumped that day, and what I was thinking, but nothing seemed to help. It was just one unbelievable day in my life where, for some reason, I was like a different high jumper, better than I ever was again. I'll never forget that great jumping day, the way it felt to soar over the bar, and the way my teammates and coach cheered me. I never was a great high jumper, but I do have that one special day to remember.

The Big Scare

I remember I was six years old, in kindergarten, and living in Hanford the day my brother scared the heck out of me. It was such a big scare that I've never forgotten it, and my brother laughs about it to this day. It wasn't funny at the time, and I hated my brother for it. My brother was two years older, and we were alone at our house for a couple hours while my parents went shopping on a Saturday morning. I had a pretty lively imagination back then, and it didn't take a whole lot to scare me. I always slept with a light on, and the slightest sound could send me out of my bed and down the hall to my parents' room. My brother knew I was a bit of a scaredy cat, and with my parents gone, he had the perfect opportunity to scare me. I had to go bathroom that morning, so I went into our one bathroom, closed the door, and sat on the toilet. It didn't take long before my brother ran to the bathroom door, opened it, and screamed, "There's a lion in the house. Run for your life!" And he ran for his life, leaving me sitting on the toilet. As a six year old in a moment of panic, I didn't think for a second about the illogic of a lion being in our house or the possibility of my brother trying to scare me. All I knew was that there was a lion in the house and it was probably coming to eat me. I jumped off the toilet seat, pants around my ankles, and ran out of the bathroom, down the hall, and towards the back door, falling every few steps as my pants tripped my ankles. Finally I made it to the back door, knowing the lion must be only a few steps behind me, opened the door and ran out, immediately falling down the back steps onto the yard. Then I heard my brother's howling laugh as he saw me lying on the ground, pants around my ankles, naked bottom in the air, toilet paper still stuck you know where. I knew in an instant that my brother had made it all up to scare me as he had done many times before. He was a little devil and I hated him at that moment, but all I could do was lie on the ground and cry. Even at the young age of six, the humiliation of being tricked, of falling down the steps, and of lying half naked on the ground was too much to take. I wailed like I had been stung by a hive of bees. Eventually my parents came home, and I couldn't wait to tell on my brother. He got punished good, but I knew it was never enough to keep him from doing it again. Tormenting me was one of his greatest pleasures. Today I can see the humor others get out of picturing me running out of the bathroom bare butted, toilet paper flying, falling every few steps, but at the time the feeling was pure terror. To this day when I go into the bathroom, my brother will occasionally say, "Watch out for the lion," the old tormenter's grin on his face. I still don't find it funny.

An Important Lesson

In high school when I was a senior, my friends wanted to punish a girl because she had taken my friend's boyfriend from her. My friend Eva was in love with the guy, and they had plans to get married and have a big family. She was always talking about how happy she was going to be when she became the wife of the man she loved. One shocking phone call from Emmanuel destroyed that dream forever. One Sunday Eva called me crying, telling me that Emmanuel had broken up with her and was with another girl. The girl was from another town and Eva didn't even know her. She said that she didn't want to live without him, that he was everything to her. For days, she was devastated. She did not eat or talk to anyone; all she did was cry. I felt awful for her. What could we do to help her? I thought. Perhaps taking her out to a dance to try and have some fun would help. Eva, however, was in no mood to cooperate. Instead, she wanted revenge on the girl that had taken the only man she loved. That scared me because all of our friends agreed with her that revenge was justified, except for me. However, I didn't want to tell them that I wouldn't go along with their plans. I didn't want to let my friends down because they would think I was betraying them. Besides, I didn't know what kind of revenge Eva was talking about, perhaps just telling the other girl that Emmanuel still loved Eva or sending the girl an anonymous card saying that Emmanuel was cheating on her. When I heard them say that they should kill the girl so Emmanuel would return to Eva, it left me numb. Oh my God, I thought. Is Eva really capable of doing something like that to someone that had done her no personal harm? Are my friends so crazy that they would even consider killing the girl and not consider the consequences? There is no way I am going to go along with them, I thought, and I told them so. I backed out, and I wanted nothing to do with the problem. The next day Eva called and informed me that she had bought the gun to kill Emmanuel's new girl friend. I tried to talk to her and tell her that what she was doing was wrong, but there was no way of talking her out of it. This was not the person I had grown up with. It was liked she had been possessed by an evil spirit. I decided I couldn't let my friend ruin her life forever, so I called Emmanuel and told him what Eva was planning on doing. At first he thought I was joking, but I convinced him otherwise. He called the police, and the police conducted an investigation, including talking to Eva and all of her friends and confirming that Eva had bought a gun. She ended up going to jail for six months for plotting a potential murder. Eva has not seen me or spoken to me since I called Emmanuel. That bothers me because we were best friends, but at least she is out of jail and won't spend the rest of her life in prison for killing someone. Eva may thank me someday for what I have done for her. Thank God that I did not go along with her plan. What would have become of my life? The last thing I heard was that her family moved out of the area. I hope and pray that Eva learned that an obsession for somebody else can destroy your life. I believe that when a person doesn't love you, you just have to let go, as hard as that may be. If Emmanuel didn't love Eva anymore, I wondered, why did she even want to be with him? I also learned to trust my own instincts and not go along with my friends if I know they are wrong. What I did was hard for me, but it was the right thing to do. I have a clear conscience, and I hope that someday I'll see my friend again.

Revision Activity 1.10

Check the paragraphing in your paper. If you did no paragraphing, paragraph your paper similarly to how you paragraphed the sample papers, changing paragraphs as you moved to something new in your draft. If you paragraphed your paper, see what changes might be made to improve your paragraphing, including dividing overly long paragraphs or combining two or more short paragraphs. Share papers with a classmate and evaluate each other's paragraphing based on how smoothly it moved you through the writer's thoughts.

Revision Activity 1.11

Write the second draft of your paper, including all improvements you made in description, sentence wording, and paragraphing. In addition, if you discover other things to change or add to improve the draft, feel free to do so. Then exchange second drafts with a classmate. Read each other's draft to see if there is anything you don't understand or if you have questions that the draft leaves unanswered. Give suggestions to your classmate, and based on your classmate's input, revise your draft further if you feel it can be improved, incorporating all changes into your second draft.

Revised sample draft - deletions lined out; additions in bold)

Emily

When I returned home from 3rd grade one afternoon, I was greeted with the news that my younger sister was sick and in the hospital. I could tell by my mother's looks that she was concerned, and she said I would be staying with grandma ~~some evenings~~ while she was at the hospital **with Emily**. I asked if I could go and see ~~Emily~~ at the hospital, and mom said, "Not right now, honey. But you can see her in a few days."

~~For~~ The next days ~~it was~~ **were** very lonely in the house without my sister, who was my best friend and playmate. My mom was somber most of the time, and I would hear her talking with grandma in ~~low voices~~ **a hushed voice**. In bits and pieces I learned that my sister had had a high fever ~~and had~~ **followed by** a seizure, ~~in fact several of them~~ **and then several in succession**. Mom said that the doctors were helping Emily and controlling the seizures, but that her brain had been hurt. I didn't really understand what any of it meant except that it seemed serious and I became very worried. "Emily may not seem like her old self for awhile," mom warned me. "It will take her time to recover."

~~I learned~~ Much later, when I was old enough to understand, **I learned** that Emily was a victim of status epilepticus, a relatively rare **childhood** condition resulting in multiple seizures which can severely impair the brain. She would have seizures on and off for the rest of her life, the**ir** frequency and severity controlled by medication, but ~~it was~~ that initial series of seizures ~~that she had as a six-year old that~~ **had** caused the damage. ~~Apparently~~ No one knows what causes the condition or why one child in thirty thousand is afflicted~~.~~ , **and** we will never know why it happened to Emily.

When ~~Emily~~ finally came home from the hospital, I was shocked by her condition although mom had tried to prepare me. ~~Em~~ **She** just lay in bed, a blank stare on her face. ~~that I had never seen.~~ She couldn't talk or walk, and she didn't even seem to recognize me. Mom said because of **the brain damage,** ~~Emily's illness, she~~ **Em** would have to relearn ~~much of what her brain sickness had erased:~~ **a great deal:** ~~being able~~ **the ability** to talk, walk, and recognize people. A therapist from the hospital ~~started~~ **began** coming to the house three days a week to help Emily with her recovery.

Very slowly, Em began to recover some motor skills, first sitting up, then standing, then taking a few halting steps. She also began making noises although they didn't form into words. Her ~~eyes began to focus better~~ **visual recognition improved,** and when she looked at me, I could ~~see some recognition in her eyes~~ **tell that she knew me.** She also began to smile ~~sometimes~~ , and with mom or me helping her, walk slowly around her room. Mom was encouraged by the progress ~~she was making~~, hoping that every day would bring more improvement.

I, however, was hoping for a miracle. Every day I woke up, I would hope that I'd walk into Em's room and my real sister would be there~~,~~ : the fun, active, loving sister I knew. I missed that sister so much and ~~sometimes I~~ would **sometimes** become angry at that "imposter" who had taken my real sister from me. I also resented that mom's life now seemed to revolve around Emily and that I was never the center of her attention. As a self-absorbed child, all I could think of was how Em's illness had affected my life and how lonely I was without Em to play with and talk to. I was also fearful that what happened to Emily could happen to me, and I was sometimes afraid to go to sleep at night, worried that I might wake up like Emily.

After months and then years, it became apparent that Emily was never going to be the person she had been. My mom, the doctors, the therapists, and the special needs' teachers did everything possible to bring Em to her highest developmental level, but there was just too much permanent brain damage for her to recover greatly. She could walk in her shuffling gate and seemed to enjoy walking from room to room around the house **or outside.** She never talked but made ~~noises~~ **sounds** which made it clear when she was happy and when she wasn't, but she had a good temperament. She **also** had a good appetite and enjoyed eating. She ~~also~~ grew to know her family again, and was always happy to see me when I came home from school. Thankfully, my mom said that Em knew nothing of her previous life or what she had been like before her illness. The only life she knew was the one she now lived. ~~so thankfully, her great loss was much more painful to our family than to her.~~

As I grew older, I learned to accept my sister as she was. I always carried a sadness for the sister that I had lost and for the normal life that was taken away from her. It was ~~truly~~ a great tragedy, and at some point I ~~knew~~ **realized** ~~that it was important~~ **the importance of** ~~to~~ help**ing** make Em's life as happy as it could be. Sometimes I would feel guilty at relative gatherings when I was having fun playing with the cousins and Em would be curled up on the sofa staring out the window, but mom assured me that Em's situation didn't mean that I shouldn't enjoy my life ~~and have fun~~. "I don't want you to live your life for Emily, honey," she said. "Emily would want you to have the best life possible, and so do I.."

My life with Emily ~~grew into a~~ **became** routine. I would come home from school and she would be happy to see me. She'd often take my hand and we would walk around the house for a while. Then we would sit on the sofa, and often she would put her head on my shoulder and stroke my hand. With all of the abilities that **she had lost** ~~her illness had taken away from her~~, she ~~had not lost perhaps the greatest:~~ **never lost** the ability to love. "I love you Em," I would tell her every day, ~~and~~ the words ~~came~~ **coming** from my heart. She never had to say a word to show her love.

Our family's life changed dramatically eleven years ago when Em became sick. It's been hard at times ~~on everyone~~ as we've all changed our routines and given up something ~~of our more active lives~~ to care for my sister. And the fact that Emily will never have a normal life weighs on all of us at times. Seeing her sitting on the sofa cuddling her baby doll can bring tears to my eyes, thinking what her life might have been. ~~like.~~ But I've learned that dwelling on such thoughts doesn't help ~~anything.~~ **anyone.**

We don't know how long we will have Emily with us, as someone in her condition may not live long into adulthood. There was a time when I spent time with Em ~~more~~ out of ~~a sort of free-floating~~ guilt, a feeling that I ~~somehow~~ bore some blame for ~~Em's~~

her condition. I also had moments when I wondered, "Why her and not me?" and felt the guilt of being the "normal" ~~person~~ **girl** that my sister couldn't be. Today, however, I spend time with Em out of ~~love,~~ a love that has grown more deeply as I have gotten older, and **I** want to appreciate every moment that I have with her. While there is little that I do for Em but spend time with her, there is a lot that she has done for me. I am no longer the self-absorbed person who was mainly concerned with how ~~anything that happened~~ **every little thing** affected me and my happiness. Through my relationship with my sister, I have grown more patient, more caring, and more loving. I don't always have to be doing for myself to find happiness or contentment. I may also have found my professional calling: ~~in life:~~ working with people with disabilities, perhaps as a therapist or speech pathologist. Because of Em, I'd like to think that I've become a better person.

Editing

The final step in completing your paper is to proofread it for errors and correct any that you find. This is the editing phase of the writing process, where you eliminate all errors from your paper, and it comes at the end of the writing process after you have made your changes in content and wording. The goal of the editing phase is to produce a polished, error-free final draft.

Of course, if you have been running the spelling check on your computer as you wrote, you may have few spelling errors. In addition, although the emphasis in the writing process has not been on correcting errors, if you found a flagrant error in spelling, punctuation or grammar usage earlier, you may have already corrected it.

The editing phase, however, is the first time you will systematically scrutinize your paper for errors, looking for the types of errors that are most frequently found in writing. When you proofread your paper - scouring it thoroughly for errors - few will escape your detection.

In each "Editing" section, you focus on different kinds of error correction, covering the most typical errors that writers make. By the end of the text, you will have covered most errors that frequently appear in writing and learned to detect and correct them if they appear in your own writing. In this section, you work on eliminating run-on sentences and on using correct irregular verb forms.

Correcting Run-on Sentences

A common error that writers make is running two sentences together rather than separating them with a period. Writers often run two relatively short sentences together whose content is related.

Readers can have problems with run-on sentences. They have expectations that a sentence will end with a period, and they rely on those periods to help move them from one thought to another. Run-on sentences can confuse readers, distracting them from the writer's ideas.

When run-on sentences are brought to most writers' attention, they can see where the period belongs to end the first sentence and make the correction. Run-on sentences are a solvable problem, one that most writers can eliminate from their papers once they are made aware of them.

Guidelines for Correcting Run-on Sentences

The following guidelines will help you avoid run-on sentences in your writing.

1. A sentence is a group of words expressing a complete thought. The end of a sentence is designated by an end mark, most frequently a period.

Example: The best place to park on campus in the late morning is behind the
library.

2. A run-on sentence most frequently involves two sentences run together as
a single sentence without a period ending the first sentence. A run-on sentence
is an incorrect sentence form that needs editing.

Example: The best place to park on campus in the late morning is behind the
library I frequently park there between ten and eleven.

Corrected: The best place to park on campus in the late morning is behind the
library. I frequently park there between ten and eleven.

3. One form of a run-on sentence, called a *comma splice*, has a comma between
the two sentences rather than a period. A comma splice is not a correct sentence
form and needs to be edited.

Example: The grass in the meadow was dry and brown, it hadn't rained all
summer.

Corrected: The grass in the meadow was dry and brown. It hadn't rained all
summer.

4. Any time you find a run-on sentence or a comma splice in your writing, you need
to correct it. To correct a run-on or comma splice, you can do one of two
things:

a. Separate the sentences by ending the first sentence with a period and
beginning the second sentence with capital letter.

Example: Joanna excels in track and field and plays stringed instruments, her
brother Theo has the same interests.

Corrected: Joanna excels in track and field and plays stringed instruments.
Her brother Theo has the same interests.

b. Combine the two sentences that are run together with a joining word such as
and, but, or *because* to form one complete sentence.

Example: I enjoyed the Beyonce concert very much, Maria thought it lasted
too long.

Corrected: I enjoyed the Beyonce concert very much, but Maria thought it
lasted too long.

c. As a general rule, separate longer run-on sentences with a period and combine shorter ones with a joining word.

Example: Alyssa had one complaint about working in a store that sold incense she couldn't get the smell out of her hair.
Corrected: Alyssa had one complaint about working in a store that sold incense. She couldn't get the smell out of her hair.

Example: Harold liked working as a security officer, he drove a new car around all day.

Corrected: Harold liked working as a security officer because he drove a new car round all day.

Editing Activity 1.12

The following paragraphs contain some run-on sentences and comma splices. Correct these sentences by separating longer sentences and combining shorter sentences.

Example: The overflow from the river had left large puddles of water along the river bank that turned stagnant the puddles became prime breeding grounds for mosquitoes. Families living around the river attended meetings of the county board of supervisors to alert them to the problem.

Corrected: The overflow from the river had left large puddles of water along the river bank that turned stagnant. The puddles became prime breeding grounds for mosquitoes. Families living around the river attended meetings of the county board of supervisors to alert them to the problem.

Casual Dress

Over the years, the way that Americans dress has become more casual and informal. A good example was the way that people were dressed at my grandfather's church last Sunday I went with him as I was visiting for the weekend. As always, my grandfather dressed in a coat and tie as he has done all his life. However, he was the only person at the church in a tie, only a few were wearing coats. The majority of men wore colorful short-sleeved shirts not tucked in. Quite a few wore shorts instead of long pants, there were also a number in sandals. Although I didn't see many men in t-shirts, I wouldn't be surprised to see more in the future. While the women appeared to be dressed somewhat better than the men, most of them wore pants instead of dresses.

    The minister obviously embraced the casual dress, his outfit included khaki pants, an open-necked shirt, and loafers. You couldn't distinguish him from the churchgoers until he stood before us. The casual dress also contributed to the loose, laid-back atmosphere inside the church and the relaxed, informal church service that took place. This was very different from the church my grandfather grew up in, where everything was very formal and solemn, he hasn't completely adjusted to the change. He also has no intention of removing his coat and tie to fit in.

Editing Activity 1.13

Proofread your latest draft for any run-on sentences or comma splices, and correct any you find by inserting periods or combining sentences with joining words. Then exchange papers with a classmate and proofread each other's drafts for run-ons and comma splices.

Irregular Verbs

Since you wrote your paper about a past experience, you no doubt wrote in the past tense, the verb tense used to write about things that have already occurred. While most writers have little trouble with the regular past tense verbs, which uniformly end in ed (e.g. walked, talked, climbed, baked), there are a group of verbs called irregular verbs that follow no rules and form their past tenses in different ways (e.g. slept, drank, driven, won).

Irregular verb forms give writers some problems since they don't follow a single pattern and must be committed to memory. Many irregular verbs also have two different past tense forms: one for the simple past tense, and one for the past participle, a form which includes a helping verb before the main verb (e.g. had drunk, have driven, has eaten, have swum).

Irregular Verb List

The following list of irregular verbs includes the most commonly used and misspelled verbs. The verbs are grouped by similarities in their spelling in the past tense and past participle forms.

The following verbs have the same form for the past tense and past participle:

Present Tense	Past Tense	Past Participle
bring	brought	brought
build	built	built
burst	burst	burst
catch	caught	caught
cut	cut	cut
find	found	found

Present Tense	Past Tense	Past participle
has	had	had
lay (place down)	laid	laid
lead	led	led
quit	quit	quit
read	read	read
set	set	set
sit	sat	sat
think	thought	thought

The past participle of the following verbs ends in "en:"

choose	chose	chosen
drive	drove	driven
eat	ate	eaten
fall	fell	fallen
get	got	gotten
give	gave	given
ride	rode	ridden
rise	rose	risen
speak	spoke	spoken
take	took	taken
write	wrote	written

From the past tense to the past participle, one vowel changes from *a* to *o* or from *a* to *u* in the following verbs.

become	became	become
come	came	come
begin	began	begun
drink	drank	drunk
ring	rang	rung
run	ran	run
shrink	shrank	shrunk
sing	sang	sung
swim	swam	swum

For the following verbs, the past tense ends in *ew* and the past participle ends in *own*, with the exception of *drawn*.

blow	blew	blown
draw	drew	drawn
fly	flew	flown
grown	grew	grown

| know | knew | known |
| throw | threw | thrown |

The following commonly used irregular verbs follow no particular pattern.

do	did	done
go	went	gone
see	saw	seen
lie (lie down)	lay	lain

Past Tense and Past Participle

The following distinctions between the past tense and past participle verb forms will help you use and spell them correctly.

1. The past tense verb form is used to write about an action that occurred or a condition that existed in the past. It is not preceded by a helping verb.

    Examples: Yesterday I *wrote* an e-mail to my cousin.
    Last Friday *was* the hottest day of the summer.

2. The past participle verb form is used to write about an action that occurred or a condition that existed over a period of time, and that may continue in the present and the future. The past participle verb form is always preceded by a helping verb such as *has, have,* or *had.*

    Examples: I *have written* an e-mail to my cousin every week this month.
    Julie *has taken* care of her invalid aunt for several weeks.
    Miles *had grown* tomatoes on his apartment balcony every summer.

3. Whether you use the past tense or past participle depends what you are expressing in a particular sentence. For example, note the distinction in meaning between the three following sentences.

    Yesterday I *drove* to school for the first time in a month.
    I *have driven* to school more than I *have ridden* my bike this semester.
    I *had driven* to school every Friday until my roommate started giving me rides.

The first sentence uses the past tense verb *drove,* and indicates an action that occurred in the past. The second sentence uses the past participle verb *driven* with the present tense helping verb *has,* and indicates an action that occurred over a period of time and may continue into the future. The third sentence uses the past participle verb *driven* with the past tense helping verb *had,* and indicates an action that occurred over a period of time but no longer occurs. As you can see, past tense and past participle verb forms carry different meanings, and writers use them in different situations.

Editing Activity 1.14

Fill in the blanks in the following sentences with appropriate irregular verbs from the list. Remember to use the past participle verb form when the blank is preceded by a helping verb (*has*, *had*, *have*).

Example: No one has <u>driven</u> as many miles to school this semester as you have.

1.   I have _____ great care not to tear my new disposable contact lenses.

2.   No American has _____ the English Channel in the last twenty years.

3.   A flock of geese have _____ over our apartment every day this month.

4.   The concert _____ with a tribute band playing Jimmy Hendrix' music.

5.   I have _____ to doubt your interest in sharing an apartment with him.

6.   Mona had _____ to work with her brother until his car broke down.

7.   Home prices had _____ more in 2005 than at any time in the past twenty years.

8.   My T shirt _____ two sizes when I washed it in hot water.

9.   Homer's young daughter gleefully _____ into the room.

10.   I hadn't _____ too far into my calculus homework until I realized that I had no idea what I was doing.

11.   The enrollment of new students has _____ very smoothly since the college established its on-line enrollment site.

12.   I _____ your doorbell several times before you heard me.

13.   Have you _____ everything possible to get the cheapest airplane tickets?

14.   Rudy hadn't _____ a solo before an audience since junior high.

15. No one has _____ more letters to her state senator than Alma.

16. I should have _____ that it would be impossible to find a parking space around the ferry building.

17. You _____ a very difficult major, but you are certainly up to the challenge.

18. Franklin hasn't _____ in a restaurant for over a year.

19. We _____ the horses down the rocky trail rather than try to ride them.

20. I _____ your sweater back that I borrowed last week.

21. Have you _____ any thought to subletting your back room?

22. Gretchen _____ the musical Hairspray in four different cities.

23. I have never _____ so many squirrels in one area of Central Park.

24. Juliette had _____ down for a nap this morning, but by late afternoon, she was already drowsy.

Editing Activity 1.15

Proofread your latest draft for errors involving irregular verbs and make the necessary corrections. Then run a final spell check on your paper and proofread your paper carefully for spelling errors and make corrections. Finally, exchange papers with a classmate and give them a final proofreading for errors.

Editing Activity 1.16

Write the final corrected draft of your paper to share with classmates.

Writing Summary

In each unit, your first writing assignment takes you step-by-step through the writing process, including activities that help you revise and edit your drafts. In the final "Writing Summary" section, you write a second paper working more independently.

The purpose of this second assignment is to give you more writing practice, an opportunity to write on a second life experience, and a chance you apply what you have learned from the unit about effective writing. Ultimately, this assignment, like all activities in the text, is designed to improve your writing and build your writing confidence.

Writing Assignment 2

Select a second experience to write about that you remember well. Select a very different experience from your first topic, one that made a different kind of impact, evoked different emotions, and occurred at a different stage in your life.

Prewriting

To help you consider potential topics for your paper and to generate some material for your first draft, free write for five-ten minutes on two or three different experiences that you recall well. Write whatever comes to your mind without concern for order, logic, or correctness.

Sample free writing

I had a friend in junior high who was very different from me. He was a Korean guy from a different neighborhood who I had little in common with except our love of sports. He was a really good athlete and I was pretty good too, so we were together a lot on the playing fields. We became friends, but we didn't hang out together except during sports because we ran with very different kinds of people. One day I remember thinking, this is stupid, never hanging out with K.J. at recess or lunch break, so I told him let's go eat lunch, and we did. Other days I'd hang out with him at recess and we always found things to laugh about. But one day all that changed. For no reason, he began acting cold to me, like he hardly knew me. One day I walked by him when he was with some of his friends, and he said something under his breath that I didn't catch and they all started laughing at me. One day I caught K.J. in the bathroom and asked him what was wrong, what did I do. He said nothing, that that's just the way it was, that he couldn't hang out with me. I realized that his buddies had gotten to him, and that he had had to make a choice: my friendship or theirs.

Drafting Guidelines

Write your first draft, keeping the following in mind.

1. The purpose of your first draft is to get the experience on paper as clearly as you recall it. Don't worry about your sentence wording or whether you make an occasional error.

2. Provide some setting and background information as a lead-in to the experience.

3. As you write, you are leading to the heart of the experience: whatever happened that made the impact on your life. Bring the experience to life for readers by describing it in detail.

4. The experience no doubt was an emotional one. Include your feelings and thoughts during the experience as you recall them so that readers can sense what you went through.

5. Conclude the draft with what happened as a result of the experience and your analysis of why the experience was so memorable: the impact it had on your life.

6. Write your draft in paragraphs, changing paragraphs as you move to something new in your paper: a different time, a different place, a different aspect of the experience.

7. Keep you reading audience - your classmates - in mind as you write.

8. Title your draft in a simple manner that tells what it is about.

Sample First draft

Lost Friendship

When I was in junior high, I mainly ran around with the guys that I had grown up with. However, while playing sports, I got to know a guy who was from a very different background, and we became good friends.

K.J. was a Korean guy from a different neighborhood who ran around with his own buddies that I didn't know. They hung out in different parts of the school from us, and our paths seldom crossed. However, K.J. and I were together every day on the sports fields playing football, basketball, and baseball, and we were both good athletes. We also both liked to mess around and make people laugh, so we got along pretty well.

One day I decided to hang out with K.J. at lunch time. I didn't think anything of it, and just said, "Let's go eat together," so we did. Soon we were also hanging out together at recess once or twice a week and having a good time. I still hung out with my buddies too, but not exclusively anymore. I liked being with K.J..

Then one day something strange happened. For no reason that I knew of, K.J. started to ignore me. He didn't talk to me and acted like he hardly knew me. I couldn't figure it out and started wondering what I could have done wrong. One day I walked by him and his buddies by the shop building, and I heard him say something under his breath, and then they all looked at me and laughed. I was mad and bewildered at the same time, not knowing what he had said or why they were laughing, but I knew K.J. was making fun of me. It really hurt.

Finally one day I caught up with him in the bathroom, just the two of us, and asked him, "What's wrong man? Why are you acting like that?" "It's got nothin to do with you," he said. "We can't be friends no more. That's just the way it is." "I don't understand," I said. "Did I do something to you?" "You don't get it, man," he said. "That's the way the world goes." And he walked out.

That was the end of K.J. and my friendship, and I'm still sad about it today. As I thought about what he had said, I began to understand that his friends had put him back in his place where they felt he belonged, with them. I'm sure they had made it pretty rough on him for hanging out with me. He felt the peer pressure and made the decision he felt he had to make. I couldn't be mad at him, and in his place, I probably would have done the same thing. But it still seemed wrong to me. I had always been pretty independent in the choices I made, and that experience made me even more determined to make friends where and with who I wanted to. I realized how wrong it was for people not to be friends because they come from different backgrounds or different ethnic groups, or for peer pressure to determine who you hung out with and who you didn't. I also realized that the less you knew about people, like my not knowing K.J.'s buddies and their not knowing mine, the more distrustful and alien you felt towards them. K.J.'s friends didn't dislike me for who I was, they disliked me because I wasn't one of them.

I saw K.J. a couple times in high school and said hi, but then he vanished and I didn't see him for several years. Then one day out of no where I saw him at a gas station, walked over and said hi. He gave me his big smile, and it was one of the moments that you remember. All the b.s. world of junior high fell away, and we talked like friends for a few minutes. We never mentioned what happened in the past, and when I left I said, "It's really good to see you, K.J.." "You too, man," he said, and I knew he meant it.

Revision Guidelines

After setting aside your draft for awhile, read it over to see what improvements you can make. Use the following guidelines to evaluate your draft.

1.   Read each sentence to make sure it says what you want clearly and concisely. Revise sentences to improve their wording and smoothness, and eliminate unnecessary words or phrases.

2. Review your draft to see where you might add some description to bring the experience to life for readers: describing the setting, people involved, the action, and your thoughts and feelings at crucial times.

3. Review your paragraphing. Change paragraphs as you move to new parts of your paper: a different time, a different place, a different incident/ Divide overly long paragraphs and combine two or more short, related paragraphs

4. Read the draft a final time with your readers in mind to see if there is anything that you can change to make the paper more interesting : adding a particular detail, clarifying the impact the experience had on you, or adding something new about the experience that just cameto your mind.

Finally, write the second draft of your paper, including all changes you have made.

Sample second draft

Lost Friendship

When I was in junior high, I ~~mainly~~ ran around with the guys that I had grown up with. However, while playing sports, I got to know ~~a guy~~ **someone** who was from a very different background, and we became good friends.

K.J. was a Korean ~~guy~~ **boy** from a different neighborhood who ran around with his own buddies ~~that I didn't know~~. They hung out in different parts of the school from us, and our paths seldom crossed. However, K.J. and I were together every day ~~on the sports fields~~ playing football, basketball, and baseball, and we were both good athletes. We also ~~both~~ liked to mess around and make people laugh, so we got along pretty well.

One day I decided to hang out with K.J. at lunch time. I didn't think anything of it, and just said, "Let's go eat together," so we did. Soon we were also **having fun** ~~hanging out~~ **being** together at recess once or twice a week ~~and having a good time~~. I still hung out with my buddies ~~too~~, but not exclusively ~~anymore~~. I liked being with K.J.

Then one day ~~something strange happened~~ **I got a real shock**. For no reason that I knew ~~of~~, K.J. ~~started to~~ **just** ignored **me**. He didn't talk to me and acted like he hardly knew me. I couldn't figure it out and started wondering what I could have done wrong. One day I walked by him and his buddies by the shop building, and I heard him say something under his breath, and then they all looked at me and laughed. I was mad and bewildered ~~at the same time~~, not knowing what he had said or why they were laughing, but I knew K.J. was making fun of me. It really hurt.

Another time in front of his friends he called me out to fight. I'd never said or done a bad thing to him, yet it was like he hated me. All I said was, "I don't want to fight you K.J. I thought we were friends." Then I walked away.

Finally one day I caught up with him alone in the bathroom, and asked him, "What's wrong man? Why are you acting like that?" "It's got nothin to do with you," he said. "We can't be friends no more. That's just the way it is." "I don't understand," I said. "Did I do something to you?" "You don't get it, man," he said. "That's the way the world ~~goes~~ **is. Just leave me alone**." And he walked out.

That was the end of ~~K.J. and my~~ **our** friendship, and I'm still sad about it today. As I thought about what K.J. had said, I began to understand that his friends **had pressured him not to hang out with me**. ~~put him back in his place where they felt he belonged, with them.~~ ~~I'm sure~~ **I imagine** they had made it pretty rough on him. ~~for hanging out with me.~~ He felt the peer pressure and made the decision he felt he had to make. I couldn't be mad at him, and in his place, I probably would have done the same thing. But it still seemed wrong to me. (*Begin new paragraph here.*) I had always been pretty independent in the choices I made, and that experience made me even more determined to make friends where and with whom I wanted ~~to~~. I realized how wrong it was for people not to be friends because they come from different backgrounds or different ethnic groups, or for peer pressure to determine who you **liked** ~~hung out with~~ and who you didn't. I also realized that the less you knew about people, ~~like my not knowing Jessie's buddies and their not knowing mine~~, the more distrustful and alien you felt towards them. K.J.'s friends didn't dislike me for who I was, they disliked me because I ~~wasn't one of them~~ **was different**.

I saw K.J. a couple times in high school and said hi, but then he vanished and I didn't see him for several years. Then one day ~~out of no where~~ I saw him at a gas station, walked over and said ~~hi~~ **hello**. He gave me his big smile, and it was ~~one of the moments that you~~ **a moment I'll always remember**. All ~~the b.s. world~~ **the problems** of junior high fell away, and we talked like friends for a few minutes. We never mentioned what happened in the past, and when I left I said, "It's really good to see you, K.J.." "You too, man," he said, and I knew ~~he~~ **we both** meant it.

Editing Guidelines

Proofread your latest draft for errors following these guidelines.

1. Check your draft for any run-on sentences or comma splices. Separate longer run-ons or comma splices with a period, and combine shorter ones.

2. Check your irregular verbs to make sure you have used the proper forms.

3. Run the spell check on your word processing program and proofread your paper carefully to catch and correct any spelling errors.

When you finish correcting any errors, write the final draft of your paper.

Readings

Walking Out

by Barbara Ehrenreich
(from *Nickeled and Dimed*)

To make ends meet, I was working as a housekeeper in the hotel and a server in the adjacent restaurant. Another housekeeper warned me that no one so far had succeeded in combining housekeeping with serving at Jerry's. "Some kid did it once for five days, and you're no kid."

With that helpful information in mind, I rush back to trailer number 46 at Terrace Gardens Trailer Park, which has neither terrace nor garden, down four Advils, shower, stooping over to fit into the stall, and attempt to compose myself for the next shift. The only unforseen obstacle to my smooth transition from job to job is my tan Jerry's slacks, which had looked reasonably clean last night when I hand-washed my Hawaiian shirt but proved by daylight to be mottled with catsup and ranch dressing stains. I spend most of my hour-long break between jobs scouring the stains out of the pants and then drying them over the hood of my car in the sun.

Back at the restaurant, I assure myself that I can do this two-job thing, in theory, if I can drink enough caffeine. I am not tired at all, I conclude, though it may be that there is simply no "I" left to do the monitoring. What I would see if I were more alert to the situation is that the forces of destruction were already massing against me.

Then it comes, the perfect storm. Four of my tables fill up at once. Four tables is nothing for me now, but only so long as they are obligingly staggered. As I bev table 27, tables 25, 28, and 24 are watching enviously. As I bev 25, 24 glowers because their bevs haven't even been ordered. 28 is four yuppyish types, meaning everything on the side and agonizing instructions as to the chicken Caesars. 25 is a middle-aged black couple who complain, with some justice, that the iced tea isn't fresh and the tabletop is sticky.

But table 24 is the meteorological event of the century: ten British tourists who seem to have made the decision to absorb the American experience entirely by mouth. Here everyone has at least two drinks - iced tea *and* milk shake, Michelob *and* water (with lemon slice in the water, please) - and a huge, promiscuous orgy of breakfast specials, mozz sticks, chicken strips, quesadillas, burgers with cheese and without, sides of hash browns with cheddar, with onions, with gravy, seasoned fries, plain fries, banana splits. Poor cook! Poor me! Because when I arrive with their first tray of food after three prior trips just to refill bevs, Princess Di refuses to eat her chicken strips with her pancake and sausage special since, as she now reveals, the strips were meant to be an appetizer. Maybe the others would have accepted their meals, but Di, who is deep into her third Michelob, insists that everything else go back while they work on their starters. Meanwhile, the yuppies are waving me down for more decaf and the black couple looks ready to summon the NAACP.

Much of what happens next is lost in the fog of war. Our cook starts going under. The little printer in front of her is spewing out orders faster than she can rip them off, much less produce the meals. A menacing restlessness rises from the tables, all of which are full. Even the invincible Ellen is ashen from stress. I take table 24 their reheated main courses, which they immediately reject as either too cold or fossilized by the microwave.

When I return to the kitchen with their trays (three trays in three trips) Joy confronts me with arms akimbo: "What *is* this?" She means the food - the plates of rejected pancakes, hash browns in assorted flavors, toasts, burgers, sausages, eggs. "Uh, scrambled with cheddar," I say. "No!" she screams in my face, "is it a traditional, a super-scramble, or an eye-opener?" I pretend to study my check for a clue, but entropy has been up to its tricks, not only on the plates but in my head, and I have to admit that the original order is beyond reconstruction. "You don't know an eye-opener from a traditional?" she demands in outrage. All I know, in fact, is that my legs have lost interest in the current venture and have announced their intention to fold. I am saved by a yuppie (mercifully not one of mine) who chooses this moment to charge into the kitchen to bellow that his food is twenty-five minutes late. Joy screams at him to get the hell out of her kitchen, and then turns and hurls an empty tray across the kitchen for emphasis.

I leave. I don't walk out, I just leave. I don't finish my side work or pick up my credit card tips, if any, at the cash register or, of course, ask Joy's permission to go. And the surprising thing is that you *can* walk out without permission, that the door opens, that the thick tropical night air parts to let me pass, that my car is still parked where I left it.

There is no vindication in this exit, no screw-you surge of relief, just an overwhelming dank sense of failure pressing down on me and the entire parking lot. Trying to endure the long shifts and relentless concentration, my job situation had become a test of myself, and clearly I had failed. Not only had I flamed out as a housekeeper/server, I had forgotten to give George his share of the tips, and for reasons perhaps best known to hardworking, generous people like my co-workers Gail and Ellen, this hurts. I don't cry, but I realize for the first time in years that the tear ducts are still there and capable of doing their job.

With half of my income lost, I move out of the trailer park rather than wait to be evicted. I always knew, like millions of Americans living on minimum wages, that I was just a job loss away from living in my car or in some flop house. It finally sunk in that I couldn't live the rest of my life like this, and I refused to keep falling back on my mom like some wayward teenager. The only thing I was certain of was that my life would never change unless I got off of the minimum-wage treadmill and somehow found my way back to school. I had no idea how I was going to do that, but it appeared the only speck of light in an endlessly dark night.

Questions for Discussion

1. What background information is provided to help readers understand the author's situation leading up to "the perfect storm?" Why is this information important to readers?

2. The main incident in the essay - the four-table fiasco at the restaurant - is awash with details about the food and the customers. What is the significance of the details?

3. What is the essay's viewpoint on the situation that minimum-wage earners face in America? Do you agree, and why?

4. What conclusion does the author reach at the end of the essay? How do you think she arrived at this conclusion?

5. Have you had any personal experiences that this essay reminds you of? If so, what did you learn from them?

Comes the Darkness

by Vanessa Vega

The darkness starts coming for me on Monday. Much like the flu, it hits the base of my spine first. The slight but undeniable tingling that won't go away. I have a chill to my bones that I can't seem to escape, even though I take two to three hot baths a day trying to alleviate it. My patience is nil. My sense of humor, gone. My desire to go anywhere or do anything has left me.

I throw myself into a flurry of activity; if I run hard and fast enough maybe I can beat it this time. Sometimes that works. But not this time. By Wednesday, the darkness is in my dreams. I am hurt, I am alone, I am dead. By Thursday I start to shake. I know what is going to happen and I feel powerless to fight it. The darkness waits for me and I can't seem to escape. By Friday morning I have shut down. I am so far into myself that if I were to try to withdraw anymore, I would implode.

At work, I can't seem to match the words coming out of my mouth with the voice in my head. People smile at me, look confused, and then walk away.

I am so tired. I don't want to do this. I desperately try to think of errands I have to do before I go home. There aren't any. Once I get home I check the mail. Maybe there will be something inside that needs my immediate and undivided attention. Junk mail. As I walk in the door, I pray for a phone message, any message, any note or urgent plea for my help. Anything to save me from the darkness, to save me from myself. But not today. Today, there is only the darkness, and it waits for me.

Like all rituals, mine is exhausting and demanding. Nothing can interfere with it or preempt it or it doesn't count. I don't want to be interrupted, so I walk into the bathroom and lock the door. Naked, I stand and take a long look at myself. I look carefully at my eyes. I'm not there, but the darkness is. I look at my breasts. My thighs. My stomach. My face. And then I see my arms. They hang there, trembling. Waiting.

I hear a voice. Clear. Commanding. Unmistakable. It is my own voice, insecure and relentless. *You know you have to do this. No, I don't. Yes you do. If you were better than this, you wouldn't be here. I don't need to do this anymore. Oh yes, you do. No one wants to hear your problems. No one cares that you're out of control. You're a burden and people don't have time for this. Stop screwing around and just do it. I'm stronger than you are. I've been waiting for you all week. It's time.*

The tears haven't started yet but they will. I reach under the sink and carefully lay out my tools: cotton balls, alcohol, scissors. I run my wrists and arms under the faucet. I use soap to make sure everything is clean. I have to. It's the rules. Now the tears come. I open my eyes and look into the mirror. All of my insecurities come through in a venomous inner dialogue. *I hate you. I hate you. I hate you. I hate you for being so weak. I hate you for what you're about to do. I hate you for what you've already done. You're a shitty wife. A marginal teacher, at best. So now you think you can be a writer. If that were true, you'd be doing it, not standing here thinking about it. You think the world cares about your past? Your pain? Your ideas? Stop kidding yourself. Face it. Nobody cares. You're a freak. Give up. Give in. Stop jerking around and do this. Do what you know the best. Hurt.*

It's time. I look at my wrists and see the scars that I've put there over the last twenty years. I cry. I am living a lie. When I made my first cuts I swore the would be my last. That if I could just get over the hump, the need for scissors and razor blades and knives would be over. One day, I said, I would be in a better place. Yeah, right.

I have to be careful where and how I cut. If I screw this up, I will end up in the ER and then I'll be committed. Maybe I should be. Maybe I'm crazy and don't even know it. I take the scissors in my left hand and hold my right arm stiff. The darkness surrounds me and I let it carry me away.

Time stands still. I don't know how long I've been cutting. Part of me can see my arm, but there isn't any pain, and so I don't know if it's real. My arm has gone from white to pink to red. I want to stop, but then I wonder if it's enough. If it's not, the darkness won't leave, and I will have to do this all over again. So I keep going. I know the parts of me that I hate the most are just under the surface. I have to find them and destroy them.

I don't know why or when I stop. The scissors are lying on the counter top and I'm holding my arm to my chest. It burns, but I'm afraid to look at it. I don't want to see what I've done. But I do. Pathetic.

I'm back in my body now. My arm stings and I panic. It's getting late. I have to cleanup everything before anyone gets home. I frantically start the shower so if anyone comes home, that's where they'll think I am. I clean the blades and hold them up to my eyes. I wonder why they hate me so much. Part of me hates them back for not doing a better job. One day, perhaps they'll kill me. But today is not that day.

The cotton balls are at the bottom of the trash can. The sink is rinsed out and clean. The scissors are clean and put away. There is nothing that can give me away. Except my arm. Except my wrist. Except me.

Questions for Discussion

1. How does the author bring readers into the personal nightmare she is living? What details prepare you for where the narrative is heading?

2. What is the purpose of the "internal dialogue" in paragraphs six and seven?

3. Why does the author cut herself? How might growing up with a father who spanked her brutally and made her feel worthless have affected her?

4. What impact did the essay have on you? What emotions did it illicit? Why do you think the author chose to write about her situation?

Unit Two
Influences

Throughout our lives we encounter people who influence us in different ways: parents, grandparents, spouses, siblings, friends, teachers, coaches, co-workers, supervisors, clergy, and so on. Some times the influence is obvious and direct, and other times it is more subtle, affecting us in ways we may not fully understand until later in life.

Writers often write about people who have helped shape their lives, for better or for worse: a wonderful grandmother, an absent father, a caring teacher, a trouble-making friend, a special older brother, an impossible boss. In this unit you will write about one such person, someone who has made an indelible imprint on your life.

In writing this paper, you will bring a person to life for readers and reveal your relationship with him or her by providing examples that capture that relationship. You will also analyze and share with readers the influence this person has had on you and the impact that he or she has made in your life.

There are several purposes for this writing assignment. First, it allows you once again to draw on your own background and experiences to write your paper. Second, it provides you a different writing experience from Unit 1. You are now focusing your writing on another person rather than yourself, and you are analyzing a relationship rather than a personal experience. Third, you employ a new type of writing development: using examples from life to help characterize your subject and show your relationship with him or her. This unit's writing assignment provides some new challenges that will add to your growth as a writer.

As in the first unit, you use the writing process in the text to prepare, write, and improve your drafts, beginning with prewriting activities and concluding with proofreading and editing. In each section you are also introduced to new elements of effective writing and review what was covered in the previous unit. The purpose of the regular review activities is to ingrain in your mind key elements of effective writing so that they become a natural part of your writing process.

Prewriting

During each "Prewriting" section, you prepare to write the first draft of your paper. Prewriting activities can help you accomplish a number of things: selecting a topic, developing some material for your draft, analyzing your thoughts and feelings about the topic, and deciding how you might organize your thoughts on paper.

Topic Selection

To help you decide on a person to write about, think about some of the people who have been important in your life: family members, friends, teachers, co-workers, supervisors, coaches, and so on. Keep in mind those people who have made the biggest impact on your life and that you would most like to write about.

Free Writing

As you did in Unit 1, you will do some free writing to consider different people you might want to write about and develop some material for your paper. Free writing is a good way to recall memories about people, explore your feelings, and decide whom to write about.

Prewriting Activity 2.1

Free write for ten minutes on two or three people that have made an impact on your life. The purpose of the free writing is to help you decide on a topic, generate some material for your paper, and think about your relationships with different people.

Sample Free Writing

#1
I guess everyone has a teacher that they had a crush on when they were little. I still remember the name of my third grade teacher, Mrs. Sinclair. It may have been Miss Sinclair, I don't remember. She was pretty and young and had dark shiny hair. She wa slender and wasn't very tall, and I remember that she smiled a lot. She was nice to all the kids in the class, and she was nice to me all the time and I really liked her a lot. One time though I did something to upset her and I felt crushed. Kids were going to the front of the room one at a time to do something, recite a poem and make a short speech or tell what we did on the weekend or something. When it was my turn, rather than just get up and walk to the front of the room, I tried to be funny and make everyone laugh. Mostly I think I was trying to impress Mrs. Sinclair, but it didn't turn out that way. I'd walk half way to the front of the room then say something like, Oops, I forgot something, and run back to my seat and pretend to get a piece of paper.

Then I'd walk back about half way and say Oops I forgot something, and ran back again. By now the kids were laughing and I was laughing and I figured Mrs. Sinclair must be laughing, but when I stopped to run back to my seat the third time, she said sternly, "Hector, stop that right now and get to the front of the class. I don't want any more clowning around from you." I was shocked and I could feel my face burning. My eyes were beginning to water and I fought back the tears. I went to the front of the class and meekly did whatever I was supposed to and then walked back, my head down. I felt humiliated and sick to my stomach and I didn't think Mrs. Sinclair liked me any more. I actually remember going home for the next few nights and having trouble sleeping because of what happened and how Mrs. Sinclair had jumped on me. So in school I tried extra hard to be good and win her over, and of course, all the big problems were just built up in my mind and she hadn't given it a seconds thought. She was her nice self again and I didn't give her any trouble the rest of the year. I think I liked her even more after that incident and I remember liking her for the whole year. It was a real childhood crush.

#2

Growing up, my mother was the most important person in my life. I didn't think much about it at the time, but she did everything for me. She made me breakfast, she always had my clothes clean and laid out for me, she took naps with me in the afternoon, and she took care of me when I got sick. She was also always there to give me a hug or a good night kiss. When I had a problem, it was mom I always went to. One time I got in trouble with another kid in the neighborhood. She had a new doll and was showing it off to us kids, so I took it to look at it, and when she wasn't looking, I buried it in the dirt on the lot we were playing in. I just did it as a joke, but when I went back to dig it up, I couldn't find it. She was furious and I was in big trouble, so I ran home. Mom came back to the lot with me with a shovel and dug around until she uncovered the doll, and we returned it to her. That's the kind of mom she was. And I don't ever remember her getting mad at me, even when I did something like that. She was my hero, and as long as she was around, I always felt safe and loved. Every kid should grow up with a mom like mine.

#3

One person that comes to mind almost immediately was my dad's friend Bow Wow, who had an unpronounceable Polish name. He was a real character, a bigger-than-life type of guy who would bound into your life and then bound out again. He had all of this energy and enthusiasm and you couldn't help but like him. He was far from perfect, however, and he'd have these big dreams and launch into something but seldom finish anything. He was also someone who was full of surprises and you'd never know what to expect from him next. He was actually famous in his own way, or at least glommed onto some well-known people, but he was also a bit of a loser. It was that huge gap between what he projected and who he really was that was both fascinating and disturbing. I really never knew who the real Bow Wow was.

Prewriting Activity 2.2

Select a person to write about from your free writing or a different person that has
come to mind. Select someone that you would like to write about, that you have clear
memories of, and that has been influential in your life.

Clustering

Clustering, aka "branching" or "mapping," is a structured prewriting technique that
helps you generate ideas for a particular topic and consider how those ideas are
related. Beginning with a central topic, in this case the person you are writing about,
you write a down a few general things that come to mind about this person - e.g.
 personality traits, characteristics, abilities, certain memories - and circle or draw a
square around each idea. These initial ideas may trigger more specific thoughts
related to each main idea. As you write down these thoughts, you create a clustering
diagram, drawing lines to connect related ideas:

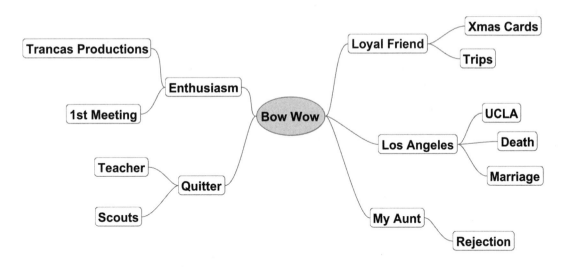

Notice that the writer began with five central ideas related to Bow Wow - loyal friend,
my aunt, Los Angeles, quitter, and enthusiasm - and then added more specific
thoughts for each central idea that would help develop it.

From your own clustering diagram you may generate some main ideas for your
paper and some supporting ideas, examples, and details to develop your paragraphs.
While clustering may not provide you with everything you eventually include in a
paper, it will help you generate ideas and consider how you may organize and develop
them.

Prewriting Activity 2.3

To generate ideas for your upcoming paper, create a clustering diagram for the person you are writing your paper on.

Sample clustering diagram:

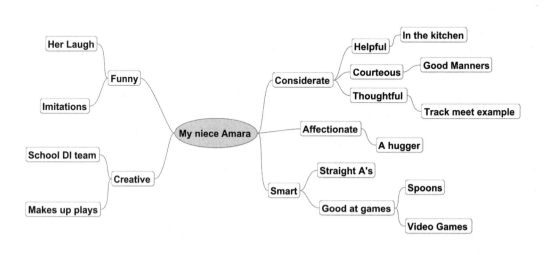

First Drafts

Now that you have selected a person to write on and done some free writing on your subject, you are ready to write the first draft of your paper. One of your challenges is to bring this person to life for readers, to make him or her distinct from anyone else. One way to do this is to provide examples from life that best characterize your subject, which is a focus for this paper.

Providing Examples

As you write your first draft, you will include qualities that your subject possesses and the relationship that you have with him or her. In both cases, the best way to help distinguish this person from others is to provide examples from life that set him or her apart. Providing examples helps to personalize your paper, creates interest for readers, and presents the clearest picture of your subject and your relationship with him or her.

   For example, it is not uncommon for a student to write, "My grandma has always been there for me whenever I needed help." Of course, this statement could be written about many people and doesn't distinguish one grandma from others. By itself, the statement doesn't mean a lot to readers.

   However, if this statement were followed by a specific example from life, we would understand a great deal more about the person and her relationship with the writer. For example, consider the following two paragraphs that begin in the same manner.

> My best friend Sylvia has always been there for me when I needed help. Once I got pretty drunk at a party, it was very late, and I was going to drive my car home. Sylvia said, "There's no way you're going to drive home like that. Give me your keys." Like drunk people often do, I said something like, "I'm fine. I can drive. There's no problem," but she wouldn't listen. She took my keys, got me in the passenger side, and drove me home. Being drunk, I just stumbled into the house and said goodby, not even wondering how she was going to get home. As it turned   out, she walked home, about six blocks, at 2:00 a.m. in the morning. That's the amazing kind of friend that Sylvia was.

> My best friend Wyndell has always been there for me when I needed help. I was always the little guy with a chip on his shoulder. I decided when I was pretty young that I didn't like getting picked on because I was little. I was little, but I was tough, so I wouldn't take any bull off anyone. Luckily, my buddy Wyndell was usually around, and he wasn't a fighter, but he was a peacemaker. More than once I took on more than I could handle, standing up to a guy who was twice my size, and Wyndell, who was a big guy himself, would step in before any punches were thrown. He'd say something like,

"Come on guys, let's go throw the football," or he'd laugh and say, "Come on. I'll fight both of you with my eyes closed." Usually guys like to find a way out of a fight without losing face, and Wyndell had a knack of stopping a fight without putting anyone down. Of course, I was the one he was doing it for, and he kept me out of a lot of fights until I got older and didn't have to prove myself to anyone.

As you can see, the two very different examples in the paragraphs are what bring meaning to the first sentence in each paragraph. They bring people to life, create interest for readers, show the relationships between subjects and writers, and reveal the unique characteristics of people that make us all different.

Guidelines for Using Examples

The following guidelines will help you use examples effectively in your writing.

1.   Provide examples to show a particular quality that a person possesses.

    Example:

    Mr. Fritz had more energy than any teacher I'd ever had. It seemed like he bounced into class rather than walked. His whole face would just light up with enthusiasm and he'd say something like, "This history stuff is great, isn't it?" When he lectured, he'd be all over the front of the classroom, and you couldn't take your eyes off of him. Then all of a sudden he'd be talking from the back of the room, and everyone's head was turned. He was like a showman as much as a teacher, and he'd go non-stop for the entire period. At the end of the class he'd say something like, "Now that was fun! See you tomorrow, historians!" You couldn't walk out of Fritz' class without a smile on your face.

2.   Provide an example or examples to show the relationship between you and the subject.

    Example:

    My father had a way of making me feel very small. When he'd get mad at me, he'd just ignore me. Our family went on one trip and dad got mad at me for some reason. He didn't get mad or yell, he just quit paying me any attention. He put all of his attention for the next days on my sister, and it was like I didn't even exist. He let her sit up front with him, help pick out the motels we stayed in and the restaurants we ate in, and he put her in charge of the travel map. I felt like the lowliest person on earth, and I hated that trip. I hated my dad too, but I also craved the attention from him that I didn't get.

3.   Whenever you write a general statement about your subject or your relationship with him or her, provide an example to show readers exactly what you mean.

Examples:

My brother is one of the strongest people I know. (Provide examples showing his strength.)

Mrs. Hatcher took every opportunity she had to put me down. (Provide an example of one such opportunity.)

Wilson never met a stranger. (Provide an example or examples of how he acted around people he didn't know.)

My mom was one of the most patient people ever. (Provide an example or examples of her patience.)

Clarice would help any stranger who was in need. (Provide an example of one such situation.)

Drafting Activity 2.4

For practice and to develop some potential material for your draft, provide an example for one of the qualities or characteristics of your subject that you may include in your paper. Write a sentence that reveals the particular quality, and then provide an example or examples to develop the paragraph.

Sample paragraph with examples

When I was with Rupert, there was always the danger of getting into trouble because he was a little crazy. One night we were just driving around and there were all these orange safety cones along one side of the road to keep people off the unpaved shoulder. Rupert thought it would be fun to see how many cones he could knock down, and that's what he did. Another time when I was driving, he stuck his rear out the side window and started mooning other cars. We were in a crowded parking lot one night where cars were packed together tightly, so he decided to get to our car by walking on the tops of the other cars, never touching the ground. There is no doubt that alcohol fueled Rupert's crazy antics, and it's amazing that he never got caught.

Drafting Activity 2.5

Write the first draft of your paper keeping the following guidelines in mind.

Drafting Guidelines

1. Write with the purpose of helping readers get to know this person like you do. Include things that typify the kind of person he or she is, and make use of your prewriting materials.

2. As you write, include your relationship with the person so that readers can understand your feelings towards him or her.

3. Include examples from life throughout your draft to show readers what the person is like, to create interest, and to reveal your relationship with him or her.

4. As you write, change paragraphs as you move to something new your draft: a new quality or characteristic of the person, a new example, a different aspect of your relationship.

5. Conclude the draft by revealing the influence the person has had on your life.

6. As mentioned earlier, writing is a recursive activity where writers continually reread sentences to help them decide what to write next. Reread what you have written regularly to keep the writing momentum going and figure out the best way to proceed.

7. Keep your readers for this paper in mind as you write: your classmates and instructor.

8. Title the draft in a simple manner that tells what the paper is about.

Sample First Draft

Bow Wow

Dad's new friend Bow Wow bounded into the house like a big dog and shook my hand until it almost fell off. Dad introduced me as his son Freddie and Bow Wow said, "Freddie T.! You look like a football player to me. You're gonna play in college someday!" I was only eight years old at the time.

Dad had met Bow Wow, whose real name was Wojahovich Wachowski, which no one could every pronounce, playing volleyball at the YMCA. Bow Wow was new to our small town and dad befriended him. With his unbridled enthusiasm, Bow Wow said he was going to start up the biggest boy scout troop in the state, and he showed me his scout master badges. I wasn't much of a joiner, but it was hard not to get caught in Bow Wow's enthusiasm, so I became a Boy Scout.

The one thing I remember from my scouting was the time Bow Wow planned a scouting campout for his eight scout members, a few hundred short of the biggest scout troop he had planned to muster. Driving at night in a rented van, we never did find the camping grounds and ended up staying the night in a Motel Six. Upbeat as always, Bow Wow convinced us this was even better than camping and led us all down to the swimming pool and got us up for the free continental breakfast the next morning. I only discovered later that Bow Wow had little money and had had my dad wire him some cash to pay for the motel. Bow Wow's scouting troop lasted about three months.

Bow Wow was a college graduate and as vice-principal of an elementary school, dad was responsible for hiring teachers. They were badly in need of teachers for the fall, and dad hired Bow Wow on a "provisional" credential, with Bow Wow promising to complete the course work to get a regular credential by the next year. True to form, Bow Wow never enrolled in a class.

Bow Wow launched into his teaching role like he did everything else, with great enthusiasm and a genuine love for kids. As far as dad knew, he was doing well with his class and the students really seemed to like him. Staying power, however, was not one of Bow Wow's greatest attributes, and he only lasted one semester. He begged off with some story of a sick sister that he had to take care of in Southern California, so sadly, he had to leave Decatur.

Before he left, however, he tried to marry my aunt. Aunt Kay worked at a bank where Bow Wow had a small account, and he asked her for a date. Pretty soon he was taking her out regularly and buying her presents, driving her around in a fancy car that he had rented. After a two-week whirlwind romance, Bow Wow asked Aunt Kay to marry him. Caught up in Bow Wow's boundless enthusiasm and laser-like attention, she was seriously considering it until my dad interjected himself and said, "Over my dead body!" So Aunt Kay rejected him and Bow Wow was out of town the next day.

Bow Wow sent us Christmas cards for a couple years, never with a return address and always with additional postage to be paid - Bow Wow's idea of a joke I suppose - and then out of the blue he sent us a letter. He was in Hollywood, he had married a celebrity journalist, lived in Beverly Hills, and started a film company called Trancas Productions, which was going to specialize in horror films. He invited us out to Hollywood to see the sights. Dad thought this was some kind of a joke, so he wrote to Bow Wow asking for specifics: an address where he lived and a date we could come out. To dad's dismay, Bow Wow responded.

Everything was true. Bow Wow was the fourth, and not last, husband of the celebrity journalist, and they lived in a big, fancy house in Beverly Hills. Actually, Bow Wow was mainly relegated to a smaller back house where he worked and had his bed, so we never got to go inside the mansion. He took us to his Trancas Productions site, which was a big, practically empty warehouse he had leased with seed money from his wife, and true to form, he said he was going to get Hollywood's greatest actors and make the greatest horror films true to the "vintage" genre of the old Dracula and Frankenstein movies. He had finally found his calling. We wished him luck and thanked him for the tour.

The celebrity journalist divorced Bow Wow after about a year, and later in a published autobiography gave him exactly one sentence, referring to him as that "crazy Pole that I wasted a year of my life with." If Trancas Productions ever made a movie, it never made it to the big screen, and I could never find anything online about a "Trancas Productions" existing. Same old Bow Wow.

We kept getting the Christmas cards for years, never with a return address and always short of postage. Then one day I was watching an Illinois-UCLA football game and saw a heavy-set guy prowling the UCLA sidelines with a big UCLA sweatshirt on. I called dad over and said, "Doesn't that look like Bow Wow to you?" Sure enough it was, a little older and heavier but with that same exuberance, slapping players on the back and acting like he was one of the guys. Bow Wow had reinvented himself again.

Dad did some research and found out through the UCLA athletic publicity department that Bow Wow was like an unofficial mascot for the team. At first he had hung around the practice field and then began attending every practice and getting to know all the players. The team basically "adopted" Bow Wow and gave him a spot on the sidelines. Dad sent a letter to Bow Wow through the UCLA football department, and to our dismay, we got a return letter and an invitation to stand on the sidelines with him at a game. Soon we received two sidelines passes from the football department, and we were off to California once more.

Bow Wow greeted us the day of the game, as always, like his two best friends. He took us to the before-game training meal, where I got to meet a few of the players. We spent a great afternoon on the sidelines, UCLA won, and Bow Wow was in a splendid mood. After the game, however, he said he had to do something across town, so we took our leave, learning nothing more of Bow Wow's mysterious life. But it had been a great day for dad and me.

A few years later, the last thing we learned about Bow Wow was his death. From the UCLA publicist's office, we were sent a newspaper clipping about the death of one Wojahovich Wachowski, a longtime friend of UCLA and its football program. He had been found dead in a small rented house, with a huge mound of junk piled in his front yard and his house scattered everywhere with UCLA memorabilia. The article said that the UCLA football program and players mourned his loss and will miss him greatly.

Bow Wow's ending was certainly bizarre but not really that surprising to me or my dad. Bow Wow never stuck to anything in his life, so for him to end up in a little rented house with a junk pile for a front yard was perhaps fitting. His last years, attending UCLA football practices and roaming the sidelines of every game, were probably his happiest. He always wanted to do great things, and being associated with UCLA and football was probably the closest he came, even as an unofficial mascot. He had finally found his calling.

Revision

Now that you have completed your first draft, set it aside for a time before reading it to see what might be improved. After distancing yourself from your paper, you can read it more objectively and identify more clearly what you have done well and what you might do better.

Revising drafts is a part of the writing process shared by all writers. After you get your ideas on paper, you can begin to fine tune your sentence wording, add details or examples where they will strengthen the paper, retool your paragraphing, make changes that will add to the readers' interest or understanding and, if necessary, reorganize parts of the paper. The purpose of revision is to improve your paper, and you will usually find ways to do it.

In each "Revision" section, you review the elements that were covered in previous units and are introduced to new elements that help writers revise their drafts effectively. In this section, you continue to work on improving sentence wording, adding details, and improving your paragraphing, and you are introduced to a new writing feature: transitional wording.

Transitional Wording

In the most effective writing, sentences and paragraphs are tied together in ways that show the relationship among the different parts of the paper and that connect those parts to the whole. One of the most effective ways to show the relationships among sentences and paragraphs is through *transitional wording*: words and phrases that tie a writer's thoughts together and show how they are related.

Transitions can serve several functions in a paper: to show how events are related in time, how different ideas are related to one another, how one paragraph relates to another, how one sentence relates to another, or how a process moves from step to step. The use of simple, well-placed transitions such as *next, in addition, second,* or *finally* provide signposts that guide readers through a paper, indicating what comes next and its relation to what has come before.

Commonly Used Transitions

The following transitions include a variety of words and phrases writers use to connect their ideas.

1. Transitions that show the order in which ideas are presented, the steps in a process, or the events in a sequence: *first, second, next, then, now, finally.*

2. Transitions that add one idea to another: *furthermore, in addition, also, moreover, additionally, on top of that, beyond that, besides that.*

3. Transitions that introduce an example: *for instance for example, such as.*

4. Transitions that indicate a conclusion: *finally, lastly, as you can see, in conclusion, in summary.*

5. Transitions that show a contrast between ideas or events: *however, on the other hand, nevertheless, nonetheless, on the contrary, despite, in spite of, whereas.*

6. Transitions that show a cause-effect relationship - one thing occurring as the result of another: *therefore, consequently, thus, as a result, to that end, because of that.*

7. Transitions that emphasize a particular point or idea: *in fact, actually, of course, in reality, needless to say.*

8. Of the transitions, you may be least familiar with the following:

    moreover: even more importantly (similar to beyond that or on top of that)

    Example: Jules is an excellent student; *moreover*, he is a wonderful human being.

    consequently: because of that (similar to therefore or thus)

    Example: There was a power outage in the neighborhood; *consequently*, all houses were dark inside.

    nevertheless: similar to in spite of, despite that, or nonetheless

    Example: It was raining hard all morning; *nevertheless*, we still went to the soccer game.

    as you can see: based on what has been written; judging from what has come before.

    Example: Yesterday it was 95 degrees with clear skies. Today it is only 72 degrees with high winds and clouds. *As you can see*, the weather this time of year is quite variable.

9. Notice that when a transition ties two sentences together, it is preceded by a semi-colon (;), a punctuation mark which unites two related sentences. Here are some examples:

The last subway train ran a half hour ago; *therefore*, we'll have to catch a bus downtown.

Ike had problems on his last calculus exam; *however*, he's still doing well in the class.

Lucinda has had a head cold for a month; *despite that*, she hasn't missed a day of work.

The following paragraphs contain a number of transitions in italics. Notice how they tie ideas within and between paragraphs together and aid the reader's understanding of the writer's living situation.

Apartment Woes

The apartment that my roommate and I rented didn't turn out to be a good deal. *First*, the walls are so thin that we hear the neighbors on both sides and above us, making it hard to study at night. *Second*, the water pressure is really low, so it takes forever to wash and rinse our hair. *On top of that*, in the morning we lose our hot water in a matter of minutes, so the second person to shower often gets cold water. We've gone to showering at night when there is less demand on the water.

Then there is the problem with the landlord. He is supposed to fix anything that goes wrong in the apartment. *However*, when we need him, he can seldom be found. When we finally get a hold of him and tell him about the problem, he takes forever to get around to it. *As a consequence*, we've had a leaky kitchen faucet for weeks.

On the other hand, the apartment is in walking distance to school, and the rent is very reasonable. *Therefore*, we'll stick it out at least for this year. Apartments near the school aren't easy to get into, so we basically took the best one we could get. *Moreover*, anything is better than living in the dorms for a second year. Having our own apartment and the freedom that goes with it is a big improvement despite the problems.

Revision Activity 2.6

Fill in the blanks with appropriate transitional words or phrases from the list to tie the sentences and paragraphs of the following paper together.

Example: Nothing we tried was ridding the apartment of cockroaches; <u>therefore</u>, we had a professional exterminator come out and do the job.

The New Arena

The seating in the new on-campus arena is terrible. The 18,000 seat arena has been publicized as one of the best on the East Coast, a great place to watch a college basketball game or a concert. _____, the reality does not live up to the hype.

_____, the seats are narrower than you'd expect. You are crammed into a seat, and if you have large people sitting on either side, you feel like they are spilling over into your seat. It is not comfortable sitting in an undersized seat, and everyone complains about it.

_____, the leg space between rows of seats is not adequate. If you are relatively tall, you have to scrunch up your knees to put your feet on the floor. Crossing your legs is almost impossible since you'll hit the person in front of you or your crossed leg will end up in the person's space beside you. _____, everyone sits like little toy soldiers, and it gets very uncomfortable. _____, every time someone walks in front of you, you have to stand up to let them by. People are standing up and sitting down all night long as others in their row arrive late, go for food, or to the bathroom. _____, your view of the basketball game or other event is blocked regularly by people standing to let others by.

_____, the arena is an uncomfortable place to sit for two or three hours. _____, there is no solving the problem since all of the concrete rows would have to be knocked out and redone. The tight seating is the result of one thing only: greed. The college wanted to cram as many seats as possible into the available space to sell the most tickets for the greatest revenue. They did this at the expense of every student or other person attending a game or concert, and _____, a lot of people are staying away. They haven't filled the arena yet, but if they had put 15,000 comfortable seats into the arena instead of 18,000 uncomfortable ones, they would fill it regularly.

Revision Activity 2.7

The following draft contains no transitional wording. Insert transitions in places that will tie sentences and paragraphs together effectively.

Example:

My computer takes forever to start working. It's relatively new, but it still takes up to ten minutes before I can get online, open my e-mail, or get into Word Perfect. I have to turn it on and then go do something else for ten or fifteen minutes before I can get onto it.

Once it starts working, it's great. I can move from one program to the next in no time, and it's the fastest computer I've owned. There must be computers that don't take forever to warm up like mine. Since it's only a year old, I'll be keeping it for quite a while, and I don't see any solution to the problem. The computer works fine, but it's slow to get going. I'll just have to live with it.

Revised (transitions in italics):

My computer takes forever to start working. It's relatively new, but it still takes up to ten minutes before I can get online, open my e-mail, or get into Word Perfect. *Consequently*, I have to turn it on and then go do something else for ten or fifteen minutes before I can get onto it.

On the other hand, once it starts working, it's great. I can move from one program to the next in no time, and it's the fastest computer I've owned. *However*, there must be computers that don't take forever to warm up like mine. Since it's only a year old, I'll be keeping it for quite a while, and I don't see any solution to the problem. The computer works fine, but it's slow to get going. *Despite* the problem, I'll just have to live with it.

Song Writer

I enjoy writing songs. I have been doing it on and off for the past three years and have written a couple dozen songs, mostly heard only by myself and my cat. I enjoy the process when I'm in the mood, and it's my one creative outlet.

When I was around ten, my dad taught me a few chords on our old piano that form the basis for most pop songs. Once I learned the chords, I discovered that with some practice and trial and error, I could play most of my favorite songs. I added new chords as I worked on more challenging melodies, and I progressed to applying the chords to melodies of my own creation.

When I'm in the mood, usually after listening to some good music, I'll go to the piano and experiment with the first notes of a melody that bang around in my head. Sometimes those first few notes lead nowhere, and other times I'm able to build on them and create a melody that I can use for a song. Composing the melody is the fun part. Writing the lyrics for the song is tough. I'm not a great lyricist, and I struggle to find an idea for the song, the best rhyming words to help tell the story, and a catchy, repeatable refrain line that most songs are anchored by. Often the words sound fake or corny, so I constantly revise for the song to have a real emotional feel. Writing lyrics is draining for me. When I finish there's a definite sense of accomplishment although I'm never completely satisfied.

I consider myself only a modest talent when it comes to song writing, and I have no illusions that I'll be the next Jewel or Taylor Swift. Like most songwriters, I dream about writing that one magical song that the world falls in love with, but the chances are one in a million. I remain content to write mainly for myself and my cat, who often sits on the piano bench when I compose. For the songs I write, a silent critic is probably the best kind.

Revision Guidelines

The following guidelines will help you revise your draft effectively.

1. Reread your draft to consider the *perspective* you have provided readers about the

person you are writing about. Does the draft provide the clearest, most accurate portrayal of the person, that particular essence that you wish to convey to readers? What might you add or change to ensure that readers view your subject in the way that you want them to?

2. Read your draft to see what you might add to make it clearer or more interesting for readers. Are there examples you can add to help show readers the qualities and characteristics that your subject possesses or that help them see the relationship between the person and yourself? Are there details you can add that will help readers see, hear, and feel what you want them to?

3. Reread each sentence to see if its wording can be improved. Delete words and phrases that are unnecessary or repetitive, replace questionable words with more appropriate ones, reword sentences to eliminate awkward phrasing, and make vaguely worded sentences clearer. Your goal is to make every sentence as smooth, clear, and concise as you can.

4. Review your paragraphing to see whether you change paragraphs when you move to something new in your paper: a different quality of your subject, a new example, or a new aspect of your relationship. In addition, if you have any overly long paragraphs, divide them into two, and if you strong two or three short paragraphs together, combine them.

5. Read your draft to see whether you have used transitional wording to tie sentences and paragraphs together. Insert appropriate transitions in places where they would help readers understand the relationship between your thoughts and between different paragraphs.

6. Read your conclusion to make sure readers understand the impact that this person has on your life, and make any changes that would strengthen your conclusion or help readers understand the impact.

Revision Review

Before revising your draft, complete the next three review activities to practice making revisions following the guidelines presented.

Revision Activity 2.8

With a partner, read the following paragraphs and make note of places in the draft where an example or detail could be added to make the draft clearer, more interesting, or more informative.

My Niece

I love my little niece, but she is developing some habits that don't endear her to other children or adults who don't know her well. One of those habits is wanting to be in control. No matter who she is with, she is the one who has to decide what they are going to do.

She always has lots of ideas and quickly throws them out, so she often gets her way. However, when she is around older children or children her age who are also strong willed, there can be problems. As a result, some children aren't too thrilled to play with her.

Another bad habit she has developed is bragging, and she finds plenty to brag about. This can really bother other children, and they often react to her bragging negatively. Her mother is aware of the problem and working with her on it.

My niece is a pretty, affectionate child with good manners. She also has a great sense of humor. Hopefully she will grow out of her bad habits, or be broken of them, so that her good qualities will shine through.

Revision Activity 2.9

Revise the following paragraph to improve sentence wording. Reword any sentence that is overly long, repetitive, awkward, vague, or has some questionable word choices.

Examples:

The runner that is running in the outside lane has the advantage until the turn, when he loses that advantage.

Revised: The runner ~~that is running~~ in the outside lane has the advantage until the turn~~, when he loses that advantage~~.

Theresa didn't make out an application for the job as a student assistant to the registrar until it was too late and the application deadline had passed.

Revised: Theresa ~~didn't make out an application~~ *failed to apply* for the job ~~as a~~ *of* student assistant to the registrar ~~until it was too late and the application~~ *before* the deadline. ~~had passed.~~

The last two weeks of the summer were the hottest on record in the valley that were ever recorded in history. You could step outside in the morning to get the morning paper and be covered with beads of perspiration in a matter of a minute or so. We had fourteen days in a row of temperatures that were over 100 degrees. To make matters worse, there were power shortages in the area that were brought on by the heavy usage of air conditioning units, and many people were without air conditioning for part of the time. At least six deaths in the valley were caused by or at least their cause was devoted to heat prostration caused by lack of air conditioning. All six were senior citizens. In addition, the air was saturated with humidity at a record rate, and so what was actually 100 degrees felt more like 110 with the combination of heat and humidity. It was the most miserable two weeks of weather I had ever engaged in.

Revision Activity 2.10

Paragraph the following first draft by marking off the beginning of each new paragraph. Change paragraphs when the writer moves to something new in the draft.

A Scary Uncle

I didn't see my Uncle Prine very often since he lived half way across the country from us. But the few times that I did see him as a young boy left a lasting impression on me. My family lived in Arizona and Uncle Prine lived in Tennessee. We drove cross country two or three times during my childhood to visit my dad's relatives in Tennessee. We saw lots of aunts and uncles and cousins, but no one stood out quite like Uncle Prine. When dad would say, "We're going to Uncle Prine and Aunt Lucy's house for a couple nights, the hairs would stand up on the back of my neck. All you had to do was look at Uncle Prine to tell that this was one crazy man. He had these wild looking blue eyes that could stare right through you, and he kept them partially hooded by eyelids that made him look like a snake ready to attack. He had a huge bulb for a nose and his nose and entire face were an angry red color all the time. His fat lips always had a smirk on them like a joke was coming and it was going to be on you. The only place I ever remember seeing Uncle Prine was sitting in a rocker on his front porch. That way he could patrol all the goings and comings from the house. And every time my sister and I would go outside to play or come back inside, I knew Uncle Prine would have something to say, his eyes lit up like firecrackers. "Boy," he'd say, "I wouldn't be goin to the back yard to play today." Being only six years old, I'd always take the bait. "Why not, Uncle Prine?" I'd ask. "Because there's alligators back there this morning, and they'd bite your feet off." I'd just stand there on the porch, half petrified, and then he'd break into this loud, awful cackle and say, "Got you good boy. You turned white as a sheet." And he'd cackle some more. Then he'd say, "Get out to that back yard. Any dummy knows there ain't no alligators in town." And I'd slink down the steps, burned again. You'd think I wouldn't have fallen for Uncle Prine's scare tactics after a while, but you'd have to see Uncle Prine and hear him to understand why I did. One time I was going into the house and there was Uncle Prine as usual sitting in his chair, just waiting for his prey. As I walked up the steps he literally leaped out of his chair, astonishingly fast for an old man, and blocked the door. "Don't go in there Boy!" he shouted. "Don't go in there!" He was shaking all over and looked like he had seen ten ghosts. "What's wrong, Uncle Prine?" I asked. "The Bogeyman's in there, and if you go in, he's going to cut out your heart and eat it. That's why I'm out here." Well, that was too much for me, and I started crying. You'd think my crying would have softened him up, but not Uncle Prine. Here came that mad cackle again, and the more I cried, the louder he cackled. "Got you good that time boy. You Western boys still believe in the Bogeyman? There ain't no Bogeyman, boy. Only your Aunt Lucy in there, and she ain't no Bogeyman." Well, Uncle Prine never changed, but I did. I got older, and when I was nine, we went back again. It was the same old Uncle Prine on the porch, but I was ready for him this time, or so I thought. "How you doin', boy?" he asked me, that smirk on his mouth and gleam in his eye. "I'm doin good, Uncle Prine, I'm doin real good," I said. "That's good Boy, that's real good," he said. Things were quiet for a day or so, and I could tell he was sizing me up, like he was circling his prey to figure out the best way to attack. This time though I would be ready and waiting. I went outside the next morning and Uncle Prine said, "Boy, I wouldn't go into the back yard this morning. We got snakes back there." I thought, is that the best you can do Uncle Prine? Can't you come up with anything scarier than that? "Sure," I said to my uncle with a smile. "I'll be real careful," and went around to the back where the swings and slide were. I began swinging when all of a sudden I saw something slithering on the ground in the grass area beside the swings. I let out a scream, jumped off the swing, and ran for my life. Uncle Prine had snuck around back for a look at the fun, and I could hear his cackling as I ran for safety. Turns out he had turned a couple of harmless garter snakes loose near the swings that morning and just waited for me to call his bluff. I couldn't believe he'd go to all that trouble just to scare me, but Uncle Prine was one demented man, and when he died a couple of years later, I can't say that I was terribly sad.

Revision Activity 2.11

Revise your first draft by applying the revision guidelines presented. Then exchange drafts with a classmate, or a small group of classmates, read each other's paper, and make any suggestions that you feel will improve the paper. Then write your second draft, incorporating all of the changes that you made.

Sample Draft Revisions

Bow Wow

My dad's new friend Bow Wow bounded into the house like a big dog and shook my hand until it almost fell off. Dad introduced me as his son Freddie and Bow Wow said, "Freddie T.! You look like a football player to me. You're gonna play in college someday!" I was only eight years old at the time.

Dad had met Bow Wow, ~~whose real name was~~ **with the unpronounceable real name of** Wojahovich Wachowski, ~~which no one could every pronounce,~~ playing volleyball at the YMCA. Bow Wow was new to ~~our~~ town and dad befriended him. **Bow Wow was a big guy with a ruddy face, thick black eyebrows, and a buzz cut.** With his unbridled enthusiasm, Bow Wow ~~said~~ **told us** he was going to start up the biggest boy scout troop in the state, and he showed me his scout master badges. I wasn't much of a joiner, but it was hard not to get caught in ~~Bow Wow's~~ **the** enthusiasm, so I became a Boy Scout.

~~The one thing~~ **What** I remember from my scouting **days** was the time Bow Wow planned a ~~scouting campout~~ **camping trip** for his eight scout members, a few hundred short of the biggest scout troop he had planned to muster. Driving at night in a rented van, we never did find the camping grounds and ended up staying ~~the night in~~ **at** a Motel Six. Upbeat as always, Bow Wow convinced us this was even better than camping, ~~and~~ led us ~~all~~ down to the swimming pool **for a dip**, and got us up for the free continental breakfast the next morning. I only ~~discovered~~ **learned** later that Bow Wow had little money and had ~~had~~ **to call** my dad **to** wire him some cash to pay for the motel. Bow Wow's scouting troop lasted about three months.

Bow Wow was a college graduate and as vice-principal of a **small** elementary school, dad was responsible for hiring teachers. ~~They were~~ **The school was** badly in need of teachers for the fall, and dad hired Bow Wow on a "provisional" credential, with Bow Wow promising to complete the course work ~~to get~~ **for** a regular credential by the next **school** year. ~~True to form, Bow Wow~~ **He** never enrolled in a class.

Bow Wow launched ~~into~~ his teaching ~~role~~ **career** like he did everything else~~,~~ **:** with great ~~enthusiasm~~ **exuberance** and a genuine love for kids. As far as dad knew, he was doing well with his class and the students really seemed to like him. Staying power, however, was not one of Bow Wow's greatest attributes, and he only lasted one semester. He begged off with some story of a sick sister that he had to take care of in Southern California, so sadly, he had to leave Decatur.

Before he left, however, he tried to marry my aunt. Aunt Kay worked at a bank where Bow Wow had a small account, and he asked her for a date. Pretty soon he was taking her out regularly, ~~and~~ buying her presents, **and** driving her around in a fancy **rental** car ~~that he had rented~~. After a two-week whirlwind romance, Bow Wow asked Aunt Kay to marry him. Caught up in Bow Wow's ~~boundless~~ enthusiasm and laser-like attention, she was seriously considering it until my dad interjected himself and said, "Over my dead body!" So Aunt Kay rejected him and Bow Wow was out of town the next day.

Bow Wow sent us Christmas cards ~~for a~~ **the next** couple years, never with a return address and always with additional postage to be paid - Bow Wow's idea of a joke. ~~I suppose - and~~ **Then** out of the blue **one day** he sent us a letter. He was in Hollywood, he had married a celebrity journalist, lived in Beverly Hills, and started a film company called Trancas Productions, which was going to specialize in horror films. He invited us out to Hollywood to see the sights. Dad ~~thought this was some kind of~~ **knew this had to be** a joke, so he **called Bow Wow's bluff,** ~~wrote to Bow Wow~~ **writing and** asking for specifics: an address where he lived and a date we could come out. To dad's ~~dismay~~ **surprise**, Bow Wow responded.

Everything was true. Bow Wow was the fourth, and not last, husband of the celebrity journalist, and they lived in a big~~, fancy~~ house in Beverly Hills. Actually, Bow Wow was ~~mainly~~ relegated to a smaller back house where he worked ~~and had his bed~~, so we never got to go inside the mansion. He took us to his Trancas Productions site, which was a big, ~~practically~~ **nearly** empty warehouse he had leased with seed money from his wife, and ~~true to form,~~ he said he was going to get Hollywood's greatest actors and make the greatest horror films ~~true to the "vintage" genre of~~ like the Dracula and Frankenstein movies **of old.** He had finally found his calling. We wished him luck, ~~and~~ thanked him for the tour, **and wondered on our flight home how long the latest incarnation of Bow Wow would last.**

The celebrity journalist divorced Bow Wow after about a year, and later in a published autobiography gave him exactly one sentence, referring to him as that "crazy Pole that I wasted a year of my life with." If Trancas Productions ever made a movie, it never made it to the big screen, and I could never find anything online about a "Trancas Productions" **ever** existing. Same old Bow Wow.

We kept getting ~~the~~ Christmas cards for years, never with a return address and always short of postage. Then one day I was watching an Illinois-UCLA football game and saw a heavy-set guy prowling the ~~UCLA~~ sidelines with a big UCLA sweatshirt on. I called dad over and said, "Doesn't that look like Bow Wow to you?" Sure enough it was, a little older and heavier but with that same exuberance, slapping players on the back and acting like he was one of the ~~guys~~. **coaches.** Bow Wow had reinvented himself again.

Dad did some research and found out through the UCLA athletic ~~publicity~~ department that Bow Wow was ~~like~~ an unofficial mascot for the team. At first he had hung around the practice field, ~~and then began~~ attending every practice and getting to know ~~all~~ the players. **Eventually** the team ~~basically~~ "adopted" Bow Wow and gave him a ~~spot~~ **place** on the sidelines. Dad sent a letter to Bow Wow through the UCLA football department, and to our ~~dismay~~ **shock**, we got a return letter and an invitation to stand on the sidelines with him at a game. Soon we received two sidelines passes from the football department, and we were off to California once more.

Bow Wow greeted us the day of the game, as always, like his two best friends. **It was like no time had passed since we last saw him.** He took us to the before-game training meal, where I got to meet a few of the players. We spent a great afternoon on the sidelines, UCLA won, and Bow Wow was in a splendid mood. After the game, however, he said he had to do something across town, so we took our leave, learning nothing more of Bow Wow's ~~mysterious~~ current life. But it had been a great day for dad and me.

A few years later, ~~the last thing~~ we learned **our last thing** about Bow Wow. From the UCLA publicist's office, we ~~were sent~~ **received** a newspaper clipping about the death of one Wojahovich Wachowski, a longtime friend of UCLA and its football program. He had been found dead in a small rented house **in West Los Angeles**, with a huge mound of junk piled in his front yard ~~and his house~~ **and UCLA memorabilia** scattered **throughout the house**. ~~with UCLA memorabilia~~. The article said that the UCLA football program and players mourned his loss and ~~will~~ **would** miss him greatly.

Bow Wow's ending was certainly bizarre but not really that surprising to me or my dad. Bow Wow never stuck to anything in his life, so for him to end up in a little rented house with a junk pile for a front yard was perhaps fitting. His last years attending UCLA football practices and roaming the sidelines of every game were probably his happiest. He always wanted to do great things, and being associated with UCLA and the football program was probably the closest he came. **He was the most interesting character I'll probably ever know, and in his own way, a most loyal friend.**

Editing

Now that you have revised your paper to improve its content, wording, and paragraphing, you are ready to proofread it for errors and make any necessary corrections. The goal of the editing phase is to produce an error-free final draft to share with readers.

While editing your paper for errors is typically the final step in the writing process, it is no less important than the others. No matter how interesting or thought-provoking a paper may be, readers also judge your writing on its correctness. If a paper is filled with spelling, punctuation, or grammatical errors, readers may judge the writing rather harshly since such errors distract from the writer's ideas.

It is not surprising that readers are troubled by writing errors. They are used to reading predominantly error-free writing, whether it be textbooks, newspapers, magazines, novels, or non-fiction books. They are used to focusing on content and not being bothered by run-on sentences or misspelled words. As writers, we owe it to readers to provide them with the best writing we can. We also owe it to ourselves to write correctly to put our ideas in the best possible light.

In each "Editing" section, you review what you learned in the previous unit, are introduced to some new editing considerations, and proofread your draft for errors following the editing guidelines provided.

Sentence Fragments

In the first editing section, you proofread and edited your draft for run-on sentences: two or more sentences run together without a period. A second punctuation problem involves inserting a period before the sentence ends, creating an incomplete sentence called a sentence fragment. While sentence fragments are not as common as run-on sentences, they do create problems for some writers.

The following guidelines will help you avoid sentence fragments and correct those you find.

1. A sentence fragment is an incomplete sentence. It does not express a complete thought or idea, and it leaves readers with an unanswered question. Here are some examples of sentence fragments.

    Because you are such a hard worker. (What will happen?)
    Sitting outside on our new rocking chairs. (Who was sitting?)
    After we finish cleaning out the garage. (What will happen?)
    The woman wearing the green and white running shoes. (What about her?)

2. Most typically, fragments are created by separating one half of a sentence from the other by a period. If you remove the period, you have a complete, correctly punctuated sentence. Here are some examples, with the fragment underlined.

The manager is going to promote you. <u>Because you are such a hard worker.</u>
(The second half is a fragment which belongs with the first sentence.)

Corrected:
The manager is going to promote you because you are such a hard worker.

<u>Before I go to the park and play softball</u>. I am going to get a lot of work done around the apartment.
(The first half is a fragment which belongs with the sentence.)

Corrected:
Before I go to the park and play softball, I am going to get a lot of work done around the apartment.

Alvin really enjoys watching cooking shows. <u>Especially the ones with audience participation.</u>
(The second half is a fragment which makes no sense without the previous sentence.)

Corrected:
Alvin really enjoys watching cooking shows, especially the ones with audience participation.

I enjoy doing many things in the winter. <u>Skating on the frozen pond in the park, going to hockey games, drinking hot chocolate, and warming myself by a fire.</u>
(The list of activities – skating on a frozen pond, going to hockey games, drinking hot chocolate – is not a sentence. It needs to be attached to the sentence before it.)

Corrected:
I enjoy doing many things in the winter such as skating on the frozen pond in the park, going to hockey games, drinking hot chocolate, and warming myself by a fire.

3. To correct a sentence fragment, do one of the following:

    a. Attach the fragment to the sentence it belongs with by deleting the period.

    Example (fragment underlined)

    You wear the most interesting outfits. <u>While I wear the most boring.</u>

    Corrected:
    You wear the most interesting outfits while I wear the most boring.

b. Add words to the fragment to make it a complete sentence.
   Example (fragment underlined)

There's a lot we can do without spending money. <u>For example,
window shop at the mall, hike to the top of Barker Hill, or bike across town to
the pier.</u>

Corrected:
There's a lot we can do without spending money. For example, we can window shop at the mall, hike to the top of Barker Hill, or bike across town to the pier.

Editing Activity 2.13

Eliminate any sentence fragment by either deleting the period that separates the fragment from the sentence it belongs with, or by adding words to the fragment to make it a complete sentence.

Examples

No one should stand around the excavation site. Until the cyclone fence is erected.

Corrected:
No one should stand around the excavation site until the cyclone fence is erected.

Alphonse is a formidable looking man. Tall and muscular, with a thick chest and arms.

Corrected:
Alphonse is a formidable looking man. He is tall and muscular, with a thick chest and arms.

1. The cafeteria food has improved. Since the school privatized the operation.

2. Instead of a school-run cafeteria with your usual food. The cafeteria is now a food court with a number of different vendors selling food.

3. Today you can get practically any kind of food you want. For example, Mexican, Chinese, Japanese, or Italian.

4. The cafeteria also looks much different today. At least a dozen food booths around the walls of the cafeteria, with seating in the middle.

5. The cafeteria is more crowded than ever. Especially between noon and 2:00 p.m.

6. Although I don't eat there very often. I've always enjoyed my food when I've gone.

7. The cafeteria has taken away a lot of lunch business from the fast food restaurants in the area. Because it has a number of fast food choices itself.

8. The purpose of changing the cafeteria was to keep more students on campus for lunch by offering a variety of good food. Which seems to be working out well.

Editing Activity 2.12

Correct any sentence fragments in the following paragraph by deleting a period that separates the fragment from the sentence it belongs with or by adding words to the fragment to form a complete sentence.

Example

The shift key on my computer keyboard keeps sticking. Any time I hit it accidentally. When it is stuck in the down position. I can't type at all. Everything gets highlighted when I want to highlight a single word or sentence. My keyboard is old, and I think I need to replace it.

Corrected

The shift key on my computer keyboard keeps sticking any time I hit it accidentally. When it is stuck in the down position, I can't type at all. Everything gets highlighted when I want to highlight a single word or sentence. My keyboard is old, and I think I need to replace it.

Scheduling Problems

Getting the classes you need in a particular semester is difficult. Especially if are trying to schedule them around your work. If you are working, you may only have certain times you can take classes. For example, before noon, after 2:00 p.m., or just in the evening. The most difficult time to schedule classes is in the morning. Because that is the most popular time. Most students like to finish their classes by noon or early afternoon, so morning classes close fast. Late afternoon classes are the easiest to schedule since many students are working or just don't want to be in class. However, they are sometimes difficult to get into because fewer late afternoon classes are offered. If you can go only in the evening, you are lucky to get into two or, at the most, three classes. Meaning that it will take many semesters to complete your course work. Many working students take many years to complete even two years of college course work. Which also makes college more expensive.

Comma Usage

Using commas correctly is an important part of effective writing. Fortunately, there are some basic punctuation rules that govern the use of commas within sentences. In this section you are introduced to those rules and then apply them to your draft.

The main purpose for using commas is to show readers where to pause within your sentences. These pauses create a reading rhythm that helps readers follow your thoughts most clearly, and they often indicate something new to follow in the sentence. Commas are also inserted in places where their absence could change and misconstrue the meaning of a sentence for readers.

For example, read the following paragraphs, the first containing no commas and the second with commas inserted correctly into sentences.

> When you drive across the campus you run into a number of problems. First there are a number of roads that dead-end into a building or a grass area so you have to turn around. Next there are a number of one-way streets but there is no pattern to them which makes it baffling getting to where you want to go. In fact after trying to get across campus many different ways I still haven't found a way to drive from one side to the other without going out to one of two main roads adjacent to campus. I have finally come to the conclusion which I have no doubt is correct that the university doesn't want you to cross the campus using internal roads but instead they want you to use the outside roads and keep the internal roads free for students seeking parking spaces. I guess that makes sense but it would sure be nice to have at least one internal road that goes all the way across campus.

> When you drive across the campus, you run into a number of problems. First, there are a number of roads that dead-end into a building or a grass area, so you have to turn around. Next, there are a number of one-way streets, but there is no pattern to them, which makes it baffling getting to where you want to go. In fact, after trying to get across campus many different ways, I still haven't found a way to drive across campus without going out to one of two main roads adjacent to the school. I have finally come to the conclusion, which I have no doubt is correct, that the university doesn't want you to cross the campus using internal roads, but instead they want you to use the outside roads and keep the internal roads free for students seeking parking spaces. I guess that makes sense, but it would sure be nice to have at least one internal road that goes all the way across campus.

Notice how each comma in the second paragraph creates a reading pause that prepares you for the next idea in the sentence and makes it easier to follow the writer's thoughts.

Comma Usage Rules

The following general rules will help you use commas effectively in your writing.

1. Use commas to separate three or more items joined by *and* or *or*, or to separate two or more words that *modify* (describe in some manner) the word they precede.

   Examples:

   Post, Kelloggs, and Sunnyside Select all had their bite-sized shredded wheat cereal on sale.
   Your back pack could be in the bedroom closet, in the hall closet, or on the back porch.
   The shortest, thinnest girl on the basketball court was also the fastest.
   Halloween fell on a cold, windy night.

2. Use commas to separate introductory groups of words which lead to the main thought in a sentence.

   Examples:

   If you don't tie the string of the balloon to your niece's wrist, it will fly away from her.
   Trying to study for the test, Angie shut herself up in her bedroom and put on her ear plugs.
   While I was crossing the street at the intersection, a motorcycle turning to the right almost hit me.
   In the middle of the darkest night of the year, Felix walked in his sleep from his room to the next door neighbor's back door.

3. Use commas to separate groups of words at the end of a sentence which follow the main thought, relate to it in some manner, and frequently begin with which or an *ing* or *ed*-ending word.

   Examples:

   The favored horse for the Kentucky Derby wouldn't get in the starting gate, *rearing* up and beating at the gate with its hooves.
   One little boy at the party covered his face with birthday cake frosting, *which* didn't seem to bother anyone.
   Allison finally left the store that was having the big discount sale, *frustrated* by the length of the check-out lines.

4. Use commas to separate the two halves of a *compound sentence* (two sentences

connected by a *coordinate conjunction*) by inserting a comma after the last word before the conjunction (and, but, for, so, yet, or).

Examples:

I'm going to the midnight concert at the campus pavilion, *but* no one else from my dorm wing is going.
The wind blowing off of Lake Erie was extremely cold, *and* we were wearing nothing but shorts and t-shirts.
Retail sales were up for the quarter for most major retail chains, *yet* the stock market continued its descent.

5. Place commas around a group of words beginning with *who, which,* or *whose* that provide information that is not essential for the sentence to make sense (called a non-restrictive *relative clause*). The sentence could stand alone and make sense without the group of words.

    Examples:

    The Empire State Building, *which* was once the tallest building in the world, no longer is among the top five tallest buildings.
    Detective Longtree, *who* works for Scotland Yards in London, has been a detective for over forty years.
    The sound of a dripping faucet, *which* I hear every night in my apartment, can drive a person mad.

    Note: If the group of words beginning with *who, which,* or *whose* provides essential information for the sentence to make sense (called a *restrictive relative clause*), do not insert commas. (Examples: The man *who* works in the library is my next-door neighbor. The book *which* you requested is on order in the book store.)

6. Use commas after introductory transitional words or phrases and before and after "interrupting" words and phrases within a sentence that require a reading pause.

    Examples:

    First, there were no cooking utensils in the cabin. *Second*, there was no silverware.
    In conclusion, I'd like to thank everyone who made today's auction a big success.
    The owner of that red Honda, *by the way*, is a Toyota salesman.
    Most of the damage, *fortunately*, was superficial and didn't harm the house's structure or foundation.

7. Often a sentence will need multiple commas due to situations where more than one comma rule applies.

Examples:

That particular jersey comes in red, white, or black, but the college store,
unfortunately, only has the small size left.
(Commas are used within a series of three or more items, after the last word
before a coordinate conjunction in a compound sentence, and before and after an
"interrupter.")

When I decide whether to enroll in summer school, which might take a week or
two, I'll let you know, but in the meantime, feel free to enroll without me.
(Commas are used after an introductory group of words, before and after a
non-restrictive "which" clause, before a coordinate conjunction in a compound
sentence, and after a second introductory group of words - in the meantime -
beginning the second sentence within the compound sentence.)

8. There are also situations where writers tend to use commas when they aren't
    needed. As a general rule, don't use commas in the following situations.

    a. In the middle of a sentence when the word connecting the two halves of the
        sentence is a *subordinate conjunction* (*because, while, as, if, when, since,
        whenever, unless*).

    Examples:

    You can return the hedge clippers *whenever* you want to.
    I don't want you to come to the tupperware party *because* you feel
    obligated.
    We're not going to attend the concert in the park *if* it's still raining.

    b. Preceding a coordinate conjunction (*and, but, so, for, yet, or*) that connects two
       words or groups of words but not two complete sentences.

    Examples:

    Julio is tired of working year after year for the college's outreach program *and*
    never getting a raise.
    Student assistants at the college looked into getting union representation *and*
    collective bargaining.
    We can carry bottled water *and* sodas into the stadium *but* not beer *or* other
    alcoholic beverages.

Editing Activity 2.13

Insert commas in the following sentences by applying the comma usage rules presented. Some sentences will require more than one comma, and one sentence requires no commas.

Example: When using any of the welding equipment in the shop please follow all the safety rules posted on the equipment which are for your protection.

Corrected: When using any of the welding equipment in the shop, please follow all the safety rules posted on the equipment, which are for your protection.

1. Judging by the quality of the soil and slope of the lot you will need to bring in a lot of top soil for your class landscaping project.

2. I would suggest bringing in at least enough top soil to provide a six-inch top to the current soil.

3. You can not begin digging trenches for the sprinkler system until you've brought in the top soil but you can lay out the design of your system in advance which will take some time.

4. Although the back area is rather small you will still need a number of sprinkler heads to provide coverage for the lawn the trees along the fence and the flowers and plants around the borders.

5. The area which requires the most watering is the lawn so you need a separate timing system for it and the other parts of the yard.

6. Since you may not be able to do the entire project by yourself I'll be glad to help but I know you are required to do as much as possible on your own.

7. I would suggest using rolls of sod for the lawn rather than grass seed because the lawn comes fully grown and with rolls of sod weeds aren't a problem.

8. The only thing you'll need to get from the landscaping department is a power hole digger which will make planting the trees easier and faster.

9. Putting in the sprinkler system will require measuring and cutting a lot of PVC pipe for the water lines but the pipe is light and easy to connect allowing you to work quickly.

10. I'd suggest giving yourself a full weekend to smooth out the top soil put in the sprinkler system and then lay out the sod and then I'd schedule a second weekend for all of the planting.

Editing Activity 2.14

Insert commas in the sentences of the following draft by applying the rules for comma usage. Some sentences will require multiple commas, and some will require none.

Example: Weather conditions in many parts of the world have become more erratic in recent years. The world has experienced warmer warms colder colds more frequent and stronger hurricanes and more tornadoes. While some weather experts attribute the changes to the natural weather cycles that have occurred throughout time others attribute the changes to man-made global warming.

Edited: Weather conditions in many parts of the world have become more erratic in recent years. The world has experienced warmer warms, colder colds, more frequent and stronger hurricanes, and more tornadoes. While some weather experts attribute the changes to the natural weather cycles that have occurred throughout time, others attribute them to man-made global warming.

The Old Dorm

The dormitory I stayed in my first year of college was an old army barracks. Many barracks buildings were converted to dorms when the college was built on the former military base many years ago and my dormitory barracks was one of the few left standing twenty years later.

The barracks consisted of an end-to-end hallway with ten small dorm rooms on each side. Each room had just enough space for two twin beds and a sink. There was no closet space anywhere so we strung a wire along one side of the room and hung our clothes. In addition since there was no space for a study desk we'd study on our beds or go to the library.

There was one bathroom for the entire dormitory with two shower stalls and two toilets. Needless to say there was often a line for the bathroom and sometimes we'd use the bathrooms in one of the newly built dorms rather than wait in line. There was also no cooling unit in any of the rooms so they got very warm in the late spring and the summer. It was also a noisy place since the thin uninsulated walls between the rooms were a conduit for sound.

Finally the dorm was in bad shape since they were planning on tearing it down soon and didn't want to put any money into it. There were holes in the walls cracked and chipped tiles on the floor and permanent mildew in the concrete shower stalls. The entire dorm had an old musty smell that always lingered and clung to your clothes. There were also holes in the walls cracks in the ceilings and cracks in the enamel sink basins. The only good thing about the dorm which was the only reason that many of us stayed was that the cost per semester was half as much as for the new dorms. As you can see no one would have lived there otherwise.

Editing Review

In Unit One, you learned to identify and correct run-on sentences and comma splices, and you learned the correct irregular verb forms for the past tense and past participle. Since it often takes more than one exposure to eliminate the most troublesome errors, there are review activities throughout the text for students who need them.

Editing Activity 2.15

In the following draft, correct errors with run-on sentences or comma splices by separating sentences with a period or combining them with a joining word. In addition, correct any misspelled irregular verbs.

Example: The mother cat had hid some of her babies behind the washing machine, we didn't realize how many kittens she had until we heared them crying.

Corrected: The mother cat had hidden some of her babies behind the washing machine, and we didn't realize how many kittens she had until we heard them crying.

Too Many Geese

A big drainage pond sat behind our apartment complex in the city, it filled with water during the rainy winter season. The pond attracted a variety of migrating birds which flied in before Christmas and left sometime in March.

We enjoyed the egrets, ducks, coots, and geese that came to visit, but we were also ready for them to leave in the spring. The problem was they would spend a lot of time on the back apartment lawn eating the grass seed, they leaved their droppings all over the lawn and concrete walkways. It was a real mess we couldn't walk back there without stepping on something.

Last winter while most of the birds were leaving in March, two pairs of Canadian geese hatched their babies. Rather than leave, they settled in to raise their brood, which consisted of six ducklings per couple. Apartment tenants started feeding them, which was a mistake they grew accustomed to their environment, and when the ducklings were old enough to fly, no one leaved.

Today we have fourteen large geese living year around behindour apartments, it is not a good situation. They keep the back area littered with their droppings, and they have drove off families by running at their children and squawking. They have became more and more aggressive, and now consider the back lawn area their territory. To make matters worse, a new brood of ducklings has hatched, and the numbers are going to keepgrowing.

The situation has got so bad that the apartment owners have brung in fish and game experts to see what can be done that was a few months ago, and nothing has happened. I seen the old movie classic "The Birds" on television, where flocks of birds start attacking people. I wonder if those geese have similar plans for us.

Editing Activity 2.16

Proofread your latest draft for errors by applying the following editing guidelines, and make the necessary corrections. Read your draft several times, looking for one type of error at a time. When you have corrected all errors, write the final draft of the paper.

Editing Guidelines

1. Check your sentences to make sure you haven't run any together or put a comma between sentences instead of a period. Correct run-on sentences or comma splices by separating longer sentences with periods and combining shorter, related sentences with a joining word.

2. Check your sentences to make sure there are no sentence fragments created by separating a part of a sentence from the sentence it belongs with. Correct fragments by attaching the fragment to the sentence it belongs with or by adding words to the fragment to make it a complete sentence.

3. Check your use of irregular verbs, making sure you have used the correct irregular forms and spelled them correctly.

4. Check your comma usage, making sure you have inserted commas into your sentences following the rules provided.

5. Check the spelling of any word you are uncertain of, or run the spell check on your word processing program, to eliminate any spelling errors.

Writing Summary

At the end of each unit, you apply what you have learned by writing a second paper without interruptions for instruction or activities. This second writing assignment provides you an opportunity to write about another influential person in your life, some additional practice in using the writing process, and another paper to share with readers.

Writing Assignment

Choose a person to write about, someone very different from the subject of your first paper, who has had a different influence on your life.

Free Writing

1. Free write for a few minutes on two or three people you are considering writing about.

Sample free writing

#1

My piano teacher had quite an influence on me although she would never know it. I wasn't a particularly good piano student and was too young to really be that interested. Mrs. Armstrong was an older woman with grey hair who lived in a nice older house with a piano in the front room. I'd go there on Mondays I believe for a half hour lesson when I was nine or ten years old. I didn't really like the lessons, I didn't like practicing, and as a result, I wasn't very good. I think she soon realized I wasn't going to be a great pianist or stick with it long, so she did something very smart. She said, "There are a few basic chords that you can learn to play a lot of songs with, and I'm going to teach you those chords. Then even if you don't keep taking lessons, you can still enjoy playing the piano." She taught me the chords, only four of them, and showed me one song that used just those chords, and I learned to play it. I quit soon after that, and quit playing the piano for some time. However, once in a while I'd go to the piano and play those chords. As I got a little older and started liking popular music, I'd take a song I liked and try to apply those chords to the melody. I would struggle a great deal, but eventually I would learn to play the song with the chords she taught me. Today I play the piano whenever I have some time and want to relax. For that I have Mrs. Armstrong to thank.

#2

One of my best friends moved to another town over a hundred miles away when we were in fifth grade. She was a real good friend and we used to do a lot of things together. We both really liked to swim and we spent lots of time at the city pool together. She was just a lot of fun to be with and she was also very ornery, like the time she slept over and wouldn't let me get to sleep almost the whole night. She was real outgoing and friendly and a lot of people liked her. The thing about Cherise was, over the years, she never let our friendship go. Once she left, I figured that was it, but Cherise was the type that would write and call once in a while. She even invited me to her house to spend time in the summer, and I did it a couple of times. I wouldn't see her or hear from her for a long time, then all of a sudden she'd be on the phone and we'd talk for a half hour. To this day she still keeps in touch although we're going to different colleges a long ways away. I would never have kept up with her the way she did with me, but I'm thankful that she did.

2. Once you have selected a person to write about, do a clustering diagram that includes some main ideas and more specific thoughts (examples, details) associated with them.

Sample Diagram:

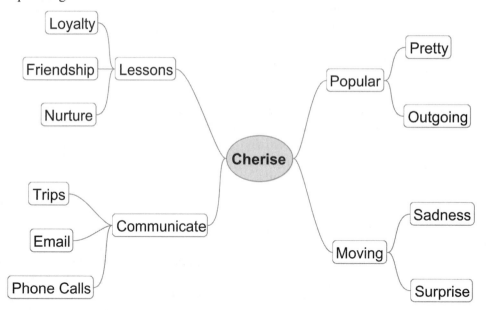

First Draft Guidelines

Write the first draft of your paper keeping the following in mind.

1.   Write your paper so that readers will get to know your subject the way you do.

2.   Write your paper so that readers clearly understand the relationship between you and your subject.

3.   Include examples to bring to life the qualities of your subject and show your relationship with him or her.

4.   Conclude your paper by relating the influence that this person has had on your life.

5.   Keep your readers in mind: your classmates and instructor.

6.   Provide a simple title that tells what the paper is about.

Sample First Draft

A Good Friend

In first grade through fifth grade, my best friend was Cherise. We went to school together, we played at each other's houses, and we spent a lot of time together in the summer. I looked up to her because she was a really good swimmer, and I wanted to be like her.

Cherise had a great personality. She was always friendly and smiling, and everyone seemed to like her. She was a very pretty girl, and people just seemed to be attracted to her. I felt lucky that I was her best friend, and I just assumed that we would always be together.

Then one day just before fifth grade started, Cherise told me her family was moving to another town where her dad had gotten a job. I was shocked and disappointed. I'd never had a friend move like that, and I never thought it would happen with Cherise. I almost felt like my best friend had died, and that I'd never see her again. I had a big hole in my life, and going back to school without her was hard.

Of course life goes on, and I began to adjust to not having Cherise around. I still missed her, but her absence wasn't ruining my life. I had other friends, I had my family, and I had activities at school. But Cherise wasn't ready to let go of our friendship. One day out of the blue she called me, and we talked for a long time, telling each other about what we were doing. I'd never even thought about calling her, assuming she was out of my life forever, and her call meant a lot to me.

That call was just the beginning of our long-distance friendship, and I'll have to admit that Cherise did the most to keep it alive. She'd call, write letters, and even invite me to spend time with her in the summer, which I did on a few occasions. Sometimes months would pass before I'd hear from her, and then she'd tell me everything that was going on in her life. It was clear that she was a popular, well-liked girl like she had always been, and as we got older, boys crept into our conversations more and more.

The same bond that made us best friends when we were young held us together as we went through high school. I have to give Cherise most of the credit for staying in touch because I was not the communicator that she was, but I was always thankful that she was. I did set her up with a date for our prom our junior year, and she drove down and we double dated. She remembered a lot of people from the old days of elementary school at the dance, and we all had a blast. She returned the favor and invited me our senior year and I went, although it felt different being with Cherise and a bunch of strangers who in some ways knew her better than I did.

Once e-mail became the way to communicate, Cherise and I e-mailed a lot, often a few times a week. We could confide things to one another that we wouldn't tell our friends in town since whatever we might say would never get back to people. We even talked about going to the same college together and rooming together, but that never worked out. She went to a college closer to her home and I went to a school even farther away. However, now that we're in college, we haven't let the change in life or the greater distance change our friendship. I'm convinced that Cherise just wouldn't let that happen, and I feel the same way.

Today Cherise and I don't communicate as regularly as we did, but the good thing about it is that we don't have to. We are both very busy and caught up in our day-today lives, but one call or one e-mail closes the distance immediately. We have an understanding built over the years, one which we never have to talk about, that I'll always be there for her and she'll always be there for me, and time or distance will never change that. To me that's an amazing kind of friendship, and one that I have her to thank for.

Cherise taught me that friendships don't have to end when people move, and she understood that at a young age. She put a lot of time into our long-distance friendship that a lot of people wouldn't have, including myself. Because of her I'm a better friend to all of my friends, and I don't take their friendships for granted. Friendships take time and work like anything else worth having, and Cherise made that clear to me by her example. I truly believe that when we are forty or fifty years old, she and I will still be in touch, no matter where we are, friends for a lifetime. Her and my friendship has to be one of the most special relationships in my life, one that I have learned to treasure.

Revision

Set your draft aside for a while so that you can see it through "fresh" eyes when you return. Then read your draft and consider revisions in the following areas:

Revision Guidelines

1. Read your draft to see if you have captured the essence of your subject and included all of the qualities that best typify him or her. Add or change whatever you think would help bring him or her to life for readers.

2. Read your draft to see if you have included good examples to show the qualities of your subject and to show your relationship with him or her. Add or revise examples where they would make your paper more interesting or informative.

3. Read each sentence to see if it says exactly what you want and is worded smoothly and concisely. Revise sentences to make them clearer, less wordy, or smoother, and replace questionable word choices with better ones.

4. Read your paragraphs to see if you have changed paragraphs as you move to different aspects of your paper: a different time or place, a different event, a different quality of your subject, a different aspect of your relationship.

5. Read your conclusion to see whether you have clearly related the influence that this person has had on you and the impact he or she has made on your life.

6. Check your use of transitional words and phrases, and add any transitions that would help tie sentences or paragraphs together more effectively.

7. Read your draft a last time with your reading audience - your classmates - in mind. What might you add or change to make your paper clearer, more interesting, more informative, or more insightful?

Sample Revision

A Good Friend

In first grade through fifth grade, my best friend was Cherise. We went to school together, ~~we~~ played at each other's houses, and ~~we~~ spent a lot of time together in the summer. I looked up to her because she was a really good swimmer, and I wanted to be like her.

Cherise had a great personality. She was always friendly and smiling, and everyone seemed to like her. She was **also** a very pretty girl, and people just seemed to be attracted to her. I felt lucky that I was her best friend, and I just assumed that ~~we would always be together~~ **it would always be that way**.

Then one day just before fifth grade started, Cherise told me her family was moving to another town where her dad had gotten a job. I was shocked and disappointed. I'd never had a friend move like that, and I never thought it would happen with Cherise. I almost felt like my best friend had died, and that I'd never see her again. I had a big hole in my life, and going back to school without her was hard.

Of course life goes on, and I began to adjust to not having Cherise around. I still missed her, but her absence wasn't ruining my life. I had other friends, I had my family, and I had activities at school. But Cherise wasn't ready to let go of our friendship. One day out of the blue she called me, and we talked for a long time, telling each other about what we were doing. I'd never even thought about calling her, assuming she was out of my life ~~forever~~, and her call meant a lot to me.

That call was just the beginning of our long-distance friendship, and I'll have to admit that Cherise did the most to keep it alive. She'd call, write letters, and even invite me to spend time with her in the summer, which I did on a few occasions. Sometimes months would pass before I'd hear from her, and then she'd tell me everything that ~~was~~ **had been** going on in her life. It was clear that she was ~~a~~ **the same** popular, well-liked girl she had always been, and as we got older, boys crept into our conversations more and more~~.~~ **, at least on her end.**

The same bond that made us best friends when we were young held us together as we went through high school. I have to give Cherise most of the credit for staying in touch because I ~~was not the communicator that she was~~ **I didn't communicate as often as she did,** but I was always thankful that she ~~was~~ **did**. I did set her up with a blind date for ~~our~~ the prom our junior year, and she drove down and we double dated. She remembered a lot of people **at the dance** from ~~the old days of~~ elementary school ~~at the dance~~, and we all had a blast.   She returned the favor and invited me **to her prom** our senior year and I went, although it felt different being with Cherise and a bunch of ~~strangers~~ **her friends** who in some ways knew her better than I did.

Once e-mail became the best was to communicate, Cherise and I e-mailed a lot, often a few times a week. We could confide things to one another that we ~~wouldn't~~ **might not** tell our friends in town ~~since whatever we might say would never get back to people~~. We even talked about going to the same college ~~together~~ and rooming together, but that never worked out. She went to a college closer to her home, and I went to a school even farther away, but ~~However, now that we're in college,~~ we haven't let ~~the~~ **that** change in **our** ~~life~~ **lives** ~~or the greater distance change~~ **affect** our friendship. ~~I'm convinced~~ **I know** that Cherise ~~just~~ wouldn't let that happen, and I feel the same way.

Today Cherise and I don't communicate as regularly as we once did, but the good thing ~~about it~~ is that we don't have to. We are both very busy and caught up in our day-to-day lives, but one call or one e-mail closes the distance immediately. We have an understanding built over the years, one ~~which~~ we have never ~~have to~~ talked about, that ~~I'll~~ **we'll** always be there for **each other** ~~her and she'll always be there for me~~, and **neither** time ~~or~~ **nor** distance will ~~never~~ **ever** change that. To me that's ~~an amazing~~ **the greatest** kind of friendship, and ~~one that~~ I have Cherise to thank for **it.**

Through her actions, Cherise taught me that friendships don't have to end when people move away, ~~and~~ **something** she ~~that understood~~ **grasped** at a young age. She put a lot of time into our long-distance friendship that ~~a lot of~~ **most** people wouldn't have~~, including myself~~. Because of her I'm a better friend to all of my friends, and I don't take ~~their friendships~~ **them** for granted. Friendships take time and work like anything else worth having, and **I learned that from** Cherise. ~~made that clear to me by her example.~~ I ~~truly~~ believe that when we are forty or fifty years old, we ~~Cherise and I~~ will still be in touch no matter where we are, friends for a lifetime. ~~Her and my~~ **Our** friendship ~~has to be~~ **is** one of the most special relationships in my life, **and I** ~~one that I have learned to~~ treasure **it.**

Editing

Proofread your second draft for errors and make the necessary corrections. Check for errors in particular in the areas covered in the following "Editing Guidelines."

Editing Guidelines

1. Check your draft for run-on sentences or comma splices, and correct them by separating longer run-ons with a period and combining shorter run-ons with a joining word.

2. Check your sentences to make sure there are no sentence fragments created by separating a part of a sentence from the sentence it belongs with. Correct fragments by attaching the fragment to the sentence it belongs with or by adding words to the fragment to make it a complete sentence.

3. Check your use of commas by applying the rules from this unit. Insert commas if they are needed and delete any commas that aren't required.

4. Check your draft for irregular verbs, making sure you have used the correct past tense and participle forms and spelled them correctly.

5. Check your spelling to make sure you have spelled all words correctly, and make the necessary corrections.

When you finish editing your paper, write the final draft to share with readers.

Readings

Writing Teacher

by Corrine Jackmon

My first year in college I took a writing course from Dr. X, a short, rather dour looking middle-aged woman with frizzy red hair, flip flops, and toenails to match her hair. The first class meeting she told us to write a paper so she could assess our writing ability.

I had done some writing in high school although not a great deal. I liked to put a lot of big words in a paper, believing that was how to impress a teacher, and I'd always gotten A's in English. I was undaunted by my first college writing assignment and whipped something out with little trouble.

When we got our papers back a week later, I was looking forward to Dr. X's praise. I figured I'd impressed her greatly with my barrage of multi-syllabic words. Instead, what I got was a sharp slap in the face. Her concluding comments at the bottom of the page read sarcastically, "Congratulations. You managed to say practically nothing in four-hundred words. Unfortunately, you are not as good a writer as you think you are."

Well, I didn't need that kind of abuse from someone who obviously didn't know what she was doing. I quit the class. At that time quitting was how I handled situations I didn't like, so I left Dr. X in my dust, hoping never to see her again.

As I discovered through other English classes, Dr. X. had been right about my writing. Going into college, I didn't know the first thing about writing. Somehow I'd gotten the notion that it wasn't what you had to say that was important but how you said it. Different college teachers nudged me gently enough in the right direction that I didn't bolt from their criticism, and my writing slowly began to improve.

I was now in my fourth year of college majoring in English. I felt I was a reasonably competent writer at that point based on the grades I'd received and favorable comments by different instructors. I had not given Dr. X. any thought for years until I saw her name in the schedule of courses for a required upper division writing course for majors. Only one section of the course was offered, so I was stuck. It was either take Dr. X's class or wait another semester and hope someone else would teach it. It wasn't much of a choice.

When I walked into her class, I was a much different person than four years ago, but Dr. X. appeared unchanged: the same dour look, the frizzy red hair, flip flops, and red toenails. And the same assignment: writing a paper to assess our writing ability. I was a much improved writer from three year ago and wasn't fearful of getting the kind of scathing evaluation I'd gotten then. I was actually rather curious as to what she'd think of my writing now.

When I got the paper back, there was red ink all over it. She found much to criticize: word choice, syntactical flow, stating of the obvious, weak metaphors, redundant conclusion. I hadn't gotten this much criticism in my other writing classes, and my first instinct was to say, "Forget this!" However, I wasn't that same immature, ego-protective college freshman, so I just set the paper aside until the next day.

When I re-read the paper with normal blood pressure, I could see Dr. X's point on some of the comments; on others, I wasn't sure what she was talking about. I decided the best thing to do was see her during an office hour and go over the paper. When I sat down in her office, she just stared at me for a while, and I felt very uncomfortable. Then she stuck a finger in my face and said, "I remember you. Freshman comp. You didn't last a week." "I can't believe you remembered," I said with a wan smile. "That was a long time ago." "You gonna run again?" she asked pointedly. "I don't want to waste my time on a quitter."

I could feel my face burning. I could also hear my dad's voice of the past saying, "You can't just give up every time something goes wrong. You won't stick to anything that way." I felt myself smiling despite myself, and I said, "I'm pretty good at quitting, I'll say that. I guess four years ago it wasn't so much what you said but how you said it. It seemed pretty cruel to me at the time."

"Cruel-schmuel," she said. "Big-headed freshmen come in all the time who know nothing but think they know everything. I give them a quick reality check." I smiled and said, "I probably needed one but it wasn't pleasant." "Anyway," I said, "I have no intention of dropping your class. I need it for my major and I want to be a good writer. I hope you can help me."

"Well, you'd better grow a thicker skin because I'll be on you like vultures on a dead possum," she said colorfully. "And by the way," she added with what may have passed for a smile, "I'm the best damn writing teacher you'll ever have. And don't even think about being a good writer. Shoot for competent." "Competent sounds good," I said.

Dr. X's writing class was the toughest I'd been in. We wrote a lot of papers and she critiqued each one in detail. Then we'd rewrite the papers until she felt we'd done as much as we could with them. I can't imagine the hours she put in reading and writing comments on every draft of every paper. I can still remember some of the more vivid comments she wrote on my papers: "That sentence just lies on the page, quivering like fat," or "You know that I know that what you said here is pure baloney. Feed me something nourishing," or "If you cut the blubber from this paper, what would be left? Moby the minnow," or "The crap detector blew a fuse on that paragraph."

All of her comments weren't harsh, however, and I thrilled over the occasional words of praise, muted as they may be: "This paper isn't as bad as I thought it would be, " or "Finally, a sentence that isn't crushed under its own weight," or "Now there's an angle I hadn't considered. Surprise me more often."

I worked hard for those meager pay-offs, but the real pay-off was bigger. I was learning more about writing than I'd ever learned before, and my writing was definitely improving: sparser, cleaner, more honest, and more insightful. I was learning that it was the thinking behind the writing that was most important, and I thought about my writing topics and how to approach them more deeply than I ever had. The one recurring comment by Dr. X. which became etched in my mind was,

"Tell me something that I don't already know." Trying to write something new, something beyond the pale of commonly regurgitated knowledge or opinion on a particular topic, was a tremendous challenge.

In the end, Dr. X became my favorite teacher. No one had ever cared about my writing enough to be perfectly honest with me, and to invest the time on my papers that she demanded that I invest myself. I spent more time in her office than any other teacher's, but I can't say that I got to know her much better. It seemed her one passion was teaching writing, and I knew nothing of her life outside the classroom, nor she of mine. All I know is that I learned more from her about writing than all my other teachers combined, and she influenced my future like no one else.

Today when I sit with a large stack of my students' papers in front of me, I think of Dr. X. Just as I expect the best writing effort from my students, I owe them my best in return. When some of my students moan, "Why are you so hard on us?" I have to chuckle a little. They have no idea what hard means.

Questions for Discussion

1. What details of looks and manner does the author provide for Dr. X. that are important for readers to get to know the teacher?

2. What examples does the author provide to show the relationship between herself and Dr. X.? How effective are the examples?

3. The author uses considerable dialogue throughout the essay. What is the purpose of the dialogue, and what impact does it have on you as a reader?

4. Discuss individuals in your life who may have seemed unduly harsh but ultimately made a positive impact. What did you learn from them?

Mama

by Jess Yim Ka-mei

What does the word "mama" mean? A lady who gives birth to babies? The one who nurtures little children into great men or women? A person who owns our flesh and blood? A soft voice, sincere face, caring eyes, gentle hands, concerned personality, someone who takes care of our meals and our clothes, who helps us with our homework, guides us through our love affairs and to our marriage… is this the description of every mom? My mom seemed to be an exception.

My mom always scolded me; even the slightest mistake would be viewed as seriously as an unforgivable crime. She never helped me study for any dictations, quizzes, tests or exams, and she sent me away whenever I asked a single question. My mom never showed appreciation for any of my achievements, from a mark of 100 in a dictation to winning a prize in an art competition. To her, nothing I did seemed to be worthy of praise. She always kept me at home, didn't let me go to my classmates' birthday parties, join school camps or picnics, or participate in extra curricular activities. I felt like a wild bird confined in a cage, and I envied other girls whose lives seemed so much better than mine.

My mom never waited for me outside school, comforted me when I was sad, or brought me to the doctor when I was sick. Once when I asked her to accompany me to the doctor's, she just replied: "Kid, how old are you? Primary three already! Just tell the doctor how you feel and that's it!" I walked to the doctor's alone that day, and when he asked me where my mother was, I responded with silence.

More than once, I wished I could have another mom. I wished for a mom who would support me in every way, give me the courage to fight my fears and provide me with faith. I wished for a mom who could share my joy whenever I achieved something; share my sorrow whenever I failed; smile with me as well as cry with me. I wished for a mom who I could depend on for my whole life. No matter how bad the world treated me, she would be there to comfort me and say, "My child, have no fear, I'll be with you forever."

Only when my mom told me her story did I realize that I hadn't understood her, and from that day forward my life changed. Her own father had been a nasty man who flirted with countless women. Her mother had been a young, innocent girl who couldn't even manage to take care of herself. When my mother was born, she was loved by nobody; she was a burden to the people who were responsible for her. Her parents didn't offer a blessing nor give her a glance before giving her up, their youngest daughter. Her foster family made her work all day long, beat her whenever they were angry, and treated her as a maid while calling her daughter. When she was three, she met her real mother and was told to call her "aunt."

As she grew, she had no opportunities to attend school, spend time with friends, go to parties, enjoy childhood, or see the wonders of life. When she was eighteen, her older sister found her, but they were never to meet again. All she ever heard from her father was the message that her sister passed on: "Never approach us again." She never tried.

Without ever knowing what a loving family was like, my mother married a poor guy and gave birth to four innocent lives. Can you blame someone who had never been loved by her family for not knowing how to express her love and affection to her children?

Then suddenly, I remembered. The box of dolls my mom bought for me when I had a high fever when I was three. Her mutterings of "put more clothes on" whenever the weather turned cold. The favorite dishes she cooked for me every birthday. The cakes she always used to bring to me whenever I studied late into the night. Her visit to the boutique that I worked in last summer. The lovely shirt that I longed for and that she bought me when she went to Japan. How could she know I loved it? How could I have missed all of the times that she tried to be a good mother and showed that she cared for me in the only ways she knew?

I'm sorry, Mom. Your daughter didn't know you before. I wish I had always known your story.

Questions for Discussion

1.   What is the purpose of the opening paragraph? How does it "set the stage" for what is to follow?

2.   What examples does the author use to show the relationship between her mother and herself in the third and fourth paragraph? How do those examples contrast with the examples in the next-to-last paragraph?

3.   What details of her mother's life before marriage affected you most strongly as a reader? Do you believe that how her mother was raised justifies how she treated her own daughter, and why?

4.   How do you feel your mother's (or father's) early life may have affected how she raised you as a son or daughter? How might your upbringing affect the kind of mother or father you may be (or are)?

Unit 3
Interests

Certain kinds of writing lend themselves best to the traditional essay form that includes a thesis statement, topic sentences, and an opening, middle, and conclusion. This traditional form is used regularly in non-fiction writing, including newspaper editorials, magazine articles, journal essays, and college writing for different courses.

Thesis-centered writing is simple in design and easy for readers to follow. That is why it has been used extensively by writers in a variety of writing situations. In the opening, the writer usually introduces her topic and includes a thesis statement expressing the writer's opinion or viewpoint on the topic. In the middle or body of the paper, the writer supports the thesis statement by providing reasons or evidence revealing why she thinks or feels the way she does. In the conclusion, the writer reinforces the thesis statement in some manner and leaves readers with some final thoughts on the topic.

In this unit, you will write a thesis-centered paper. You will also use this form for much of the writing you do in the future, whether for a history, sociology, or English class, a "letter to the editor," or a letter to a local politician. Learning to write an effective thesis-centered paper is a valuable part of the writing experience.

Your writing assignment for this unit focuses on a particular interest of yours, something that you enjoy doing or that you are very committed to. Writing about an interest accomplishes three purposes. First, it allows you to write about something that you are passionate about, which often leads to the best writing. Second, it lends itself well to the thesis-centered format, the writing focus for this unit. Third, by reading about an interest of yours, readers will learn more about you and also about a topic they may know little about.

Prewriting

In each unit, the initial prewriting activities help you prepare to write the first draft of your paper. During this section, you will select a topic to write on, decide on a thesis statement for your paper, and generate some support for your thesis.

Topic Selection

No doubt you have several interests that occupy your free time. Think about things that you enjoy doing or find rewarding, that you know a lot about, and that may be somewhat different from the next person's interests. Think about interests that reveal something about you and that might even surprise readers.

Consider different interests that you find most gratifying. They may be in the area of sports, music, politics, computers, social issues, or fashion, and they might involve collecting, performing, volunteering, working, or creating.

Prewriting Activity 3.1

Select a topic for your paper following these suggestions.

1.   Select an interest that you would like to write about.

2.   Select a topic that readers may be interested in learning more about.

3.   Select a topic about which you are knowledgeable and can write easily on.

4.   If you are considering two or three interests, select the topic that may differ from your classmates' choices.

Sample topic selection

I like wearing offbeat, funky clothes and shopping at thrift stores. That's a big hobby of mine. I've enjoyed tutoring since I was in elementary school, and it has helped me make a decision about my future career. I'm also interested in the health of our planet and try to go "green." I use paper bags instead of plastic, take public transportation when I can, and always recycle. I'm not sure what I want to write about, but those are three things to think about.

Thesis Statement

Now that you have selected a topic, the next step is to consider what you want to write about it. To that end, generating a thesis statement provides a focus for your paper, something around which to develop it.

The following points clarify what a thesis statement is and its role in how you write your paper.

Thesis Statement Guidelines

1. A thesis statement expresses the main point of your paper: the primary idea that you want to convey about your subject to readers. For example, if a writer chose doll collecting as her topic, her thesis statement might be, "While collecting dolls may seem like child's play to some, it is an interesting hobby for women of all ages."

2. A thesis statement generally reveals the writer's opinion or viewpoint on the topic: what she believes or how she feels about it. For example, on the topic of "politicians," if a writer's thesis is, "Politicians learn to say nothing in a lot of different ways," the writer's opinion of politicians is quite clear.

3. The thesis statement is usually found in the opening so that readers know what the paper is about. For example, on the topic of bird watching, the thesis statement, "Bird watching is the most exciting hobby imaginable," lets readers know that they will discover the excitement of bird watching from the writer's perspective.

4. A paper is written in support of its thesis, which is called thesis development. For example, following the thesis statement on doll collecting, the writer would relate to readers everything interesting about doll collecting. Following the thesis statement on bird watching, the writer would explain and show to readers the excitement of bird watching.

5. A thesis statement should express what a writer believes about his subject. If the thesis expresses the writer's true feelings about a topic, it will lead to the most interesting and authentic writing.

6. Papers by different writers on the same topic may have quite different thesis statements. For example, on the topic of interior design, one writer's thesis statement may be, "Interior design provides a creative outlet like nothing else," while another writer's thesis may be, "Interior design is all about geometry: combinations of shapes blending together in interesting forms." Clearly, these two thesis statements would lead to very different papers.

Prewriting Activity 3.2

Underline the thesis statement in the following opening paragraphs of different papers: the one sentence that best expresses the writer's viewpoint on the topic.

Last summer I registered on-line for the fall semester for the first time. Previously I had always gone on campus for the traditional registration in the gymnasium, waiting in line after line to try and get the classes I wanted. What a difference on-line registration made, as I sat comfortably in my room in front of the computer instead of standing in line at school. It was still frustrating when a class I wanted would show up on the monitor as "closed," but not nearly as frustrating as driving to campus to find out the same thing. On the whole, on-line registration is much better than the traditional way, and I'd recommend it to anyone.

Before going to college, I always shopped for groceries at the regular supermarkets, not worrying much about the price of one thing or another. However, when I came to college and began cooking for myself and buying my own groceries, I became very price conscious. I soon found that there are alternatives to shopping at the big-name stores. As I discovered, you can save a lot of money shopping at discount supermarkets, and you don't have to sacrifice quality. That was one of the best things I learned my freshman year.

I like all kinds of music, from the 1950's to today's. I listen to different radio stations that play oldies, classic rock, alternative, and hip hop, and I'll flip from station to station to find a song I really like. However, one day a friend of mine told me to go on-line to "You tube" and plug in the name of the artist and song I wanted to hear. I tried it, and I not only heard the song but saw a video. To hear the music that you want when you want to hear it, "You tube" is the best place to go. It couldn't be easier to use.

Today I'm sitting in the cafeteria watching every person that walks in or out. I station myself with a friend at a table with a good view of the door, and there we sit, eating a little and looking a lot. When there's a lot of traffic, our lunch stretches out quite a while. I don't know if you'd call it a hobby, but people-watching ranks as one of my favorite activities. That may sound weird to some, but to me and my friends, it's good fun. There are a lot of interesting people in the world.

Living inland my whole life, with hot summer and cold winter weather, I wasn't prepared for the weather on the coast where I'm going to school. There were no more 100 degree summer days or 20 degree winter nights. Every day the weather seemed about the same: the low 70's with mild breezes. Some seasons were a little cooler than others, but they fluctuated by just a few degrees, not the forty or fifty I was used to. Having lived on the coast for over a year, I realize that coastal weather has some real advantages.

Prewriting Activity 3.3

For practice generating thesis statements, write a potential thesis statement for any four of the following topics that expresses your viewpoint on the topic and that you could support in a paper.

Examples:

Topic: Punk rock bands
Thesis: To really understand the whole punk rock scene, you have to attend live
         performances.

Topic: Classical music
Thesis: Classical music is an acquired taste that I have never developed.

Topic: Classic cars
Thesis: Cars of the 1950's and 60's have more style than today's copycat automobiles.

1.   Topic: country music
      Thesis statement:

2.   Topic: rap music
      Thesis statement:

3.   Topic: Fast food restaurants
      Thesis statement:

4.   Topic: Cafeteria food
      Thesis statement:

5.   Topic: iPads
      Thesis statement:

6.   Topic: Twittering
      Thesis statement:

7.   Topic: Working while going to school
      Thesis statement:

Prewriting Activity 3.4

Generate a thesis statement for your topic that expresses the main idea that you want to develop in your paper. Create a thesis that reflects your viewpoint on the topic and that you could support in a paper.

Sample thesis statement

Topic: being a vegetarian

Thesis statement: Becoming a vegetarian was one of the best choices I've made.

Making a List

During prewriting, writers often make a list of ideas on their topic that they may include in their draft. For your upcoming paper, you could make a list of points that support your thesis statement and develop them in separate paragraphs in your draft.

For example, the writer whose topic was "being a vegetarian" listed the following points in support of her thesis.

Thesis statement: Becoming a vegetarian was one of the best choices I've made.

Supporting points: I eat healthier food.
I feel better.
I've lost weight.
I am committed to not eating animals.

While listing some supporting points doesn't restrict you to those ideas or obligate you to use them, it does get you thinking about your topic, provides some beginning ideas from which to develop paragraphs, and puts some ideas on paper that you can reorganize to present most effectively in a paper.

Prewriting Activity 3.5

Make a list of four or five points in support of your thesis statement.

Sample supporting points

Thesis statement: Working with the elderly is very rewarding.

Supporting points: They have great stories to tell.
They are very appreciative of any help.
They are honest and tell you what they think.
Cheering them up makes me feel better.

First Drafts

Now that you have done considerable prewriting work for your paper, you are ready to write your first draft. The drafting considerations in this section include the three parts of a thesis-centered paper - opening, middle, and conclusion - and the use of topic sentences.

The purpose of having an opening, middle, and conclusion is to make the paper as readable as possible. Readers first want to know what a paper is about, which they discover in the opening. Next, they want to know what you have to say about the topic, which they discover in the middle paragraphs. Finally, they want to understand why you wrote the paper, which they usually discover in the conclusion.

Opening, Middle, and Concluding Paragraphs

While opening, middle, and concluding paragraphs vary in nature depending on the kind of writing you are doing, they generally have one thing in common: each is distinct from the others. Readers have a clear sense of when they are moving from the opening, which introduces the topic, to the middle, where the topic is developed, to the ending, which wraps up the paper.

The following are the basic elements that characterize each of the three parts of a paper.

Opening or Introductory Paragraph(s)

1. The opening introduces the topic to readers and provides the writer's viewpoint on the topic, which is revealed in the thesis statement.

2. The opening captures the readers' interest and also reveals the writer's interest in the topic.

3. The thesis statement usually comes at or near the end of the opening and prepares readers for what lies ahead in the middle paragraphs.

4. The opening gives readers a reason for reading further, by emphasizing, for example, how serious or interesting the topic is or why readers should know more about it.

5. While openings are typically one paragraph long, they may include two or three paragraphs, with the thesis statement often in the last paragraph.

Middle Paragraphs

1. The middle paragraphs develop and support the main idea expressed in the thesis statement.

2.   The middle paragraphs provide the reasons that the writer believes as he does about the topic.

3.   In support of the topic sentence, the middle paragraphs may do several things: explain more about the topic, provide points of support for the thesis, or provide examples to further develop those points.

4.   Middle paragraphs often begin with a *topic sentence*: an opening sentence that tells what the paragraph is about. The rest of the sentences in the paragraph develop that idea. The purpose of the topic sentence is to let readers know what a paragraph is about, to highlight a supporting point for the thesis statement, and to ensure that a paragraph is developed around one central idea.

    For example, if the thesis statement for a paper is, "I enjoy playing the keyboard for relaxation," the supporting points in the middle paragraphs might include the following: forget about problems, be creative, play favorite songs, play to my mood. In the paper, these four points could be expressed in the following topic sentences, each of which would begin a separate paragraph.

    a. Playing the keyboard helps me forget all my problems for a while.
    b. I also enjoy trying out new melodies on the keyboard
    c. Playing the keyboard, I can enjoy hearing my favorite songs over and over.
    d. Whatever mood I'm in, I play music that fits that mood.

The following is an example of how one paragraph was developed based on the topic sentence it begins with (topic sentence underlined):

<u>Whatever mood I'm in, I play music that fits that mood</u>. For example, if I feel upbeat and happy, I might play something by Train or Bruno Mars. If I'm in a romantic mood, I might play some classic ballad like "Wicked Game" or something by Journey. If I'm in an introspective mood, I might play something from Green Day like "Boulevard of Broken Dreams." If I feel like moving, I'll try something by Beyonce or Rihanna. Whatever my mood, there's some music to fit it, and I always feel better after playing the keyboard.

Concluding Paragraph

1.   The concluding paragraph brings the paper to an end in a way that reinforces the thesis statement.

2.   The concluding paragraph may do any number of things: summarize the main supporting points in the paper, restate the thesis in different words, provide a final powerful point or example to support the writer's viewpoint on the topic, explain the writer's purpose for writing about this particular topic, influence the readers' attitude towards the topic, project what the future may

hold regarding the topic, or leave readers with a final powerful thought to take with them.

3.   The concluding paragraph should be more than just a summary or restatement of what has come before. It should go beyond what has been presented, leaving readers with something new to think about.

4.   Being the last thing that is read, the conclusion should make an impact on readers, leaving them with something to ponder, laugh about, be concerned with, or learn more about.

Sample Draft

The following draft provides an example of a paper with an opening that includes a thesis statement, middle paragraphs beginning with topic sentences, and a conclusion that reinforces the thesis statement and projects into the future. The thesis statement is italicized, and the topic sentences in the middle paragraphs are underlined.

Politics

A lot of people my age aren't interested in politics, but I am. I come from a politically active family, and my dad has worked locally on a number of campaigns. While many college students feel disconnected from politics and have no interested in who gets elected to what, I feel that the decisions that politicians make today can affect the future of my generation. *Younger voters have a stake in the political process, and I know from experience that we can make a difference.*
    As a child, I spent a lot of evenings in campaign offices, eating pizza and watching TV while dad was doing phone banking. I also walked precincts with him, leaving campaign flyers on people's doorsteps. I didn't really know what I was doing, but I enjoyed being with my dad and getting his praise for helping out. I also got to attend some victory parties, which meant lots of food and colored balloons. <u>I didn't know it at the time, but these experiences paved the way for my becoming politically active</u>.
    <u>There is nothing glamorous about working in political campaigns</u>. The things you have to do to win a campaign are very basic: stuff thousands of envelopes, make hundreds of phone calls, walk precincts to reach the voters, man a voter registration table, put up candidate's signs around town. Most campaign work is rather tedious, and many times I'd rather be doing something else. That's why you have to believe in what you're doing and the candidate or candidates you are working for. If you become a political volunteer for the glamour of the campaign, you won't last.
    <u>Of course, it's the ultimate pay-off that brings the excitement</u>. When your candidate wins the election, there is no better feeling in the world. You know that all of the hard work that you and many others put in helped to make the difference. When you share in the victory party with your candidate and all the supporters, it's a time of sheer jubilation. In later days, that rush is replaced with a feeling of satisfaction. All of the hard work becomes a faint memory. Before long you're ready for the next

campaign.

<u>While the political highs are thrilling, the political lows are devastating</u>. It's hard to describe the feeling of utter despondency and sadness when you are on the losing end of a long campaign. One of the feelings that always gnaws at me is guilt. What could I have done that I didn't do? Why did I go to the concert one night and skip the phone banking? However, instead of wallowing in self-pity, I just recommit myself to working harder the next time. To work in politics, you have to be an optimist.

When it comes to politics, I feel out of touch with most of my fellow students. However, as a voting bloc, I know that the 18-to-21 year olds have a lot of power. So I sit at the voter registration tables on campus, I recruit members to join our political club, I write political pieces for the school paper, and I try to get people to help on a campaign. More students are starting to see the connection between political decisions and the availability of student aid or college loans, the cost of tuition, the price of gas, and the health of our environment. As politics is a big part of my life, I think it's also going to get bigger for a lot of students. I'm going to do what I can to help make that a reality.

Notice in the opening paragraph how the writer introduces her topic, explains her interest in it, and concludes with her topic sentence. In the next paragraph she tells how she became involved, and in the three subsequent middle paragraphs, she relates what it is like to be a political volunteer. Finally, she concludes the paper by telling readers more about her political involvement and how she hopes it spreads to many college students. By the end of the paper, we clearly understand the writer's passion for politics and her knowledge of the political process.

Drafting Activity 3.6

Read the following essay. With a classmate, identify the opening, middle, and concluding paragraphs, the thesis statement in the opening, and the topic sentences in the middle paragraphs. Then analyze the content in each part of the essay and what the writer accomplishes in the opening, middle, and conclusion.

Passion for Football

Every Sunday during football season, you'll always find me in the same place most of the time: sitting in front of the television. I'm there again every Monday night, and sometimes on Thursdays. Those are the times when NFL football is on television, and I seldom miss a game. Every year I can't wait for fall to roll around so I can enjoy my favorite pastime: watching professional football.

While I like watching all levels of football, professional football is by far the best. The players are the best in the world, and the speed of the game is amazing. I like everything about the game, especially the long bomb, the big hits, the breakaway running plays, and the acrobatic catches. Professional football players are some of the best athletes around, and when they play together as a team, it is beautiful to watch.

While I'll watch any pro game, I do have my favorite teams that I prefer watching. I like the Colts because of their high-powered offense and the Steelers because of their toughness and in-your-face defense. I like the Patriots because they always perform at a high level. When any of these teams are playing, I always have a team to cheer for. The rest of the times I just sit back and enjoy the game.

I particularly like it when two games are on at a time, which usually happens on Sunday mornings. Then I can switch back and forth between games and watch two at a time. If I time it right, I can catch almost every play of both games since seldom do both games have a play occurring at the same time. Sometimes there will even be three games on at once, and I'm flipping that remote all over the place.

I watch a game differently from a lot of guys I know. I'm not like some of them who love to go to the sports bar and root for their team along with a hundred other screaming maniacs. I'm not into all that emotional stuff and high-fiving. I don't even care if no one is watching the game in the house but me. Sometimes a friend will be over to watch with me, but I'm just as happy sitting there by myself. I watch the games just to enjoy the great athletes and great plays, so that makes me different from a lot of fans.

Although some people tell me to get a life, they don't understand that watching pro football is a big part of my life. They don't really understand how much I enjoy what I'm doing, and I don't waste my time telling them. If there's anything better to do than watching Peyton Manning throw a perfect strike into the end zone through three defenders, or LaDamian Tomlinson breaking through the line and juking the linebackers, or Randy Moss leaping high to snare a pass with one hand, or Junior Seau flying across the field and smashing into a startled running back, I haven't seen it. It's like watching great artists at work.

Football season is almost over for the year, but the Colts are in the Super Bowl, so I'll have one last Super Sunday to enjoy. Then my life changes for the worse. I have nothing to do that replaces the enjoyment I get from watching NFL football, and watching a baseball game on a spring Sunday afternoon is boring with a capital B. I go through football withdrawal for a couple months, then switch gears and start getting out of the house on weekends and doing things I don't do during football season, like going to the gym.

By mid-summer, the upcoming football season is in the news again, and I read every article I can. In a way, I start preparing for the new season like the players do, by checking the playing schedule, seeing how the draft picks and free agency trades are working out, analyzing the coaching changes, and gearing up for hundreds of hours of games. By the start of the season, I've got my game face on and am hunkered down in the living room with fresh batteries in my remote. Let the games begin.

Drafting Guidelines

Keep the following guidelines in mind when you write your first draft.

1.   Write an opening, middle, and conclusion for your draft. Include your thesis sentence in the opening, and begin each middle paragraphs with a topic sentence that expresses the main idea for the paragraph.

2.   Include some of your list ideas from prewriting to help develop your paper, using them to generate topic sentences for your middle paragraphs.

3.   If you are writing on a topic your reading audience may know little about, include some explanation in the beginning of your middle paragraphs.

4.   As you write, reread your sentences to help you decide what to write next.

5.   Your writing purpose is to help your readers understand why you feel the way you do about your topic. Keep that goal in mind as you write.

6.   Your purpose in writing the first draft is to get your ideas on paper without concern for wording perfection or whether you make an occasional error.

Drafting Activity 3.7

Write the first draft of your paper keeping the drafting guidelines in mind.

Sample First Draft

Tutor

In fourth grade when the bell rang for recess, my classmates couldn't get outside fast enough to play ball or run around the playground. Not particularly good at games or sports and a slow runner, I was less enthusiastic, often watching the fun from a distance or hunting ladybugs and rolly pollys with a couple friends. Then I found out about an activity that changed my recess time dramatically.

Knowing my dislike for the rigors of the playground, my teacher told me that students could earn service points towards the Block R award by tutoring kindergarten students. She said I could do it during some recess periods. I told her I'd like to give it a try and the next recess, three of us reported to the kindergarten building.

I sat with students individually and helped them with their numbers, letters, and small art projects. I enjoyed it, and the students seemed to respond well to me. The kindergarten teacher said I was doing a good job, and before long I was spending practically every twenty-minute recess in the kindergarten room. It was a part of the day I always looked forward to.

Looking back, it wasn't too surprising that I took to tutoring. From the time I was very young, I liked playing school with my younger sister and grandparents, and I was always the teacher. Tutoring kindergarten students seemed a natural extension of my play. I earned enough service points that year that along with my grades and other activities, I earned my Block R plaque, a great accomplishment for me. I also enjoyed my "students" shouting out to me across campus or waving to me in the cafeteria. I had many little friends.

I continued my tutoring for the remainder of elementary school, working with first graders as a fifth grader and with second graders as a sixth grader. Admittedly some of my classmates let me know that they thought it a little strange that I preferred tutoring to recess, but no one made fun of me. I was also getting a lot of positive feedback from teachers, and some teachers would request me specifically to work in their classrooms. I also continued racking up the Block R service points, but by this time I would have kept tutoring without them. I remember one teacher saying, "Imelda, you are a born teacher," an observation I would never forget.

In middle school there was no tutoring program similar to elementary school, and I found fewer opportunities to work. Once a week middle school students could volunteer to tutor at the elementary school for an hour, and I did that, but it was far from the regular tutoring routine I had in elementary school, and I missed that. However, once I got into high school, I had a plan.

I felt confident in my tutoring abilities by this time, particularly in reading, writing, and math, the three areas that students most needed help. Reading was my first love and something of a specialty for me, and I spent a lot of time learning about reading instruction, including phonics, sight word memorization, and contextual clues. Since I wasn't doing any after-school activity at the time, I asked my mom about me starting an after-school tutoring business. I could earn a little money and continue doing what I enjoyed. She said to give it a try although we were both skeptical that I'd get any students to tutor.

I advertised in the local paper for tutoring elementary age students in reading, writing, and math, and I got a few phone calls. I would meet with the mothers of prospective students at my house, with my mom present, and tell them my qualifications and years of experience. The students would be coming to me since my mom didn't want me going all over town to different people's houses. I started out with just a couple students, but the business grew as I continued to advertise and word of mouth began spreading that students and parents were happy with the results. Soon I was tutoring three-four days a week, sometimes taking two students at a time with similar skill levels.

I continued my tutoring business through my junior year of high school and then experienced my first burn-out. I had been tutoring kids since the fourth grade and I felt I needed a break. My enthusiasm for the work was dropping, and the tutoring sessions were becoming more like drudgery. I wanted to relax and enjoy my senior year, spend more time with my friends, and have no after-school obligations. So I put tutoring out of my mind, thinking perhaps that it had run its course for me.

I learned that you sometimes have to get away from something that you have done for a long time before you realize how much it meant to you. I had a full year to recharge my battery, and by the time I started college, tutoring seemed like a good idea again. However, I wanted to try something different this time, and the college provided the opportunity. The college hired peer tutors to work with students who were working below college level to help bring them up to grade level. Prospective tutors were interviewed and also did mock tutoring sessions. I decided to specialize in reading instruction, my greatest love and aptitude, and during the mock sessions, showed off the considerable teaching skills I had developed over the years. The head of tutorial instruction was impressed, and I was hired.

Over the past two years, I have gotten as much tutoring work as I wanted and made a number of friends. I realized that I instilled some of my passion for reading with my students as well as helping them develop their skills, and I often left books with them that I thought they might like. Although I had expected for some time that my future career lay somewhere in the area of teaching, my college tutoring brought a clearer focus to what I wanted to do.

I enjoyed tutoring my peers, but I knew that my first love was working with elementary age children, and I knew that I had a good rapport with them. I also realized that while I loved working with students one-on-one or in small groups, that working with a class of thirty students might not be my strong suit. Finally, I knew that teaching reading was what I loved the most and did the best, and it was something I could imagine doing the rest of my life.

After doing some research, I learned that most school districts had one or more reading specialists who went from school to school working with individual students or small groups on a pull-out basis. In addition, they helped to develop and coordinate reading programs in the district, conduct reading staff development, and assess student progress in reading. I couldn't think of a job that I would enjoy more or was better suited for.

After I get my liberal studies degree in two years, I will apply to a reading specialist credential program at a nearby college whose program has a good reputation. To have that direction in my life gives me a very good feeling, particularly as I see classmates who have no idea what they want to do or major in. Who knows. If I had been more athletically inclined and enjoyed recess like most students, I may have never gotten into tutoring, which sent my life in the direction it's going. And I still hearken back in the fifth grade to one teacher's comment, "Imelda, you are a born teacher." Maybe I am.

Revision

Now that you have written the first draft of your paper, you are ready to make any changes you feel will make it more interesting, informative, complete, or better written. Writing the first draft is a major step towards completing your paper, but there is still work to be done.

Often writers feel a sense of completion after finishing a first draft, and aren't anxious to jump in and start revising it. That is a good reason to set your draft aside for a few hours or even overnight. Then when you take a fresh look at it, you may feel more motivated to improve the paper. You will also find yourself less enchanted with what you wrote and realize that some changes are probably in order.

Think of your writing process as creating a sculpture. In the first draft, you have chiseled out the rough form of your sculpture, and viewers can clearly see your intended figure: a child with a cat in her lap. In the second draft, you use a finer chisel and more refined sculpting skills to turn the roughly formed figure into a finely featured work of art. Neither writer nor artist can create a finished product in a single step

In the "Revision" sections, you are introduced to new elements of revision and also apply what you learned in previous units to help revise your draft. In this section, the new revision consideration is organizing your paper.

Organization

An important element of an effectively written paper is its organization: the order in which its content is presented to readers. In a well-organized paper, ideas are presented in an order that best conveys the writer's ideas. There is a logic to the organization, and the ideas in one paragraph follow naturally from the previous paragraph and lead sensibly into the next one.

While different types of writing favor particular organizational schemes, there is one organizational constant in most writing. Writers begin with an opening that introduces their topic, continue with a middle that develops what they have to say about the topic, and end with a conclusion that "wraps up" the paper for readers, providing a sense of completion. This basic organizational scheme has stood the test of time, providing writers with the most efficient structure for communicating with readers. Within this basic framework, however, there are other organizational decisions you make with any paper that you write. The following guidelines will help you make the best choices as you determine the most effective way to present your ideas.

Organizing Guidelines

1.   Narrative papers that tell a story usually have the most straightforward organization. The story is told in chronological order, with events presented in the order that they occurred. This is the organizational scheme you used in your first paper in Unit 1.

2.   Papers often contain a number of points or ideas that support the thesis statement of a paper. These points should be presented in their most effective order, usually one of the following:

     a. Start with the most important point and conclude with the least important.
     b. Start with the least important point and conclude with the most important.
     c. Start and conclude with the two most important points and sandwich the other points between them.
     d. Group related points together in sequential paragraphs.

     The order in which you present your points will depend on what you believe is the most effective and logical presentation of ideas, based on what you want to accomplish in the paper.

3.   Certain types of papers lend themselves to a particular organizational scheme. For example, in a problem/solution paper, which you will write in a later unit, a typical organizational pattern includes introducing the problem, presenting its causes, explaining its effects, and providing possible solutions.

4   Often in a paper, you will use the middle paragraphs to do different things: explain more about the topic, provide examples supporting your thesis statement, present reasons why you feel as you do about the topic, or present other information related to the thesis statement. In such cases, you would order your ideas based on these considerations:

     a. What is the most logical, natural order for the ideas to be presented in?
     b. What is the most effective order for readers to follow your thoughts?
     c. What order would best accomplish your writing purpose?

     For example, if readers need to learn more about your topic, it is best to provide that information before getting into the supporting points for your thesis statement.

5.   While you might decide on a rough organizational scheme during your pre-

writing planning, you often need to get your thoughts on paper before discovering the best way to organize them. On rereading a first draft, a particular paragraph or sentence may appear out of place, so you move it to a location where it fits better.

It is important to check the organization of your paper during the revision process to see how effectively you have ordered your ideas. Sometimes moving a paragraph or two to a different location can significantly improve a paper, and using a word processing program, moving paragraphs or sentences is a simple task.

Revision Activity 3.8

For the following two topics, arrange the supporting points in the order you would present them in a paper. Be prepared to explain the order you choose.

Topic: Rugby

Thesis statement: Rugby is a great sport that most Americans know little about.

Supporting Points: Requires great stamina and running ability
Extremely fast, tough sport
Tremendous individual skills of top players
Originated in Europe
Basic rules of the game
Exciting to watch

Topic: Elementary school teacher

Thesis statement: Being an elementary school teacher is a challenging job.

Supporting Points: Discipline problems to deal with
Long hours
Teaching non-English speaking children
Responsible for children testing at grade level
Helping children who have bad home lives
Endless paper work to fill out from district and state

Revision Activity 3.9

Read the following first draft and reorder the paragraphs in a more effective way.
Escaping the Gang

I am one of nine children, the son of Mexican immigrants. My family moved around a lot when I was young. Once after we went to back to Mexico, our family split up. My dad stayed in Mexico where he was working and my mother moved the rest of us to Los Angeles. My father was going to join us later. I never saw him again.

I am one of the lucky ones. I escaped from gang life, I'm not in prison, and I'm still alive. Every day I see young kids hanging out on the street and I know where their lives are heading. That's why I spend time at the youth center on weekends talking to kids and playing with them. I know the lure of gang life and also how gangs ruin lives. If I can help one kid stay out of gangs, maybe I've saved a life.

We eventually moved to a small two-bedroom apartment, the first of many that we lived in. There were a lot of other poor kids like me around, and they became my friends. We began hanging out in the streets, sometimes very late. I had a lot of anger in me, especially towards my father, and I vented it by getting into fights. Some of the guys that befriended me were gang members. When you're young, you don't judge people who are nice to you, and I had someone to back me up and to pass the time with. My mom was busy trying to keep nine children clothed and fed.

When you are young, you really don't know what a gang is about. Once you are older, things change. People start shooting at you. You can't go certain places because you'll get jumped. And when you get hit by members of another gang, you have to retaliate. My homeboys and I would go on patrol searching for rival gang members. We'd smoke weed to get up our courage, and then we'd see a couple guys and jump out of the car and fight, hitting them with bats and "jacking" their stuff.

By the time I was in fifth grade I had begun to steal, breaking into homes with my homeboys and grabbing video games or any cash we could find. By the time I was a freshman, I was "jumped" into my gang, getting pounded for several minutes by some gang members. I fought back and got in some punches, just to show I wasn't going down like a punk. I passed the test.

I got kicked out of high school for being a trouble maker and went to continuation. Luckily, there were some teachers there who didn't give up on me. I got my high school diploma. However, once I got out of school, I had more time to hang out with my homeboys. We broke into homes, and when we weren't stealing, we smoked marijuana and drank beer. We'd steal booze from a liquor store and trade it on the street for some weed. We'd spend most of the day getting drunk and high.

My life fell apart after my homeboys and I robbed a clothing store. Someone got our license number, and soon police were rounding up my friends. I left the area and stayed on the run for a few weeks. Finally, I turned myself in because I missed my girlfriend. I was convicted of grand theft and sent to county jail with other gang members. Being in jail got my attention. I wondered whether I'd end up rotting in prison ten years from now. I didn't want that, and I decided to drop out of the gang.

I told an officer I was dropping out, and I was moved to another center to "protect" me. I made it through, and once I got out, I was put in touch with Jorge, a former gang member who was director of New Hope. I got in a program where I learned to manage my anger, fill out a job resume, and stay clean. After I got through the program, Jorge lined me up with a job. He also probably saved my life.

Today I look at my time in jail as a blessing because I had the opportunity to see what I was doing wrong. I'll be on probation for three years and I can't mess up. My old friends still want to hang out, but I've got too much going for me to lose it.

When I talk to the young guys, I tell them straight up what it's like. I tell them the temptations are great, but they need to be strong and stay away from the street life. I tell them to respect their moms and to care about school so they don't ruin their lives. Some of them listen to me; some of them don't. I keep trying because I know they want to have a future like everyone. They just don't know how to get there.

When I see young kids on the street, I feel for them. I know how poor they are and how lonely it can get. I also know that being around older guys seems exciting. They are your role models, and when they give you attention, it's a big deal. You don't imagine what it's like once you start stealing, gang banging, and getting shot at.

Most importantly, I take an interest in them. I talk to them and listen to them. I spend time with them so they know that I care. Maybe I'm a role model for some of them, and if I had had someone like me in my life when I was growing up, things might have been different. I hope it is for them.

Revision Guidelines

The following guidelines will help you revise your draft effectively.

1. Reread your draft to determine whether readers will understand clearly what the topic means to you: i.e., the enjoyment, sense of satisfaction, excitement, or sense of accomplishment it may bring. Revise your draft in ways that help readers understand your passion for the topic.

2. Check your opening paragraph to make sure you have clearly introduced your topic, created some interest for readers, and included your thesis statement. What might you add or change to make your opening even more interesting for readers?

3. Check your middle paragraphs to make sure that each paragraph begins with a topic sentence expressing its main idea, and that each paragraph relates to and supports the thesis statement in some manner. Also check the

organization of your paragraphs, and decide whether any paragraphs or any sentences within a paragraph could be moved to a more effective location.

4.   Check your concluding paragraph to make sure that it provides readers with a sense of completion, relates to your thesis statement, and adds something for readers beyond what you have already written. What can you add or change in the conclusion to make it one of the strongest parts of your paper?

5.   Read each paragraph to see if there is anything you can add - an example, a reason in support of your thesis, a specific detail or description, an explanation - to make the paper more interesting, informative, or complete.

6.   Check your use of transitional wording to tie sentences and paragraphs together. Add any transitions (e.g. first, second, also, in addition, finally, therefore, however, etc.) that will help readers understand your ideas and how they are connected.

7.   Check your paragraphing to make sure you have changed paragraphs when you move to something new: a different part of the paper, a new supportive point, a different example, a different time, place, or event. Divide overly long paragraphs into two, and combine very short paragraphs containing related material.

8.   Check the wording of each sentence, and revise sentences to make them clearer, smoother, and more concise by eliminating unnecessary words or phrases and rewording awkward or unclear sentences.

9.   Reread your draft a last time with your readers' response in mind. What final changes might you make to heighten their interest in your topic or further their understanding?

Revision Activity 3.10

With a classmate, or a small group of classmates, read the following first draft and apply the revision guidelines. Make note of changes that you would recommend the writer make in her next draft.

Crazy for Windmills

Driving along a country road or through a suburban neighborhood, I'm often looking for something that most people seldom notice. I never noticed them either until my young niece started pointing them out to me one day. She loved finding new windmills, and I'd help her look for them after picking her up at school. Now even when she's not in the car, I catch myself looking for windmills.

What you probably don't realize until you look is that there are windmills everywhere. You will find them in country pastures, beside barns, on hillsides, in back yards and front yards, and even on the tops of buildings. You will also find that windmills come in all different shapes and sizes.

I became more interested in windmills as I learned more about them. They've been around for hundreds of years in various parts of the world, and many of the better known ones dot the landscapes in Holland, Norway, Russia, and Greece. They have served various purposes over the years, including grinding grain into flour, pumping water from wells, and creating electricity, all using the power created by the wind turning their blades and the shaft connected to them.

The windmills in the United States and in Europe are very different in looks as well as function. I find them both attractive but favor the European mills. Interestingly, you can find European style windmills in the US, most of them ornamental but a few of them functional. I have yet to see an American styled windmill in Europe based on hundreds of pictures of windmills I've seen on the Internet.

I've even started collecting windmills. I have a charm bracelet with small windmill trinkets on it, and relatives will add to the collection on my birthday.
I bought a table light windmill from a collectable store whose blades turn when you turn on the light. I also have a couple small American windmill replicas sitting in my room that I put together from kits.

Outside our house I have some decorative back-yard windmills. One is silver and red and stands about seven feet tall. Another is a wooden replica of a Dutch windmill that is about four feet tall. The last one is a black five-foot American windmill that I can see from my bedroom window.

With my niece's help, I even wrote a small children's book for her which she illustrated with drawings of windmills. It was a story about a girl who loved windmills and an old windmill she named Old Windy that was going to be torn down for a housing development. The story has a happy ending, and my niece had a good time illustrating it and taking it to school to share with her class. She is quite an artist for her age and is even taking some art instruction from a local teacher/artist who holds art classes after school.

One great thing about being a windmill hound is that a long trip is never boring. My niece went with me and our family on a two hundred mile trip across the state recently. My niece and I spent almost the entire trip looking for and finding windmills, and we found over thirty on our way. We get excited over any windmill we find, but we particularly like the big ones, and if they are spinning, that's a bonus.

On this particular trip, we saw what has to be one of the tallest American windmills anywhere.

One of the highlights of our windmill experiences was when I took her to a place called Windmill World on the outskirts of a small town about an hour from where we live. The old man who owns Windmill World builds windmills for farms and ranches across the country, and he has over fifty windmills on this property. For a windmill fanatic, seeing fifty windmills in one place is as good as it gets. We spent over an hour looking at the windmills and talking to the man, who was thrilled to find people who loved windmills as much as he does. In the end he gave each of us a windmill kit to build a two-foot ornamental American windmill. That was the perfect ending to a great outing.

I can't separate my enthusiasm for windmills from my niece's because we are in this thing together. We have gone on-line and found a couple of windmill museums in the US, one in Oklahoma and one in Texas. Our goal in the near future is to visit both museums on one trip. We may be the only two people in the country with such a goal.

Revision Activity 3.11

Revise your draft by applying the revision guidelines presented. Then exchange drafts with a classmate and suggest any further revisions that you feel would improve each other's paper. Finally, write the second draft of your paper, including all improvements you have made in content, wording, and organization.

Sample Revised Draft

Tutor

In fourth grade when the bell rang for recess, my classmates couldn't **wait to** get outside ~~fast enough~~ to play ball or run around the playground. Not particularly good at games ~~or sports~~ and a slow runner, I was less enthusiastic, often **just** watching the fun ~~from a distance~~ or hunting ladybugs ~~and rolly pollys~~ with a couple friends. Then I ~~found out about~~ **discovered** an activity that changed my recess time dramatically.

Knowing my dislike for the rigors of the playground, my teacher told me that students could earn service points towards the Block R award by tutoring kindergarten students. ~~She said I could do it~~ during some recess periods. I told her I'd like to give it a try and the next recess, three of us reported to the kindergarten building.

I sat with students individually and helped them with their numbers, letters, and small art projects. I enjoyed it, and the students ~~seemed to~~ responded well ~~to me.~~ The kindergarten teacher said I was doing a good job, and before long I was spending ~~practically~~ **almost** every ~~twenty-minute~~ recess in the kindergarten room. It was ~~a part~~

~~of the day~~ **something** I always looked forward to.

Looking back, it wasn't too surprising that I ~~took to~~ **enjoyed** tutoring. ~~From the time I was very~~ **At a** young **age**, I liked playing school with my ~~younger~~ sister and grandparents **who babysat me**, and I was always the teacher. Tutoring kindergarten students ~~seemed~~ **was** a natural extension of my play. I earned enough service points that year ~~that along with my grades and other activities, I~~ **to get** my Block R plaque, a great accomplishment for me. I also enjoyed my **kindergarten** "students" shouting ~~out~~ to me across campus or waving to me in the cafeteria. ~~I had many little friends.~~ **It made me feel good.**

I continued ~~my~~ tutoring ~~for the remainder of elementary school~~ **in fifth and six grade**, working with ~~first graders as a fifth grader and with second graders as a sixth grader~~ **first graders and second graders.** ~~Admittedly~~ Some ~~of my~~ classmates let me know that they thought it ~~a little~~ strange that I preferred tutoring to recess, but no one made fun of me. I was also getting ~~a lot of~~ positive feedback from teachers, ~~and~~ some ~~teachers~~ **who** would request me ~~specifically~~ to work in their classrooms. I also continued racking up the Block R service points, but by ~~this time~~ **then** I would have kept tutoring without them. I remember one teacher saying, "Imelda, you are a born teacher," ~~an observation~~ **something** I would never forget.

In middle school there was no tutoring program similar to elementary school, and I found fewer opportunities to work. Once a week middle school students could volunteer to tutor at the elementary school for an hour~~, and~~ **which** I did ~~that~~, but it was far from ~~the~~ **my** ~~regular~~ **former** tutoring routine, ~~I had in elementary school, and~~ **which** I missed. ~~that.~~ However, once I got into high school, I had a plan.

I felt confident in my tutoring abilities by this time, particularly in reading, writing, and math, ~~the three areas that~~ **where** students most needed help. Reading was my first love and ~~something of a specialty for me~~ **favorite tutoring subject**, and I spent a lot of time learning ~~about reading instruction, including~~ **about** phonics, sight word memorization, and contextual clues. Since I wasn't doing any after-school activity ~~at the time~~, I asked my mom about ~~me~~ starting ~~an after-school~~ **a** tutoring business. I could earn a little money and continue doing what I enjoyed. She said to give it a try although we ~~were both skeptical~~ **weren't sure** that I'd get any students. ~~to tutor.~~

I advertised in the local paper ~~for~~ **to** tutor~~ing~~ elementary ~~age~~ students in reading, writing, and math, and I got a few phone calls. I would meet with the mothers of prospective students at my house with my mom present, and tell them my qualifications and years of experience. The students would be coming to me since my mom didn't want me going ~~all over town~~ to different people's houses. I started out with just a couple students, but the business grew as I continued to advertise and word of mouth ~~began spreading~~ **spread** that students and parents were happy with the results. Soon I was tutoring three-four days a week, sometimes taking two students at a time with similar skill levels.

I continued ~~my~~ tutoring ~~business~~ through my junior year of high school and then experienced my first burn-out. I had been tutoring kids since the fourth grade and ~~I~~ felt I needed a break. My enthusiasm ~~for the work~~ was dropping, and the tutoring sessions were becoming ~~more like~~ drudgery. I wanted to relax and enjoy my senior year, spend more time with my friends, and have no after-school obligations. So I put tutoring out of my mind, thinking perhaps that it had run its course. ~~for me.~~

I learned that you sometimes have to get away from something ~~that you have done for a long time~~ before you realize how much it meant to you. I had a full year to recharge my battery, and by the time I started college, tutoring seemed like a good idea again. However, I wanted to try something different this time, and the college provided the opportunity. ~~The college~~ **They** hired peer tutors to work with students who were working below college level **in particular subjects.** ~~to help bring them up to grade level. Prospective tutors were~~ **I was** interviewed and also did a mock tutoring session. I decided to specialize in reading instruction, my greatest ~~love and aptitude,~~ **strength,** and during the mock session, showed ~~off~~ the considerable teaching skills I had developed over the years. The head of tutorial instruction was impressed, and I was **one of the few freshmen who were** hired.

Over the past two years, I have gotten as much tutoring work as I wanted and made a number of friends. ~~I realized that~~ I **try to** instill~~ed~~ ~~some of~~ my passion for reading ~~with~~ **in** my students ~~as well as~~ **along with** helping them develop their skills, and I often ~~left~~ **leave** books with them that I ~~thought~~ **think** they might like. Although I had **long** expected ~~for some time that~~ my future career lay **in** ~~somewhere in the area of~~ teaching, my college tutoring **helped me to decide** ~~brought a clearer focus to~~ **specifically** what I wanted to do.

I enjoyed tutoring my peers, but ~~I knew that~~ my first love was working with elementary ~~age~~ children, ~~and I knew that I~~ **whom I always** ~~had a good rapport~~ **got along well** with. ~~them.~~ I also realized that while I loved working with students one-on-one or in small groups, ~~that~~ working with a class of thirty students **seemed daunting.** ~~might not be my strong suit.~~ Finally, I knew that teaching reading was what I ~~loved~~ **enjoyed** the most and did ~~the~~ best, ~~and it was~~ something I could imagine doing the rest of my life.

After doing some research, I learned that most school districts had one or more reading specialists who went from school to school working with individual students or small groups on a pull-out basis. In addition, they helped to develop and coordinate reading programs, ~~in the district,~~ conducted reading staff development, and assessed student progress ~~in reading~~. I couldn't think of a job that I would enjoy more or was better suited for.

After I get my liberal studies degree in two years, I will apply to a reading specialist credential program at a nearby college. ~~whose program has a good reputation.~~ To have that **career** direction **feels very good** ~~in my life gives me a very good feeling~~, particularly ~~as~~ **when** I see classmates who have no idea what they want to do. ~~or major in.~~ Who knows. If I had been more ~~athletically inclined~~ **athletic** and enjoyed recess ~~like most students~~, I may have never gotten into tutoring, which sent my life in ~~the~~ **its current** direction. ~~its going.~~ And I still hearken back ~~in~~ **to** the fifth grade ~~to~~ **and** one teacher's comment, "Imelda, you are a born teacher." ~~Maybe~~ **Perhaps** I am.

Editing

In the final phase of the writing process, you rid your paper of any errors that could distract readers from its content. Error detection and correction come at the end of the writing process because there is little point in editing a paper for errors while you are still working on its content and wording. You proofread your paper after all revisions have been made so that you are working with the final product.

In each "Editing" section, you are introduced to new elements of punctuation, grammar usage, or spelling that give writers problems, and you review what you have learned in previous units in order to apply all of your editing knowledge to your latest draft. In this section, you are introduced to subject-verb agreement, and you review what you have learned about run-on sentences and comma splices, sentence fragments, irregular verbs, and comma usage.

Subject-Verb Agreement

An important element of correct grammar usage is subject-verb agreement: making sure that you use the correct present tense verb form, depending on whether the subject is singular or plural. When you use the correct verb form, the verb agrees with its subject.

Subject-verb agreement is not difficult for most writers when the subject and verb are beside each other in a sentence. However, when they are separated by a group of words, or when their order is inverted, with the verb coming first, writers can have problems. This section will be devoted primarily to the more problematic constructions.

For example, in the sentence "That smell nauseates me," it is obvious that the verb form nauseates, ending is s, agrees with the subject smell. If the s were left off of nauseates, the sentence, "That smell nauseate me," would sound wrong to most writers. However, in the sentence, "That smell from the sewer farm beside the housing projects nauseate me," the verb form nauseate may not sound as bad, although it is still incorrect. The separation of a subject and verb in a sentence often makes it more difficult to "hear" the correct verb form.

Subject-Verb Agreement Rules

The following basic rules and guidelines will help you avoid subject-verb agreement problems in your writing.

1. The *subject* of a sentence is what the sentence is about: the main person, place, thing, or idea on which the sentence is centered.

Examples (subject underlined):

Your <u>aunt</u> from Wisconsin is a very friendly person.
The <u>separation</u> of subject and verb in a sentence makes selecting the correct verb form more difficult.
In the end, a person's <u>wealth</u> is a poor indicator of happiness.

2.   The *verb* in a sentence expresses an action or a state of being. It tells what the subject is doing (action) or the condition of the person or thing (state of being).

Examples (verb italicized, subject underlined)

The <u>separation</u> of subject and verb *creates* agreement problems for some writers.
The <u>mouse</u> constantly *darts* out of the closet and down the hallway.
Your <u>aunt</u> from Wisconsin *is* tired from her long flight.

3.   Subject-verb agreement involves present tense verbs: verbs that express something that is happening or existing in the present. The following agreement rules apply to present tense verbs.

   a. If the subject of the sentence is singular (one person, one place, one idea), the present tense verb ends in "s."

   Examples (subject underlined, verb italicized):

   My baby <u>niece</u> *enjoys* banging on the piano.
   The <u>Empire State Building</u> *is* no longer the tallest building in the world.
   My <u>roommate</u> *works* in a delicatessen on weekends.

   b. If the subject of the sentence is plural -two or more persons, places, or ideas - the present tense verb does not end in s. (Exception: verbs already ending in s like dress, press, or guess.)

   Examples:

   My baby <u>nieces</u> *enjoy* banging on the piano.
   The <u>Empire State Building and Sears Tower</u> *are* no longer the two tallest buildings in the world.
   My <u>roommates</u> *work* in a delicatessen on weekends.

c. The subject pronouns *you* and *I* are treated as plural when applying the agreement rule.

Examples:

I *like* early morning classes.
You *enjoy* evening classes.

4. When there is a group of words separating the subject and verb, ignore these words when determining subject-verb agreement. (An exception is explained in 6.a.)

Examples:

The boys in the back of the room seldom *participate* in discussion.
The women working in the cold storage plant on "N" Street *belong* to the retail employees' union.
The woman who works in several different store departments *is* seventy years old.
Only one of the men *works* the night shift year around.

5. When a sentence begins with *There* + a *to be* verb (is, are, was, were), the subject comes after the verb, so find the subject to determine the correct verb form. (Note: The verbs *was* and *were* are the only past tense verbs to which the subject-verb agreement rules apply. *Was* is used with singular subjects, and *were* is used with plural subjects.)

Examples:

There *is* a full moon tonight.
There *are* very few stars in the sky tonight.
There *were* several students absent on the day of the concert.

6. Four other subject-verb agreement situations warrant your attention.

a. If the subject *most, more, some, a lot,* or *all* is followed by a *prepositional phrase* (most of the cake, more of the men, some of the rules, a lot of money, all of the lobsters), the last word in the prepositional phrase determines the correct verb form.

Examples:

Most of the spectators *sit* under the covered bleachers. (Since spectators is plural, the verb sit does not end in s.)
All of the cake *needs* to be eaten before tomorrow. (Since cake is singular, the verb needs ends in s.)

b. In some sentences, two or more verbs go with the subject. In such cases, each verb must agree with the subject.

Examples:

My cat always *mews* under my bedroom window in the morning and then *scratches* on the window screen to awaken me.
The eastbound train that *runs* from Hanford to Bakersfield *is* often late.

c. In some sentences, there are two or more pairs of subjects and verbs. In such cases, each present tense verb agrees with its subject.

Examples:

The moon *is* yellowish-white when it *rises* above the horizon, but it *turns* a pale orange as it *moves* higher.
While Josh *vacuums* the hallway carpet, you *mop* the bathroom floor.

d. If a relative pronoun such as *that, who*, or *which* precedes the verb, the verb must agree with the subject that the relative pronoun refers to.

Examples

The men who *pour* foundations for the houses being built in the neighborhood *work* very long hours.
The one garage sale item that *attracts* me the most *is* the reading lamp.

Editing Activity 3.12

Underline the subjects and circle the verbs in the following sentences, and be prepared to explain why each verb ends or doesn't end in *s*.

Example: Joan and I *walk* to school in the fall, but we usually *drive* in the winter when the <u>weather</u> *gets* colder. (subjects underlined, verbs in italics)

1. The sudden sound of a car alarm in a parking garage always startles me.

2. One of the reasons that I go to movies frequently is that I enjoy getting out of the house on weekends.

3. There are several large bins behind the apartment building that we dump our trash in.

4. Students who do the most reading often possess the best vocabularies.

5. Concert attendees in the back of the arena have the least expensive seats.

6. The aroma of barbecued hamburgers lingers in our back yard.

7. The lottery for student basketball tickets is at 9:00 a.m. tomorrow in the cafeteria, but few students seem to know about it, and those students that know appear rather indifferent.

8. A lot of students really like the cafeteria's donuts because by the time I get there in the morning, the donuts are all gone.

9. The colorful ornaments that you put on the Christmas tree give it a festive look.

10. The head of my golf club loosens every time I hit the ball near the bottom of the club, so I try to hit the ball in the center.

Editing Activity 3.13

Underline the subject or subjects in each sentence, and then underline the correct verb forms in parentheses.

Example: <u>Julian and Lucy</u> (<u>try</u>, tries) hard when <u>they</u> (<u>play</u>, plays) doubles in tennis but seldom (<u>win</u>, wins).

1. One of your friends (enjoy, enjoys) teasing me about my collection of rubber bands.

2. There (appear, appears) to be several large pigeons nesting in the eaves of the

science building.

3.   The sounds coming from the upstairs apartment (indicate, indicates) that
     someone (are, is) in trouble.

4.   Most of the wedding cake (were, was) eaten, but few of the anchovy
     appetizers (were, was) touched.

5.   My best guess from analyzing the early election returns (are, is) that all of the
     incumbent board members on the voting ballot (are, is) likely to win.

6.   Maxine and Sue (realize, realizes) that their friend Nagumi, who frequently
     (attend, attends) campus functions with them but (go, goes) to another school,
     (like, likes) her school very much, and despite their pleas for her to switch
     colleges, (plan, plans) to stay where she (are, is).

7.   In the back of the classroom by the double doors (sit, sits) a guy who (sleep,
     sleeps) through most of the class and sometimes even (snore, snores).

8.   Most of the people who (attend, attends) presidential debates (mill, mills)
     about outside the auditorium after the debate and (discuss, discusses) the
     candidates' performances.

9.   The debate over whether the recent global warming (are, is) man-made or part
     of the natural weather cycle (appear, appears) to favor the side who (believe,
     believes) that man and his creations (are, is) responsible.

10. Most meteors from distant space that (fall, falls) towards earth (burn, burns)
     up in the atmosphere long before they (get, gets) close to our planet.

Editing Activity 3.14

Proofread the following draft for any subject-verb agreement errors, and make the
necessary corrections.

Example: The plans for the new performing art center is impressive, but there is no
          timetable in place for its construction.

Corrected: The plans for the new performing art center are impressive, but there is no
          timetable in place for its construction.

The foul smells emanating from the garbage bin beside the apartment spreads across the complex and leaves everyone feeling nauseous. No person in the apartments are to blame, but everyone suffers from the effect.

The problem is that garbage collection for the apartments occur on a two-week cycle. You can imagine the combination of unpleasant odors that come from dirty diapers, rotting food, and souring milk products that sits in the garbage bin for two weeks. Each day the odor gets worse, and by the end of the week, the smell is beginning to creep inside the apartments. Besides that, by the end of the second week, the garbage bin are overflowing, and garbage is strewn on the ground and dragged around the complex by dogs.

The answer to our garbage problems are, of course, a weekly garbage collection schedule by the city. For some reason the city does a weekly collection at individual houses in the area but collect at the apartment complexes every other week. That seems unfair to all of the apartment residents and make little sense when you consider that the garbage trucks are in the neighborhood every week.

Editing Review Activity 3.15

Before editing your latest draft for errors, proofread and edit the following draft by correcting any errors involving run-on sentences or comma splices, sentence fragments, irregular verbs, or comma usage.

Example:

The once beautiful river was now a dry river bed with the smell of dead fish fouling the air, the dam builded above the river had cut off the river's flow filling a reservoir with water to be used for farm irrigation.

Corrected:

The once beautiful river was now a dry river bed with the smell of dead fish fouling the air. The dam built above the river had cut off the river's flow, filling a reservoir with water to be used for farm irrigation.

Parking Woes

Parking at the college was getting worse every semester. As more and more students enrolled. To park in one of the main lots for an 8:00 a.m. class, you had to get to the school by at least 7:30 which was hard for a lot of students. If your first class was at 9:00 a.m. your only chance of finding an on-campus parking space was if someone from an 8:00 a.m. class left the lot, which didn't happen frequently.

If you couldn't park on campus you had to park on one of the streets adjacent to the campus that allowed parking, or you had to park in the large dirt lot across from campus which also filled with cars by early morning. A lot of students had to park more than a mile away and walk to campus, and for them getting to class on time was difficult, teachers complained about late students but it wasn't their fault.

The other option that a surprising number of students taked was to park illegally on campus they would park in "teacher only" lots which often had available spaces in "administration only" parking lots in ten-minute parking green zones and in loading zones. Sometimes the students would get away with it and sometimes they'd get ticketed. It was strictly a game of chance, for some students it was an expensive game.

Finally the college done something to ease the terrible parking crunch they built a five-story parking garage behind the Event's Center at a significant cost but it was the only thing they could do. Now almost all students can park on campus. And have no more than a five minute walk to class. The number of students who are late to class has gone down markedly and everyone seems more relaxed including the teachers and administrators.

Editing Guidelines

When you proofread your paper for errors, read it several times, looking for a particular type of error each time. If you try to find all types of errors in one reading, you may overlook some. The more proficient you become at proofreading, and the fewer errors you make, the easier it becomes to identify and correct your errors in fewer readings.

The following guidelines will help you proofread and edit your papers effectively.

1. Check your sentences to make sure you haven't run any together or put a comma between sentences instead of a period. Correct run-on sentences or comma splices by separating longer sentences with periods and combining shorter, related sentences with a joining word.

2. Check your draft for any sentence fragments: incomplete sentences with a period after them. To correct fragments, attach them to the complete sentence they belong with, or add words to make them complete.

3.   Check your use of irregular verbs, making sure you have used the correct irregular forms and spelled them correctly.

4. Check your comma usage, making sure you have inserted commas into your sentences following the rules presented in the text.

5. Check the spelling of any word you are uncertain of, or run the spell check on your word processing program, to eliminate any spelling errors.

6. Check all present tense verbs to make sure that they agree with their subjects, following the rules presented in this section.

Editing Activity 3.16

Proofread your draft following the guidelines presented and make the necessary corrections. Next, exchange papers with a classmate, proofread each other's drafts, and point out any undiscovered errors. Then write the final draft of your paper to share with classmates.

Writing Summary

At the end of each unit, you write a second paper, applying what you have learned to this point in the text. The purpose of this assignment is to allow you to work independently through the writing process, to write without interruptions for instruction or activities, and to gain more experience writing thesis-centered papers.

Writing Assignment

For your first paper in this unit, you wrote about a topic that you had a keen interest in, something that you enjoyed doing. For this paper, you are going to do just the opposite: write about something that you don't enjoy. While we can learn about writers from knowing what they like, we can also learn from their dislikes.

   For your topic for this paper, choose something that you don't enjoy, whether it be giving a speech in front of an audience, sitting through a soccer game, taking early morning classes, working on weekends, listening to presidential debates, or going to the dentist. Choose a topic that has enough substance to write a paper on, and one that your classmates might find interesting or relate to.

Prewriting

In preparation for writing your first draft, first you generate a thesis statement for your paper, and then you develop some supportive material by making a list of supporting points.

Thesis Statement

Once you have selected a topic for your paper, write a thesis statement that expresses your viewpoint on the subject and that you could support in a paper.

Sample Thesis Statement

Topic: Country Music

Thesis statement: I am not a fan of country music.

Making a List

After you have generated a thesis statement, make a list of four or five points that support your thesis and that would help readers understand why you feel as you do.

You may develop some or all of these points in the middle paragraphs of your paper.

Sample List of Supportive Points

Thesis statement: I am not a fan of country music.

List of points: Songs all sound alike
                    Corny lyrics in most songs
                    Old fashioned and out of date
                    Can't relate to the music

Drafting Guidelines

Now that you have selected a topic, generated a thesis statement, and developed some potential supporting points, you are ready to write the first draft of your paper. As you write, keep the following in mind.

1. In your opening, introduce your topic, create interest for readers, and include your thesis statement at or near the end.

2. In the middle paragraphs, support your thesis by providing the reasons that you feel as you do about the topic. Make use of your list of points, developing each in a different paragraph, and use a topic sentence to begin each paragraph.

3. Conclude your paper in a way that supports or reinforces your thesis and that also provides something new for readers. Keep your readers - your classmates - in mind as you write the conclusion.

4. Change paragraphs as you move to different parts of the paper and to different supporting points within the middle paragraphs.

5. Write without a great deal of hesitation, not worrying about perfect wording or an occasional error. Your purpose is to get your ideas on paper so that readers understand what you dislike about your topic.

Sample First Draft

Country Music

When I'm driving to work or to school, I always have the radio on listening to music. I'll change stations regularly, looking for a song that I want to hear. I like different kinds of music, including jazz, hip-hop, alternative, classic rock, and even the oldies, so there's always something on that I like. However, when I tune in to a country station, I keep moving the dial because I know that I'm not going to like the song very much. The truth is, I don't listen to country music at all because I just don't care for it.

To me, music is an emotional experience, and some music moves me and some doesn't. Country music doesn't move me at all. It is more difficult to explain exactly why, like trying to explain why I like chocolate ice cream better than strawberry. There is just nothing in the sound of country music that excites or moves me in any way.

First, I think most of the country lyrics that I've heard are corny. Like the Garth Brooks' song "I've got friends in low places," to me those are corny lyrics that you'd only hear in a country song. It doesn't sound real, and no one I know says things like that. I don't feel any connection with country song lyrics, and maybe you have to be a certain kind of country person to relate. I don't relate.

Most country songs sound the same, and I don't care for the sound. You always have that twangy guitar sound and a melody that sounds old-fashioned and boring. I never hear an interesting beat or a really cool guitar riff, nothing to make me move my feet or feel the song in my body. I know some country music singers today are trying to make an edgier, rock-sounding song, but then they're just doing a weak imitation of rock, and who wants to hear that when you can hear the real thing? The only time country gets a little interesting is when it gets away from its twangy roots, but then it isn't really country and is trying to be something that it isn't.

To me the whole country music scene seems a little phony. Here are all these guys and girls in cowboy hats and Wrangler jeans and cowboy boots, and probably none of them even know the front of a horse from the back. The audience is filled with good old boy red necks, and these aren't people I'd care to be around. I don't relate to people that like country music, and maybe that's one reason I don't like the music. To me, they are the America, love it or leave it, flag-waving Republicans that help send our country in the wrong direction. What that's got to do with country music I'm not sure, but it's a part of the mix of my dislike for the music.

I think you could cut country music out of the American music scene and everything would be just fine. I know I wouldn't miss it for a minute. I do want to make an exception, though. I went to see the Johnny Cash life story movie with Joaquin Phoenix, because I'm a big Joaquin Phoenix fan, and I liked one Johnny Cash song about killing a guy and going to prison and ruining his life. That song got to me, both the way it sounded and what it said. So I'll make that one exception, but that's it. And since Johnny Cash isn't going to be writing or singing any new songs, I'll keep tuning out the country stations.

Revisions Guidelines

Now that you have written your first draft, set it aside for a few hours or a day and then begin the revision process. As you read over your draft, make changes following these guidelines.

1. Reread your draft to evaluate how well readers will understand your negative feelings about the topic. Revise your draft in ways that help readers understand why you feel as you do.

2. Check your opening paragraph to make sure you have clearly introduced your topic, created some interest for readers, and included your thesis statement. What might you add or change to improve your opening?

3. Check your middle paragraphs to make sure that each paragraph supports your thesis sentence in some manner, and that each begins with a topic sentence expressing the main idea of the paragraph. What might you add - a new example, some added explanation, a particular detail, a new supporting point - to make your draft more interesting, informative, or complete?

4. Check your concluding paragraph to make sure that it provides readers with a sense of completion, relates to your thesis statement, and adds something new to your paper.

5. Check your use of transitional wording to tie sentences and paragraphs together. Add any transitions (e.g. first, second, also, in addition, finally, therefore, however, etc.) that will help readers understand your ideas and how they are connected.

6. Check your paragraphing to make sure you have begun a new paragraph when you move to something new in your paper: a different part, a different reason, a new example, a different time, place, or event. Divide overly long paragraphs, and combine very short paragraphs containing related material.

7. Check your organization, the order in which you present your supporting points in the middle paragraphs. Would any point or points be more effectively presented in a different location? Is there any sentence or sentences that would fit better within a different paragraph or in a different location in the same paragraph?

8. Check the wording of each sentence, and eliminate unnecessary words, replace questionable word choices, and reword awkward or vague sentences

> to make each sentence as smooth, clear, and concise as you can.
>
> Write the second draft of your paper, including all of the changes you have made to improve its wording, content, organization, and paragraphing.

Sample Revised Draft

Country Music

When I'm driving to work or to school, ~~I always have the radio on~~ **I'm always** listening to music **on the radio.** I'll change stations regularly, looking for a song that I want to hear. I like different kinds of music, including jazz, hip-hop, alternative, classic rock, and even the oldies, so there's always something on that I like. However, when I tune in to a country station, I keep moving the dial because I know that I'm not going to like the song very much. ~~The truth is,~~ **In fact,** I don't listen to country music at all because I just don't care for it.

~~To~~ **For** me, music is an emotional experience, and some music moves me and some doesn't. Country music doesn't move me at all. It is more difficult to explain exactly why, like trying to explain why I like chocolate ice cream better than strawberry. There is just nothing in the sound of country music that ~~excites or~~ moves me in any way.

First, I think most of the country lyrics ~~are~~ **sound a bit** corny. ~~Like~~ For example, the Garth Brooks' song **lyrics** "I've got friends in low places" ~~to me those~~ are the corny **kind of** lyrics that you'd only hear in a country song. ~~It doesn't~~ **They don't** sound real, and no one I know ~~says things~~ **talks** like that. I don't feel any connection with country song lyrics, and maybe ~~you have to be a certain kind of~~ **only** country ~~person~~ **music lovers** can relate. I don't ~~relate~~.

Most country songs sound the same to me, and I don't care for the sound. ~~You~~ **There is** always ~~have~~ that twangy guitar sound and an **old-fashion sounding** melody. ~~that sounds old-fashioned and boring~~. I never hear an interesting beat or a really cool guitar riff, nothing to make ~~me move~~ my feet **move** or feel the song in my body. ~~I know~~ Some country music singers today are trying to make an edgier, **rock-like sound** sounding song, but then they're just doing a weak imitation of rock, and who wants to hear that when you can hear the real thing? The only time country gets a little interesting is when it gets away from its twangy roots, but then it isn't really country, **just** ~~and~~ trying to be something that it isn't.

To me the whole country music scene seems a little phony. ~~Here are~~ All these guys and girls **are dressed** in cowboy hats, ~~and~~ Wrangler jeans and cowboy boots, and probably none of them ~~even~~ knows the front of a horse from the back. The audience is **also** filled with **a lot of** good-old boy red necks, and these aren't people ~~I'd care to be around~~ **whose company I seek.** I don't **really** relate to people that like country music, and ~~maybe~~ **perhaps** that's one reason I don't like the music. ~~To me, they are the America, love it or leave it, flag-waving Republicans that help send our country in the wrong direction. What that's got to do with country music I'm not sure, but it's a part~~

~~of the mix of my dislike for the music~~.

~~I think you could cut~~ **If** country music ~~out of the~~ **was removed from** the American music scene, ~~and~~ everything would be just fine **with me**. I know I wouldn't miss it for a minute. I do want to make an exception, though. **A while back** I went to see the Johnny Cash life story movie with Joaquin Phoenix~~, because I'm a big Joaquin Phoenix fan~~, and I liked one Johnny Cash song about killing a guy, ~~and~~ going to prison, and ruining his life. That song got to me, both ~~the way it sounded and what it said.~~ **the sound and the message**. So I'll make that one exception, but ~~that's it. And~~ since Johnny Cash isn't going to be ~~writing or~~ singing any new songs, I'll keep tuning out the country stations.

Editing Guidelines

Now that you have improved the content, wording, and organization of your paper, the final step is to proofread your paper for errors to produce an error-free final draft. Proofread your draft by applying the following guidelines, and pay particular attention to the types of errors you are most prone to make. Then write the final corrected draft of your paper to share with classmates.

1. Check your sentences to make sure you haven't run any together or put a comma between sentences instead of a period. Correct run-on sentences or comma splices by separating longer sentence with periods and combining shorter, related sentences with a joining word.

2. Check your draft for any sentence fragments: incomplete sentences with a period after them. To correct fragments, attach them to the complete sentence they belong with, or add words to make them complete.

3. Check your use of irregular verbs, making sure you have used the correct irregular forms and spelled them correctly.

4. Check your comma usage, making sure you have inserted commas into your sentences following the rules in this unit.

5. Check the spelling of any word you are uncertain of, or run the spell check on your word processing program, to eliminate any spelling errors.

6. Check your verbs in each sentence to make sure that they agree with their subjects.

Readings

Helping the Homeless

by Malcolm Feeley

I help the homeless. I give money to non-profit organizations that help street people. I volunteer at shelters and soup kitchens. I pass out cards to homeless people that list local shelters. I donate food, clothing, and toys for homeless children. On occasion I take a homeless person to an AA meeting or a drug rehab center.
I don't help the homeless out of any noble or altruistic sentiment. I don't help them out of guilt. I help the homeless for one reason: they are my brothers and sisters. And yours.

I was homeless for over five years. I am an alcoholic, and I lost my job and family when drinking took over my life. I lost interest in everything but my next bottle, and before long I was on the streets living from drink to drink. Unless you are an alcoholic, it is hard to understand how a person could lose everything just to pursue the pathetic goal of staying drunk. I hit rock bottom on the streets and stayed there for five years.

Life on the streets is tough for everyone. I slept on sidewalks, under bridges, in parks, in abandoned cars, and in shelters. I panhandled for money to buy booze and rummaged through dumpsters and garbage cans behind restaurants for food and recycled cans and bottles. I was beaten up by thugs or someone who wanted my bottle more than me, and I was arrested several times for loitering. I was often sick and in and out of free medical clinics. Cold and hunger were constant companions along with uncontrollable tremors when I went too long between drinks. I figured I'd be dead in a few years.

I made a few friends on the streets, and we hung out together, sleeping in a park until we'd get kicked out, then moving under a bridge, and then back to another park. We shared bottles and food when someone didn't have anything, and we watched each other's back. We also shared our pasts - other lives once lived and how we got where we were. You can't judge a person by their life circumstance, and I met some good people on the streets: decent, honest, and yes, hardworking. I also met some bad people, as there are in all walks of life, who preyed upon their homeless brothers and sisters.

Who are the homeless people? Many are drug addicts or alcoholics like me who didn't get or seek out treatment for their disease as their lives spiraled downward. Other homeless, through no fault of their own, have lost their jobs and can't pay rent. Many are war veterans who returned with emotional or physical problems that prevented them from holding jobs or fitting back into society. Many abandoned or abused women end up on the streets, sometimes with children in tow. They often turn to prostitution to survive and drugs to escape.

People you see muttering to themselves or sitting lifelessly on a sidewalk often suffer from mental illness such as schizophrenia, bipolar disorder, or depression that goes untreated year after year. Younger people who run away from home or who believe living on the streets is an adventure are among the transient homeless who come, eventually leave, and are replaced by an endless flood of alienated youth. Many people who have lost their jobs eventually find other work and vanish from the streets. The older homeless are a more entrenched group, often living out their lives on the street.

People seldom see the homeless as individuals, and they are generally viewed as the dregs of society, unworthy of human contact. These filthy, bedraggled human flotsam and jetsam have committed the cardinal sin of our society: financial failure. Become a street person for one day, sitting on a sidewalk, and you will see in the faces of passersbys what every homeless person sees: disgust, scorn, hatred, curiosity reserved for freaks. Of course, there are always the exceptions who treat you like a human being, but most of society would rather cross the street to avoid the slightest contact. And homeless people, who already blame themselves for their plight, often perceive themselves as they are perceived by society, adding to the guilt and self-loathing many already carry.

I was one of the lucky ones. I was staying in a shelter during one bitterly cold winter week and began talking with a volunteer. He was an alcoholic who had been sober for five years. He invited me to an AA meeting and said he'd come by the next day to pick me up. I'd been invited before, but I'd never wanted to give up the only thing I lived for. This time, however, I felt particularly vulnerable, maybe because I was feeling ill or because of the frigid cold or the fatigue in my bones from five years on the street. When he came to pick me up the next day, I didn't run.

After five years of drunkenness, getting sober wasn't easy and I fell off the wagon more than once. However, the volunteer named Jim never gave up on me, so I was accountable to someone who cared about me. I had a dream that kept me going - to someday be reunited with my family - and although it was an improbable dream, it was something to hold onto. Jim finally got me into a half-way house that had the structure I needed and a part-time job with a soft drink distributing company. Eventually as I got physically and mentally stronger, I was able to work full-time and move into my own apartment. They speak of the lure of the streets calling the homeless back to their carefree, independent life, but I never heard it. That was the last place I wanted to go, and there is nothing carefree about living on the streets.

Jim helped me find out where my family was living, but their lives, naturally, had moved forward. My wife had remarried and my two teenage children were in a stable family situation with a good step-father. My ex-wife had no interest in seeing me again, and I didn't blame her. However, she let me meet with my kids in a restaurant while she and their step-dad waited next door. Just to see my kids brought a flood of emotion I couldn't restrain. I couldn't begin to tell them how sorry I was for everything I had done. I hugged both of them when I left, and it was the best feeling I had had in years. Just to be a small part of their lives is my dream come true.

I don't remember the moment when I decided to start helping the homeless, but I know they had never left my mind from the time I left the streets. They were the only family I knew for over five years, and I couldn't abandon them. So I do what I can do, never enough and with no delusion that I am making a big difference. But if I can help get one person off the streets from time to time, or make life a little more tolerable for others who may always be homeless, the gift I receive is greater than the one I give.

There are thousands of people like myself who help the homeless, but there are never enough. The homeless need our help, and there are things that we can all do. The next time you pass by a homeless person, look him or her in the eye, smile, and say, "How are you doing today?" In other words, acknowledge their humanity. I know how much that can mean.

Questions for Discussion

1. What is the thesis of the essay? How is the thesis developed as the essay unfolds?

2. What is the purpose of the paragraphs in which the author relates his own experiences on the street?

3. What impact does the author having been homeless himself have on the reader?

4. What did you learn from the essay about homeless people that you didn't know, and how may it affect your attitude towards them?

Five Women Buried Alive -- and the Media Ignore It

by Riane Eisler

Last month, the U.S. media were full of stories about the resignation of Pervez Musharraf as president of Pakistan. But another event that same week in Pakistan -- that tribesmen buried five young women alive for wanting to choose their own husbands -- got almost no coverage.

According to the Asian Human Rights Commission, the women's "crime" was that they defied tribal elders and arranged marriages to men of their own choosing in a civil court. They were abductedat gunpoint by some men and dragged off to a remote field, where they were beaten, shot, thrown into a ditch, and then, while still breathing, smothered to death with rocks and mud.

Yet not even when a member of the Pakistani parliament, Israr Ullah Zehri, defended these barbaric killings as "century-old traditions" - when he said that killing women who defy male control by wanting to chose their own husbands is necessary to "stop obscenity" - was there international outrage.

Why is this? And why is there no international outrage about the fact that violence against women and female children is indeed a "century-old tradition?"

- Every day, so-called "honor killings" of girls and women - often by members of their own families, and even when they are victims of rape - are unpunished, and even lauded, in Iran, Iraq, Saudi Arabia and other Middle Eastern nations.

- In Africa and parts of Southeast Asia and the Middle East, each year an estimated 2 million girls are genitally mutilated - another "moral" tradition that not only kills but exacts a terrible lifelong toll of disease and sexual dysfunction from those who survive.

- In China and India, millions of baby girls have been killed or abandoned. Indeed, female infanticide and medical neglect of girls can be so severe that, according to a U.N. Human Development Report, girls ages 2 to 4 die at nearly twice the rate of boys in India's Punjab state.

- According to a World Health Organization report, 20 percent of women have suffered sexual abuse as children.

- According to another U.N. report, thousands of girls are enslaved - often offered for sale by members of their own families - in the global sex industry.

- Even in these United States, more women are killed by their husbands or boyfriends than by automobile accidents.

Neither reporters nor pundits find all this violence against girls and women worthy of attention despite the U.S. media's seeming obsession with mayhem and murder. Nor have the world's religious leaders seen fit to speak out against this violence despite the fact that they often say they are against violence. It's time that we change the shameful fact that when it comes to barbarity against members of the female half of humanity, the silence of not only the press but also of political, religious and other leaders is almost deafening.

Women's organizations nationally and internationally have for years struggled to change this, and gradually human rights organizations have paid more attention to the pandemic of violence against women. But men - and particularly men who identify themselves as moral leaders - must also raise their voices. They too must voice their outrage about their "brothers" all over the world who are brutalizing women with impunity.

I co-founded "Spiritual Alliance to Stop Intimate Violence" with Nobel Peace Prize laureate Betty Williams to engage leaders from the world's religions to at long last use their moral authority to end traditions of violence against women and children. We did this not only for the sake of the millions of girls and women who are beaten, burned, mutilated or killed each year, but for the sake of all of us. Because as long as brutality against women and children is ignored or dismissed as "just" a women's or children's issue, talk of a more just and caring world will only be just talk. For millions of women across the world, there is no justice.

It is time that morality no longer be used to mask brutality and violence. It is time that women and men worldwide, including the women and men of the mass media, express outrage against the immorality of using tradition to justify mayhem and murder. If enough of us make this a top issue in our churches, synagogues and mosques, our religious authorities will eventually follow. If enough of us write letters to the editor, blog and otherwise break the silence about traditions of violence against women and children, the media - and eventually also politicians and others who make and enforce social policy - will follow worldwide.

Questions for Discussion

1. What is the author's purpose in beginning with the shocking incident presented in the first three paragraphs? What was your reaction to the incident?

2. Assuming as the author states that atrocities against young girls and women often go unreported, why do you think this occurs? How can the situation change?

3. What is the author's purpose in writing the essay? What is her primary interest?

4. Discuss abusive incidents against girls or women that you are aware of. What are the causes, and what can we all do to end such violence?

Unit 4
Beliefs and Values

One of the higher purposes to which writers apply their skills is to share their beliefs and values with readers. Through their writings, we discover what issues they feel are important, what they believe in, and what values guide those beliefs.

For example, if a writer values the health of children, she may be concerned about the issue of obesity in children. She may feel it is important that they eat nutritious foods and avoid less healthy, fattening foods. To that end, she may write an essay expressing the belief that eating at fast food restaurants is not good for children, and that the best way for them to get nutritious meals is through home cooking. What she values - the welfare of children - guides her concern for their eating habits.

In this unit, you will write about an issue of importance to you based on your personal beliefs and values. You will decide what issue to write about and what you believe about the issue. In addition, you will decide who your reading audience will be and your purpose in writing to them.

The purpose of this assignment is to expose you to a different type of writing. In the first three units, you wrote about your life - memorable experiences, influential people, and particular interests - with the primary purpose of informing your audience and engaging their interest. In this unit, rather than writing about yourself, you write about an issue that may affect you as well as others, and you move beyond informing your reading audience to influencing how they think and feel about something important.

People often have different beliefs, or viewpoints, on a particular issue. Lightening rod issues such as abortion, gun control, capital punishment, or gay marriage polarize people who hold clashing viewpoints. Because people's viewpoints differ on many issues, writing about such issues is always challenging. Getting readers to change their minds or to take action is never easy, particularly if their own values are challenged by the writer's viewpoint on an issue. However, that doesn't mean it is impossible, and some of our greatest social changes were influenced by the persuasive writings of passionate Americans: the abolition of slavery, the abolition of child labor, the right of women to vote, and the right of all children to an education.

Prewriting

In preparing to write the first draft of your issue-oriented paper, you will first spend some time deciding on a writing topic, using the brainstorming technique to generate potential topics. Next, you will decide how you feel about the issue, and express that viewpoint in a thesis statement that you will support in your paper. Finally, you will make a list of some of the reasons that you believe as you do, and also consider why some people may feel differently.

Topic Selection

For your upcoming paper, you will choose an issue that you feel is important and that people may have differing opinions on. In deciding upon a topic, consider the following:

1. What is a particular issue that interests you and that also may interest other people?

2. What is a particular issue that you know something about and have an opinion on?

3. What is a particular issue that people have different opinions on? For this paper, you are selecting a topic that everyone doesn't feel the same way about.

4. You may write about an issue from any field - sports, education, politics, fashion, technology, music, health, family, etc. - that people have differing opinions on.

Brainstorming

Needless to say, there are many issues in different fields that could be subjects for your paper. One way to consider a number of possible writing topics is to brainstorm on the topics: writing down any issue that comes to mind without evaluating it. When you brainstorm, you try to get as many ideas on paper as possible.

The purpose of this brainstorming session is to generate and consider different topic choices with the goal of deciding upon the best topic for your paper. The freewheeling nature of brainstorming helps you come up with ideas you may not have thought of otherwise, perhaps leading to a topic you hadn't considered.

Prewriting Activity 4.1

Brainstorm as many issues as you can think of within different fields. Write down any issue that comes to mind without evaluating it.

Sample Brainstorming:

Cost of textbooks	Revitalizing our downtown - worth it?
Parking on campus	Reality TV
Dark parts of campus at night	All the testing in elementary grades
Attendance at campus functions	Gangs and violence
Outsourcing American jobs	Dress codes for high schools?
Athletes getting arrested	Shootings at schools
Playoff for college football?	The way young girls dress
Violent rap songs	Juveniles tried as adults?
Free song downloading	Public vs. private schools
Woman president for U.S.?	Torn up streets in town
Should campus security carry guns?	Illegal alien problems

Prewriting Activity 4.2

From your brainstormed list and other topics you may be considering, choose an issue for your upcoming paper, keeping in mind the four suggestions for topic selection. Since this is not a "research" paper, make sure to select a topic that you know enough about to write knowledgeably.

Thesis Statement

As you recall from the previous unit, your thesis statement expresses the viewpoint on your topic that you want to develop and support in the paper. The thesis statement accomplishes a number of purposes: letting readers know what your paper is about, providing direction for you as the writer, giving your paper a focus that influences everything you write, and sharing with readers what you believe in and value.

For the thesis statement for your upcoming paper, consider how you feel about the topic. For example, if your issue were the parking situation on campus, you may believe any of the following: that there is adequate on-campus parking for students; that there is not adequate parking for students unless they get to school early to find it; that there is only a parking issue because students who live near the campus are too lazy to walk or ride a bike; or that the parking issue is so serious that students are opting to go to other local schools as a result.

As another example, let's say you are writing about a proposed downtown lake that is being considered by the city council as a way to attract people and revitalize the area. You may be in favor of the project, you may be opposed to the project, or you may feel that while building a lake doesn't sound feasible, a different kind of downtown water feature might accomplish the same purpose. The most important consideration is that you decide on a thesis statement that most accurately expresses your belief on the issue, one that you can enthusiastically and convincingly support in a paper.

Prewriting Activity 4.3

Decide on a thesis statement for your upcoming paper. Generate a statement that clearly expresses your viewpoint on the topic and that you can support and develop in a paper.

Sample thesis statements

Topic: Creating a lake in the downtown area
Thesis: Creating a lake downtown would be a big step towards revitalizing the area.

Topic: Serving beer at the on-campus pizza restaurant
Thesis: Serving beer on campus would not be in the interest of students or faculty.

Topic: Campus police carrying handguns
Thesis: In today's world, campus police should be armed with handguns.

Topic: Proposed new gambling casino
Thesis: The last thing this county needs is another gambling casino.

Thesis Support

Some writers initially believe that if they have a good thesis, the paper will take care of itself. Unfortunately, that is not the case. Some readers may disagree with your thesis and have an opposing viewpoint. Others may be disinterested in your topic and your thesis. Still others may take a "wait and see" attitude, deciding how they feel about your viewpoint after reading your paper and learning more about the topic.

How well a writer supports her thesis determines the effectiveness of a paper and its impact on readers. A good assumption to make is that every reader will need to be convinced that the writer's viewpoint is valid and sensible. Before beginning a draft, a writer should have the mind-set, "My readers don't agree with me yet. How can I write this paper so that they will agree with me by the end?"

Thesis Support Guidelines

You can support your thesis in a variety of ways.

1. By explaining the issue clearly so readers understand it.
2. By providing and developing strong reasons in support of your opinion.
3. By anticipating readers' arguments and addressing them in your paper.
4. By showing readers how they could be affected by the issue.
5. By providing possible "scenarios" of what could happen if your viewpoint is heeded and if it is not.
6. By using comparisons that support your thesis. (For example, if you support a downtown lake, you may show the success of similar projects elsewhere.)

Considering these six points, let's say that the issue for your paper is the proposed tuition increase at your college, and your viewpoint expressed in the thesis statement is that you are strongly against the increase. First, you might explain exactly how much the increase is, calculate the new, increased cost for a semester, a year, and even four years, and then calculate the increase between the current and new tuition rates for those periods of time. Readers, the trustees for the school that set policy, would know that you understand the specifics of the tuition increase and the exact financial effect it would have on students.

Next, you might develop a few supportive points for your thesis, each in a separate paragraph. Your points might include how many students can't afford a tuition increase, how students are still reeling from the last increase two years ago, how the school will actually lose money by declining enrollment, how the increase isn't justified by the school's needs, and how other similar colleges are holding the line on tuition. You might also bring in a value that you as well as trustees may hold - that college should be affordable to all Americans - and show how the tuition increase can kill the American dream for many people.

Finally, you might acknowledge that the school does have increased costs but that raising tuition is the worst way to try and cover them, and then provide alternative solutions. In addition, you might raise another point that you believe could move school trustees: that it is the job of every elected trustee to keep the college doors open for every person who elected them. In this paper, then, you would have helped readers understand the tuition issue clearly, presented and developed a number of points in support of your viewpoint, acknowledged and addressed the concern that led to the proposed increase, and involved the readers (trustees) by showing that they have an obligation that runs counter to the tuition increase.

Making a List

Making a list of supporting points for your thesis helps you consider why you believe the way you do, determine whether you have some good supportive reasons, see where the strengths of your upcoming paper may lie, and develop some material for your paper. You might even find that you can't think of many supporting ideas, and that you may be better off writing about something else.

Prewriting Activity 4.4
Make a list of supporting points for your thesis statement which you may develop in your first draft. List any point that you feel may be relevant.

Sample list

Topic:	Illegal Immigration
Thesis:	America has benefitted greatly from the economic contribution that illegal immigrants have made and continue to make.

List of points:	My grandparents' story
	U.S. agricultural success built on back of illegal immigrants
	Contribute to the economy as consumers
	Form the backbone of many rural American towns
	Commit few crimes compared to Americans
	Successors of earlier immigrants become mainstream Americans

---

Opposing Arguments

Recognizing and addressing opposing arguments is an effective way to support your thesis. If you can make readers question their own viewpoint by poking holes in their supportive arguments, they may be more receptive to your viewpoint.

For example, let's say you support the creation of a downtown lake to attract people and help revitalize the area. However, you are also aware of the opposition's arguments: that a lake project is too expensive and taxpayers will foot the bill, and that since no other plans have worked to revitalize the downtown, a lake probably won't help either. If you raise those arguments in your paper and then reveal their flaws to readers, you may win some people over who had based their opinion on those arguments.

Prewriting Activity 4.5

Come up with two or three arguments in opposition to your thesis and consider how you might counter them in your draft.

Sample arguments

Topic: Illegal Immigration
Thesis: America has benefitted greatly from the economic contribution that illegal
         immigrants have made and continue to make.

 Opposing arguments:

1.   Illegals take jobs from Americans.
2.   Illegals are an economic drain on the country.
3.   Illegals have a high crime rate.

Counters:

1.   Illegal aliens have always done the jobs that Americans won't do.
2.   Illegal aliens contribute much more to the economy than they cost the country in
     services.
3.   Illegal aliens have a low crime rate compared to their American counterparts.

First Drafts

As mentioned previously, writing about issues is different in some ways from the writing you have done in earlier units. Rather than writing primarily to inform, as you did in previous papers, you are now not only writing to engage your readers' interest but also to influence their beliefs and behavior. The writing challenge has clearly been stepped up, and the writing considerations have become more complex, an important step in continuing to develop your writing skills.

Audience and Purpose

Two primary concerns with issue-oriented writing are your reading audience and your purpose: whom you are writing for and why. For example, if you support the creation of a downtown lake in your city, you may have at least four different audiences that you may want to reach at some point: the city council members who will decide the fate of the lake project, the residents who are opposed to the lake, the residents who are indifferent or uninformed, and the residents who like yourself favor the idea. All four audiences may have an impact on whether the lake is ever built, and you might target each group for your writing.

Your purpose for writing, however, and what you write to each audience may differ depending on their attitude towards the project. For example, your purpose in writing to the council members would be to support those who favor the project and to change the minds of those who don't. Your purpose in writing to residents in opposition would be to change them into supporters or at least neutralize their influence with the council. Your purpose in writing to neutral citizens would be to inform them on the issue and get them to support the project. Your purpose in writing to residents who favor the project would be to get them to support it actively and influence the council directly.

Reading Audience

When you consider your reading audience for your upcoming paper, ask yourself the following:

1.   What people would be most interested in the issue?
2.   What people might have an impact on the outcome of the issue?
3.   What people would support your viewpoint, who would probably oppose it, and who would probably be neutral or indifferent?

Drafting Activity 4.6

Considering the preceding four questions, decide on the primary reading audience for your paper: the people that you feel should definitely read your paper. It may be your classmates, a particular group of classmates, college students in general, the school board, the college president, instructors at the school, all adults residing in the area, a certain state legislator, all music lovers, men in particular, women in particular, wild animal lovers, and so on.

Sample audience

Primary audience for paper on illegal immigrants:

The general public, whose viewpoint will help determine the direction the country takes with immigration "reform"

Writing Purpose

Going hand in hand with your reading audience is your writing purpose: what you hope to accomplish by writing to this audience. Once you determine your purpose, you can consider the best ways to accomplish that purpose, which will influence both the content and the tone of the paper. Your tone is the attitude that you convey through your writing, whether it be angry, courteous, sarcastic, humorous, enthusiastic, negative, attacking, concerned, and so on. The tone that you set in your paper, which may change in places depending on your purpose, may have as much of an impact on readers as what you have to say.

Let's say that you strongly oppose the new earlier class drop date the college is considering implementing next semester. Previously, the college allowed students to drop after the eighth week in the semester without penalty. The new proposal is for a five week drop date, with drops beyond that date resulting in an "F" for the student. In writing about this issue, you decide your best audience would be the instructors since they understand the impact of drop dates on students, and many may be sympathetic to the students on this issue.

Your writing purpose is clear: to get instructors to oppose the proposed drop date and voice their opposition to the board and administration. You are angry about the proposed change, but your anger isn't directed at the instructors, so your writing may carry a friendly, "conspiratorial" tone implying that on this issue, it is "us" (students and instructors) against "them" (trustees and administrators). When you want people on your side, you don't want to alienate them by using an angry or condescending tone.

On the other hand, if you were writing directly to the school board, your purpose and approach would be different. First, these are people who are not affected by the drop date like students are. Second, they may not agree with you that there is a problem, so you would need to educate and convince them. Third, while you were getting instructors to rally behind your cause, your purpose with the board is to get them to reconsider a policy they may have had a hand in developing. You probably want to maintain a courteous tone in your letter but at the same time show the great concern that students have with the proposal.

To decide on your writing purpose for the upcoming paper, consider the following:

1.　What do you hope to accomplish by writing to this audience?
2.　What is the most that you can realistically expect to achieve?
3.　What is the best tone for the paper in order to accomplish your purpose?
4.　How do you think you can best accomplish your purpose through your writing?

Drafting Activity 4.7

Decide on your writing purpose for your upcoming paper and the best tone for accomplishing that purpose.

Sample writing purpose

Topic:　　Illegal Immigration

Purpose:　To get readers to see illegal immigrants in a positive light.

Tone:　　Serious, committed

Drafting Activity 4.8

Read the following first draft and with a classmate and analyze it by answering the following questions.

1.　What is accomplished in the opening paragraph? What is the thesis statement?

2.　What is the purpose of the author relating the story of his grandfather? What is he trying to accomplish?

3.   What are the main supporting points for the thesis, and how are they developed?

4.   What are the opposing arguments that are raise and how are they countered in the draft?

5.   What is accomplished in the final two paragraphs? What is the writer's primary purpose in communicating with his reading audience?

6.   What is the tone of the paper - the attitude the writer displays - and how appropriate is it?

Sample First Draft (reading audience - general public)

Illegal Immigration

When I read about immigration "reform" recommendations like sending all illegal Mexican immigrants back to Mexico or not allowing children of illegal immigrants to attend public school or receive medical care, I think of my grandfather. He is one of these illegal immigrants that some people claim are ruining America: taking our jobs, living off our benefits, and committing crimes. In fact, America has benefitted greatly from the economic contribution that illegal immigrants have made and continue to make.

My *abuelo* came to America as a young man from the Mexican state of Jalisco. He came from a large, poor family and like millions of Mexicans, came to America for a better life. Later, he was joined by a brother and two sisters, but to his deep regret, he never saw his parents again although he sent them money for as long as they lived.

Had my *abuelo* had the option of entering the U.S. legally, he certainly would have done so because crossing the border illegally was risky and dangerous. However, U.S. quotas for Mexican immigrants didn't begin to cover the number of Mexicans wishing to immigrate, so my *abuelo's* options were to scratch out a life of poverty in Mexico or come to America illegally. It is not hard to understand why he, like so many Mexicans, chose the latter.

Once in America, my *abuelo* found work on the West Coast as a migrant farm laborer, moving at different times of year from the strawberry and garlic fields of Salinas and Gilroy to the grape fields of the Central Valley to the apple orchards of Washington. The work was back-breaking and the life was hard, but my *abuelo* followed the crops for ten years. In a grape field near Selma one year he met a young female worker who would become my *abuela*. They had three children, including my father Gilbert, who traveled with them as my *abuela* cut back on her work to be with the children.

My *abuelo* was a good worker and a smart man, and to his and his family's good fortune, he was given year-around work at a farm outside of Dinuba in the Central Valley. He began by pruning vines and trees in the winter, fertilizing and thinning crops in the spring, and picking grapes, peaches, and plums in the summer and early fall. He went on to do irrigating, tractoring, and machine repair work, and within a couple years he was helping to manage the farm and oversee the migrant workers. He rented a house on the farm property with two bedrooms and an indoor bathroom, luxurious lodgings to a family used to living in labor camps.

Living in one place, my dad, his sister and brother were enrolled at a Dinuba elementary school, where they began getting an education for the first time. My *abuelo* realized that education was the key to escaping a life of manual labor, and he and my *abuela* made sure that their children were in school every day and did their lessons. Given the opportunities my *abuelos* never had, the U.S. citizenship they never received, the command of English they never gained, and none of the hardships they endured, my father flourished in America, doing well in school, graduating from college, and becoming a high school counselor. Thanks to my father and mother, who works as an administrative assistant in the county schools' office, I along with my sister and brother grew up in a middle class environment with a nice house and a beautiful life, all which we took for granted.

I am currently in college, my older brother is attending law school, and my sister recently graduated with a degree in physical therapy. Our futures are very bright, and we learned to work hard from our parents, who learned from their parents, who were all illegal immigrants. Most young Mexican-American adults my age in the Valley have similar family histories, with either their grandparents or great-grandparents coming to the U.S. from Mexico illegally. They, like my *abuelos*, worked hard, sacrificed greatly, lived poorly, took nothing from the government, and scrimped and saved so that their children and their children's children would have a better life. They worked hard for low wages and helped build one of the vastest and most successful agricultural industries in the world, which today's illegal immigrants continue to do.

Recognizing the tremendous work ethic and willingness of Mexican immigrants to work for lower wages, U.S. employers also hire today's illegal immigrants in all manners of labor including housing construction, gardening, house and hotel cleaning, and a variety of mechanical work. And these immigrants will continue to follow a pattern established long ago by people like my *abuelos*: get married, raise families, send their children to school, and spawn future generations of solid, hard-working U.S. citizens.

Every objective account I've read of illegal immigrants in the U.S. bear out these facts: they contribute much more to the economy than they take from it in educational and health services; they are not welfare recipients; they don't take jobs from Americans, doing the back-breaking work that Americans won't do; they commit significantly fewer crimes proportionately than American citizens do, doing nothing that would cast a light on themselves and their status; they make food products and housing cheaper for Americans by keeping agricultural and building overhead low; and they make life easier for the middle class by mowing their lawns and cleaning their houses. And like all American immigrants past, they beget future generations of U.S. citizens who have continued to make this country greater since its existence.

Is there then an illegal immigrant "problem" in the U.S.? Certainly not in the way that it is cast by right-wing politicians. First, of course, illegal immigration is a two-way street. Illegal immigrants have not only been welcome but are recruited by employers throughout the U.S. who rely on their employment. If there were no jobs available, there would be little immigration, but employers and the American public profit greatly from the influx of illegal aliens. The first step, then, in any attempt at "reform" would be to grant citizenship to all immigrants who have lived and worked in this country for a given time, say at least five years. They have earned their citizenship by the great good they have provided our country. I do not believe that a realistic part of the "solution" is to punish employers who hire illegal aliens. First, too many American industries rely on the hard work and low salaries that illegal aliens provide. No flood of Americans is going to rush in to fill the void for the kinds of work and wages that are available.

Will there come a time when the flow of illegal immigrants surpasses America's need for low-salaried employees? I can't say, but one thing is certain: when the job availability dries up, so will the flow of illegal immigrants. People emigrate for a better life and for jobs that aren't available in their country. If those jobs aren't available in America, the incentive for immigration drops dramatically. In the meantime, current illegal aliens who are long-term U.S. residents should be granted citizenship, and every illegal alien in the country should be treated with dignity and respect. My *abuelo* and *abuela* certainly deserved that, and America is a better country because of them and immigrants like them. So right-wing politicians should quit scapegoating illegal aliens for the recessionary problems that they had no role in creating and turn their attention to real problems like the deficit and the outsourcing of American jobs. When it comes to the economy, illegal aliens have always been a part of the solution, not the problem.

Drafting Activity 4.9

Write the first draft of your paper keeping the following guidelines in mind.

Drafting Guidelines

1. In your opening paragraph, introduce your topic, create reader interest, and include your thesis statement at or near the end of the paragraph.

2. Develop the support for your thesis statement in your middle paragraphs, including some or all of the points that you listed during prewriting. As a general rule, develop each point in a separate paragraph, and begin each middle paragraph with a topic sentence that expressesthe main idea of the paragraph.

3. Towards the end of the middle paragraphs, introduce and counter one or two

opposing arguments to your viewpoint.

4. Conclude your paper in a manner that reinforces your thesis statement and makes your purpose clear, whether it be to move readers to action, to keep them from acting, or to reconsider their viewpoint on the topic.

5. Keep your reading audience and purpose in mind as you write, and try to maintain the best tone to accomplish your purpose. Keep a single question in mind: how can I best convince my readers to agree with my viewpoint?

6. While your prewriting preparation provided you with a number of ideas to develop in your draft, don't limit yourself to just those ideas as you write. Often new ideas will come to mind, triggered by what you have written. Keep your mind open to new thoughts during the drafting process, and include anything that you feel could improve the paper.

Revision

A critical part of the writing process is revising your drafts. All writers share the task, and it is an invaluable part of producing your best writing. Many writers feel that revision is the most important part of the process, and the oft-heard phrase "writing is revision" reflects that belief.

When writing your first draft, your main concern is getting your ideas on paper without a lot of thought to your wording or organization, or the effect your writing may have on readers. When you begin to revise, you shift your focus to evaluating how well you have expressed your ideas and the impact your writing may have on readers. Your focus has shifted from getting your ideas on paper to expressing those ideas in the most effective way.

In this section, you revise your draft based on revision considerations from previous units and new considerations that apply to your issue-oriented paper. You learn the importance of substantiating claims: providing evidence to convince readers of the value of your supporting points.

Substantiating Claims

When readers read and evaluate an issue-oriented paper, they seldom agree with everything the writer says without question. They may have a different viewpoint on the topic or little or no opinion, reading to decide whether they might embrace the writer's viewpoint. In either case, they may be reading with a degree of skepticism, waiting to be convinced rather than accepting the writer's thesis.

Let's say, for example, that you are writing about the drop-date change at your school that was mentioned previously in the unit. You are writing to the board of trustees for your college, and you have good reasons to believe that moving the drop date forward is a bad idea. However, the board members may be a skeptical lot since they are considering changing the drop date. They are going to take some convincing.

One reason that you believe an earlier drop date is a bad idea is that it will result in more students taking an "F" grade for dropping beyond the deadline. That is a claim that you are making: a statement you believe to be true. Board members may not agree with you, however. To convince them, you need to substantiate your claim by providing some evidence that the date change will result in what you say.

To substantiate your claim, you may learn from the office of admissions that the majority of students drop classes during the eighth and ninth week of a semester. That would help convince trustees that a five-week drop date may be too early for many students, resulting in the "F" grades you claim. You might also discover that students at another college that instituted an earlier drop date experienced a dramatic increase in "F" grades as a result, a further substantiation of your claim.

A second claim you may make is that a five-week drop date does not give students enough time to evaluate their progress in a class. To substantiate your claim, you might provide some evidence from your experience, citing different classes you have taken where little or no testing occurred during the first five weeks. You might provide further evidence by referring to the class syllabi of several teachers showing little testing occurring during the first five weeks compared to subsequent weeks.

The claims that you make in support of your thesis statement are very important. However, the substantiation of those claims - the evidence you provide to show that your claims are credible - is equally important. Unsupported claims do little to convince discerning readers, so it is important to recognize when you are making a claim in your writing and how to substantiate it.

Guidelines for Substantiating Claims

The following guidelines will help you substantiate claims effectively in your papers.

1. Provide evidence to support any statement that you make in defense of your thesis. The following are examples of such statements.

   People are friendlier during the Christmas season that at any other time. (How do you know? What evidence can you provide?)

   If global warming continues, many coastal cities will be underwater within fifty years. (What proof do you have? Who says so?)

   The best way to prepare for a test is to study an hour a day for a week before the test. (What evidence do you have? How do you know that?)

   The more experience you have revising your drafts, the easier it becomes. (How do you know that? What evidence do you have?)

2. Provide evidence that you feel would be most effective to support your claims.

   Claim: Chocolate ice cream is by far the favorite of most Americans.

   Evidence: Based on a survey of employees in ice cream parlors, on a survey of college students, and on a survey of supermarket employees.

   Claim: Biology 101 is one of the most difficult science classes at the college.

   Evidence : Based on personal experience, on the experience of other college students, and on the high drop-out rate.

Claim: Cherry tomatoes are very easy to grow.

Evidence: Based on personal experience, on the experience of neighbors, and on the opinion of horticulture instructors.

Claim: The Windmill Inn has excellent barbecued ribs.

Evidence: Based on personal experience, on the popularity of the menu item, on the comments of friends, and on comparisons with other restaurants.

3. Use any types of available evidence that would help convince readers of the validity of a claim: personal experience, the experience of others, examples, surveys, expert opinion, credible statistics, or relevant comparisons.

Revision Activity 4.10

Read the following paragraphs that support the thesis statements provided. With a classmate, identify the claim in each paragraph, the types of evidence used to support the claim, and the effectiveness of the evidence provided.

Topic: Extinction of Dinosaurs

Thesis: The extinction of the dinosaurs was caused by an asteroid crashing into earth.

Scientists have discovered a high concentration of iridium, a metal rare to earth but common in asteroids, in the sedimentary layer of rock laid down during the last era of the dinosaurs. In addition, a 150-kilometer crater was discovered near the Yucatan Peninsula in Mexico, evidence of a huge falling mass that struck the earth. Such a collision, scientists theorize, created a dust-filled atmosphere that blocked out sunlight, dropped temperatures drastically, and killed off over 70% of all plant and animal life, including the dinosaurs. Only such a cataclysmic event could destroy the creatures that had dominated the earth for hundreds of millions of years.

Topic: Cars for the future

Thesis: The auto technology is available to end our dependence on oil.

While Toyota has taken a major step in producing gas-saving hybrid vehicles, a bigger innovation is quietly taking place. A small company in North Carolina can add a second plug-in battery to the Toyota Prius car battery system. You can drive thirty-five miles on the newly installed battery before Prius' battery/gasoline system kicks in, and then plug it in overnight for another thirty-five miles. For most people, a thirty-five mile range will cover most of the daily driving they do, which would virtually eliminate gas usage. Car rental companies are lining up their fleets for conversion, and the genie is out of the bottle. The future is near.

Revision Activity 4.11

The following paragraphs contain some unsubstantiated claims that the writer needs to support to convince readers of their validity. With a classmate, identify the unsubstantiated claims that readers might question and the kinds of evidence the writer might use to substantiate them.

College Library

The school library is probably the most underused building at the college. Many times I've been in the library during the day and only a handful of students were in the huge building. At night it's even worse, and it feels eery, almost like you're in an abandoned building. One night I counted a total of five students in the building.

One problem is that students don't like studying in the library. In addition, the library's strict rules don't help the situation. The location of the library is also a problem. It is situated far from the center of campus where most classes are held. It sits on the northern end of campus near the technical and industrial buildings, a half-mile walk from most classrooms. The new student center near the middle of campus is a comfortable place to sit and study or read a magazine, so most students go there rather than trek a half mile across campus.

Finally, with most students having Internet access, there is little need for the library anymore. Perhaps technology is beginning to make traditional libraries obsolete.

Revision Activity 4.12

Revise the first draft of your paper by applying the following guidelines.

Revision Guidelines

1. Reread your paper and reevaluate your thesis and support. On careful analysis, have you taken a position on the issue that you feel is the most valid and defensible? At this point, you are not obligated to retain your current thesis if on

reexamination and reflection, you are persuaded that a different or altered position is more valid or makes more sense. If that is the case, revise your thesis and support to reflect your change of mind.

2. Check your opening paragraph to make sure you have clearly introduced your topic, created some interest for readers, and included your thesis statement. Is there anything you can add or change to make your opening more effective?

3. Check your middle paragraphs to make sure that each paragraph relates to and supports your thesis statement, that you have used topic sentences to express the main idea of each paragraph, and that you have presented your supporting points in the best order.

    In addition, make sure that you have provided effective evidence to support each claim you have made. Finally, make sure you have included one or two opposing arguments near the end and countered them effectively.

4. Check your concluding paragraph to make sure that it provides readers with a sense of completion, relates to your thesis statement, and adds something new for readers.

5. Read each paragraph to see if there is anything you can add - an example, a point in support of your thesis, a specific detail or description, an explanation, new supportive evidence for a claim - to make the paper more interesting, informative, or convincing.

6. Check your use of transitional wording to tie sentences and paragraphs together. Add any transitions (e.g. first, second, also, in addition, finally, therefore, however, etc.) that will help readers understand your ideas and how they are related.

7. Check your paragraphing to make sure you have begun a new paragraph when you move to something new in your paper: a different part, a different reason, a new example, a different claim, further evidence. Divide overly long paragraphs, and combine very short paragraphs containing related material.

8. Check the wording of each sentence, and revise sentences to make them clearer, smoother, and more concise by eliminating unnecessary words or phrases, rewording awkward or unclear sentences, and replacing questionable word choices.

9. Read your paper to make sure that your purpose is clear to readers and that you did everything possible to accomplish that purpose, including establishing a

> tone that is most appropriate for the paper.

Sample Revised Draft

Illegal Immigration

When I read about **politicians'** immigration "reform" recommendations like sending all illegal ~~Mexican~~ immigrants back to Mexico or not allowing **their** children ~~of illegal immigrants~~ to attend public school or receive medical care, I think of my grandfather. He is one of these illegal immigrants that some people claim are ruining America: taking our jobs, living off our benefits, and committing crimes. In fact, America has benefitted greatly from the economic contribution that illegal immigrants have made and continue to make.

My *abuelo* came to America as a young man from the Mexican state of Jalisco. He came from a large, poor family and like millions of Mexicans, ~~came~~ **emigrated** to America for a better life. Later, he was joined by a brother and two sisters, but to his deep regret, he never saw his parents again, **one of the greatest sacrifices that millions of immigrants have made.** ~~although he sent them money for as long as they lived.~~

Had my *abuelo* had the option of entering the U.S. legally, he certainly would have done so because crossing the border illegally was risky and dangerous. However, U.S. quotas for Mexican immigrants didn't begin to cover the number of Mexicans wishing to emigrate, so my *abuelo's* options were to scratch out a life of poverty in Mexico or come to America illegally. It is not hard to understand why he, like so many Mexicans, chose the latter.

Once in America, my *abuelo* found work on the West Coast as a migrant farm laborer, moving ~~at~~ different times of year from the strawberry and garlic fields of Salinas and Gilroy to the grape fields of the Central Valley to the apple orchards of Washington. The work was back-breaking and the life was hard, but my *abuelo* followed the crops for ten years. In a grape field near Selma one year he met a young female worker who would become my *abuela*. They had three children, including my father Gilbert, who traveled with them **and began helping in the fields at a young age.** ~~as my *abuela* cut back on her work to be with the children.~~

My *abuelo* was a good worker and a smart man, and to ~~his and~~ his family's good fortune, he was given year-around work at a farm outside of Dinuba in the Central Valley. He began by pruning vines and trees in the winter, **tying vines,** fertilizing, and thinning crops in the spring, and picking grapes, peaches, and plums in the summer and early fall. He ~~went on~~ **learned** to do irrigating, tractoring, and machine repair work, and within a couple years ~~he~~ was helping to manage the farm and oversee the migrant workers. He rented a house on the farm property with two bedrooms and an indoor bathroom, luxurious lodgings ~~to~~ **for** a family used to living in labor camps.

Living in one place, my dad, his sister and brother were enrolled at a Dinuba elementary school, where they began getting ~~an~~ a **real** education for the first time. My *abuelo* ~~realized~~ **knew** that education was the key to escaping a life of manual labor, and he and my *abuela* made sure that their children ~~were~~ **went** ~~in~~ **to** school every day and did their lessons. ~~Given the~~ **My father and his sister and brother had** opportunities my *abuelos* never had, the U.S. citizenship they never received, the command of English they never gained, and ~~none~~ **few** of the hardships they endured. My father flourished in America, doing well in school, graduating from college, and becoming a high school counselor. Thanks to my father and mother, who works as an administrative assistant in the county schools' office, I along with my own sister and brother grew up in a middle class ~~environment~~ **family** with a nice house and a ~~beautiful~~ **wonderful** life, all **of** which, **of course,** we took for granted.

I am currently in college, my older brother is attending law school, and my sister recently graduated with a degree in physical therapy. Our futures are very bright, and we learned to work hard from our parents, who learned from their parents, ~~who were~~ all illegal immigrants. Most ~~young~~ Mexican-American**s** ~~adults~~ my age in the Valley have similar family histories, with either their grandparents or great-grandparents coming to the U.S. from Mexico illegally. They, like my *abuelos*, worked hard, sacrificed greatly, lived poorly, took nothing from the government, and scrimped and saved so ~~that~~ their children and ~~their children's children~~ **grandchildren** would have a better life. They worked hard for low wages and helped build ~~one of~~ the ~~vastest and~~ most successful agricultural industry in the world, which today's illegal immigrants continue to ~~do~~ **maintain.**

Recognizing the tremendous work ethic and willingness of Mexican immigrants to work for lower wages, U.S. employers ~~also~~ **have branched out to** hire ~~today's~~ illegal immigrants in all ~~manners of labor~~ **types of jobs** including housing construction, gardening, house and hotel cleaning, garment manufacturing, and a variety of mechanical work. And these immigrants will continue to ~~follow a pattern established long ago by people like~~ **do what** my *abuelos* **did**: get married, raise families, send their children to school, and spawn future generations of solid, hard-working U.S. citizens.

Every objective account I've read of illegal immigrants in the U.S. bear out these facts: they contribute much more to the economy than they take from it in educational and health services; they are not welfare recipients; they don't take jobs from Americans, doing the back-breaking work that Americans won't do; they commit significantly fewer crimes proportionate~~ly~~ ~~than~~ **to** American citizens, ~~do,~~ **doing** nothing ~~that would~~ to cast a light on ~~themselves and~~ their status; they make food products and housing cheaper for Americans by keeping agricultural and ~~building~~ **construction** overhead low, and they make life easier for ~~the middle class~~ **millions of Americans** by mowing their lawns and cleaning their houses. And like all American immigrants past, they beget future generations of U.S. citizens who have continued to make this country greater since its ~~existence.~~ **beginning. The term "illegal" in front of "immigrant" does not devalue the contribution they make.**

Is there, then, an illegal immigrant "problem" in the U.S.? Certainly not in the way that it is ~~cast~~ **characterized** by right-wing politicians. First, of course, illegal immigration is a two-way street. Illegal immigrants have not only been welcome but are recruited by employers throughout the U.S. who rely on their employment. If there were no jobs available, there would be little immigration, but **both** employers and the American public profit greatly from the influx of illegal aliens. The first step, then, in any attempt at "reform" would be to grant citizenship to all immigrants who have lived and worked in this country for ~~a given time, say~~ at least five years. They have earned their citizenship by the great good they have provided our country. I do not believe that a realistic part of the "solution" is to punish employers who hire illegal aliens. First, too many American industries rely on the hard work and low salaries ~~that~~ **of** illegal aliens. ~~provide.~~ No flood of Americans is going to rush in to fill the void for the kinds of work **available** and wages **provided** ~~that are available~~. **Second, given the millions of employers nationwide who employ illegal aliens, not to mention the private citizens, enforcement of such a "solution" would be impossible.**

Will there come a time when the flow of illegal immigrants surpasses America's need for low-salaried employees? I can't say, but one thing is certain: when the job availability dries up, so will the flow of illegal immigrants. People emigrate for a better life and for jobs that aren't available in their country. If those jobs aren't available in America, the incentive for immigration drops dramatically. In the meantime, current illegal aliens who are long-term U.S. residents should be granted citizenship, and every illegal alien in the country should be treated with dignity and respect. My *abuelo* and *abuela* certainly deserved that, and America is a better country because of them and immigrants like them. So right-wing politicians should quit scapegoating illegal aliens for ~~the~~ recessionary problems that they had no role in creating and turn their attention to real problems like the deficit and the outsourcing of American jobs. When it comes to the economy, illegal aliens have always been a part of the solution, not the problem.

Editing

You are nearing completion of your issue-oriented paper, with little left but to clean up any errors and make a last-minute revision or two as you proofread your draft. It is important to apply the same thorough, meticulous approach you used to evaluate the wording and content of your paper to proofreading your draft for errors. An error-free final paper is certainly an attainable goal.

In this section, you review the punctuation and grammar elements covered in previous units and are introduced to two new grammar elements: subject pronouns and pronoun-antecedent agreement. Then you apply what you have learned to editing your latest draft for errors.

Pronoun Usage

Pronouns are among the most frequently used parts of speech. We use them to replace words rather than repeat the same words over and over in our writing. For example, if pronouns didn't exist, a sentence might read like this:

Jason brought Jason's dog with Jason to the restaurant, and Jason ate breakfast while Jason's dog waited outside for Jason.

Of course, such a sentence sounds ridiculous because we are used to the repeated word "Jason" being replaced by pronouns:

Jason brought *his* dog with *him* to the restaurant, and *he* ate breakfast while *his* dog waited outside for him.

Most of the time, writers use pronouns correctly because the correct forms sound right. However, when errors do occur, they usually involve subject pronouns or pronoun-antecedent agreement, where the pronoun must agree in gender and number with the word it replaces. You will learn how to avoid such errors in this section.

Subject Pronouns

Subject pronouns are only a problem when the subject is compound: two or more subjects joined by and or or. When there is only one subject, the correct subject pronoun form sounds right: I like to study late at night. He likes to study in the morning. They prefer studying together. We would never write, "Me likes to study late at night," or "Them prefer studying together."

However, when the subject pronoun is compound, the incorrect form doesn't sound as bad to some writers. For example, while you would never write, "Me like to go to outdoor concerts," some writers might write, "Alicia, Munro, and *me* like to go to outdoor concerts," rather than "Alicia, Munro, and *I* like to go to outdoor concerts."

To use the correct subject pronoun forms with compound subjects, follow these rules and suggestions.

1. A subject pronoun is a pronoun used as the subject of a sentence: *I* am tired of this heat.

2. Always use the correct subject pronoun forms in your writing: *I, he, she, it, you, they, we.*

3. Never use the following object pronouns as subject pronouns: *me, him, her, them, us.*

4. When the subject of a sentence is compound - two or more subjects joined by *and* or *or* - you use the same correct subject pronoun forms: *I, he, she, it, you, they, we.*

5. To always use the correct pronoun with a compound subject, mentally cross out the other subject(s) and decide which form sounds best by itself.

    Examples:

    Breanna, Jordan, and (we, us) went to the county fair on Sunday. (Would you say "*We* went" or "*Us* went?" The correct pronoun - *we* - is obvious when you separate it from the other subjects.)

    Matt, Fletcher, Monroe, and (he, him) enjoy eating breakfast in the cafeteria. (Would you say "*He* enjoys" or "*Him* enjoys?" The correct pronoun - *he* - is obvious when you separate it from the other subjects.)

Editing Activity 4.13

Underline the correct subject pronoun form in each of the following sentences. Example: Matt and (her, <u>she</u>) have been friends since childhood.

1. The Gomez brothers and (us, we) enjoy sitting in the end zone seats at the football game.

2. Gloria and (she, her) have roomed together for three semesters.

3. Julius, Raymond, Phyllis, Jorge, and (them, they) all tried out for the school debate team.

4. Your grandmother and (him, he) graduated from the same high school sixty years ago.

5. She, her) and (him, he) have very different opinions on whether Miriam and (me, I) should attend the anti-war rally on campus.

6. (They, them) and (us, we) always park in the same area of the dormitory parking lot.

7. Britanny and (her, she) don't look like sisters.

8. Your uncle and (him, he) gave me their tickets to Thursday's art gallery exhibition.

9. The other tourists in our group and (us, we) got on the wrong subway line and ended up in East Manhattan when we wanted to go to downtown.

10. Whenever you and (them, they) want to play backgammon again, just let me know.

Pronoun-Antecedent Agreement

The purpose of pronouns is to replace words that would otherwise be repeated needlessly. For example, the sentence, "John brought John's art portfolio with John to class," sounds odd. Therefore, we use pronouns to make the sentence sound normal: John brought *his* art portfolio with *him* to class.

Since a pronoun replaces another word, it needs to agree with that word - called its *antecedent* - in number and gender. For example, in the previous paragraph, the pronouns *his* and *him* replace the word *John* and agree with their antecedent because like John, they are singular in number and masculine in gender.

The following rules will ensure that your pronouns agree with their antecedents.

1. The following pronouns are grouped according to their number and gender.

   Singular masculine: *he, him, his, himself*

Singular feminine: *she, her, hers herself*
Singular neutral: *it, its, itself*
Plural: *they, them, their, theirs, themselves*
Plural including self: *we, us, our, ours, ourselves*

(Note: The first-person singular pronouns *I, me, my, mine* and the second-person singular/plural pronouns *you, your, yours, yourself* do not replace other words and don't create pronoun -antecedent agreement problems.)

2.   A pronoun always agrees with its *antecedent* - the word it replaces - in number and gender. Number refers to singular or plural, and gender refers to masculine, feminine, or neutral. For example, the antecedent Maria is singular and feminine, so any pronouns that replace the word Maria must also be singular and feminine: *she, her, hers, herself.*

Examples: (Antecedent is underlined and pronoun(s) are italicized.)

Sabrina brought *her* mother to college movie night. (The singular, feminine pronoun *her* agrees with its singular, feminine antecedent "Sabrina.")

Those maple trees lose *their* leaves early in September. (The plural pronoun *their* agrees with its plural antecedent "trees.")

The moon loses much of *its* luster as *it* descends towards the horizon. (The neutral pronouns *its* and *it* agree with the singular, neutral antecedent "moon.")

Vanessa and I ruined *our* concert tickets when *we* put *them* through the washing machine. (The plural pronouns *our* and *we* agree with their plural antecedent "Vanessa and I," and the plural pronoun *them* agrees with its plural antecedent "tickets.")

A pronoun should agree in number and gender with *its* antecedent. (The singular, neutral pronoun *its* agrees with its singular, neutral antecedent "pronoun.")

3.   If an antecedent may be either singular masculine or feminine (e.g. *person, student, employee*), use the pronouns *he or she, his or her,* or *himself or herself* to replace it.

Examples:

If a person believes in *himself or herself, he or she* can weather bad times.

A <u>student</u> who does *his or her* best has nothing to be ashamed of.

Note: In essay writing, when continued use of *he or she* and *himself or herself* seems awkward, you can alternate between the masculine and feminine singular forms as is done throughout the text, or change singular antecedents to plural ("<u>Students</u> do *their* best ..." instead of "A <u>student</u> does *his or her* best . . .").

4. An indefinite pronoun - *one, everyone, anyone, everybody, anybody, someone, somebody, nobody* - is always singular, so any pronoun that replaces it must also be singular.

    Examples:

    <u>Everyone </u>on the girls' volleyball team played *her* heart out tonight.
    <u>One </u>of the rose bushes lost *its* blossoms because of the frost.
    <u>Everybody</u> should bring *his or her* umbrella along on the hike.

Editing Activity 4.14

Fill in the blanks in each sentence with pronouns that agree with their antecedents. Underline the antecedent(s) in each sentence.

Examples: <u>Audrey and</u> I seldom see <u>*our*</u> roommates on weekends.
            The mother <u>cat</u> hid <u>*her*</u> newborn kittens behind the washing machine.

1. One of the barns in the area lost _____ tin roof when a tornado blew through the valley.

2. New students need to have _____ photos taken for _____ student ID cards.

3. Regina and I brought _____ sleeping bags with _____ when _____ lined up at 5:00 a.m. to get tickets to the Shakira concert at the campus arena.

4. Fred treated _____ to a double cheeseburger after _____ survived five weeks on a meatless diet.

5. Everyone needs to park _____ car in the south parking lot since _____ is the only lot on campus not being repaved today.

6. The weather will be mild for the rest of the week, and _____ should remain pleasant for most of the month.

7. Ralph and Freda bought _____ computer at a discount warehouse, and now that _____ is having problems, _____ have no warranty to cover the cost of fixing _____.

8. Amanda and Trevor don't realize how large _____ Newfoundland puppy will get, but _____ will find out for_____ in the next six months.

9. One out of every five residents living along the river had to evacuate _____ home as the water rose from the heavy storm.

10. Azaleas will start losing _____ blossoms if _____ don't get enough water, but _____ leaves will start turning yellow if _____ get too much water.

Editing Review

In the previous units, you have edited your drafts for errors involving run-on sentences and comma splices, sentence fragments, irregular verb forms, comma usage, and subject-verb agreement. Writers prone to such errors usually don't eliminate them overnight. For that reason, it is important to continue working on them, which the review activities allow you to do.

Editing Activity 4.15

Proofread the following paragraphs for errors involving run-on sentences or comma splices, sentence fragments, irregular verb forms, comma usage, and subject-verb agreement, and correct all errors.

Example

I get very sleepy during my biology lab after lunch, I can barely stay awake. Sometimes my lab partners who is also my roommates has to nudge me. When I start drifting off. I yawn the entire period and I have trouble keeping my mind on the lab experiment we are doing.

Corrected

I get very sleepy during my biology lab after lunch, *and* I can barely stay awake. Sometimes my lab partners, who *are* also my roommates, *have* to nudge me when I start drifting off. I yawn the entire period, and I have trouble keeping my mind on the lab experiment.

House Calls

In England today doctors actually still make house calls which is unheard of in America. For example in London if you have a very bad stomach ache you call a doctor. From a list of physicians that make house calls in your area. Within half an hour a doctor will be at your doorstep, he will treat you at home unless your condition requires hospitalization.

 In America the house call are a thing of the past it happens very rarely and only in the smallest towns. Americans who experience sudden onsets of pain sits endless hours in emergency waiting rooms with other patients. Any person who has went through the experience know how unpleasant it is, compare that experience to having a doctor assist you in the privacy of your home.

 Such comparisons with other health care systems have drove many Americans to question our health care practices. London is just as big as New York City so why can't American doctors make house calls? It seems that in England the doctor-patient relationship is different than in America. In England the doctor goes where he must to serve the patient, in America, the patient goes where he must to see the doctor. In England, the doctor is saw more as a public servant who serve the people, in America, the doctor is saw more as an elite person who see the people when he is available.

Editing Activity 4.16

Proofread your latest draft for errors by applying the following "Editing Guidelines," and make the necessary corrections.

Editing Guidelines

1. Check your sentences to make sure you haven't run any sentences together or put a comma between sentences instead of a period. Correct run-on sentences or comma splices by separating longer sentence with periods and combining shorter, related sentences with a joining word.

2. Check your draft for any sentence fragments: incomplete sentences with a

period after them. To correct fragments, attach them to the sentence they belong with, or add words to make them complete.

3. Check your use of irregular verbs, making sure you have used the correct irregular forms and spelled them correctly.

4. Check your comma usage, making sure you have inserted commas into your sentences following the rules from Unit 2, and that you haven't inserted commas where they aren't required.

5. Check the spelling of any word you are uncertain of, or run the spell check on your word processing program, to eliminate any spelling errors.

6. Check your verbs in each sentence to make sure that they agree with their subjects.

7. Check your pronouns in each sentence to make sure they agree with their antecedents, and make sure you have used the correct subject pronoun forms.

Editing Activity 4.17

Exchange papers with a classmate, proofread each other's drafts for errors, and make any necessary corrections. Then write the final draft of your paper to share with readers.

Writing Summary

To conclude the unit, you write a second issue-oriented paper, applying what you have learned to this point in the text. The purpose of this assignment is to give you more practice writing issue-oriented papers, to give you freedom to write more independently, and to help you internalize what you are learning to apply to future writing.

Writing Assignment

Select a second issue to write on that interests you and that people have different viewpoints on. Select a topic that you are knowledgeable about and that you would like to share with readers. Your issue may come from any field: sports, education, politics, fashion, music, health, family, your particular college or community, and so on.

Thesis Statement

Once you have selected a topic, consider how you feel about the issue, and generate a thesis statement expressing your viewpoint, which you will support and develop in the paper.

Sample Thesis Statement

Topic: Testing in elementary schools
Thesis: The overemphasis on testing in the elementary grades is hurting
            students.

Supporting Your Thesis

Make a list of four or five potential supporting points for your thesis that you could develop in a paper. In addition, list one or two opposing arguments and consider how you might counter them.

Sample Lists

Topic: Testing in elementary schools
Thesis: The overemphasis on testing in elementary schools is hurting
            students.

Supporting Points: Too much stress on children
                        Takes the fun out of school
                        Takes away from other important subjects
                        Equates getting an education with test scores

Opposing Arguments: Testing is the only way to tell how students are performing.
                        (Counter - Testing is only one form of evaluation.)
                        Testing helps raise reading and math scores for most students.
                        (Counter - At what expense to the student?)

First Draft

Before beginning your first draft, decide on your reading audience for this paper - the people that you would like to reach on this issue - and your purpose for writing to them. In addition, decide on the best tone for the paper to further your purpose.

Sample Audience/Purpose/Tone

Topic: Testing in elementary school
Audience: Local elementary school trustees
Purpose: Convince trustees that current testing program is wrong and harmful
Tone: Respectful, firm

Write the first draft of your issue-oriented paper, and consider the following guidelines.

First Draft Guidelines

1. In your opening paragraph, introduce your topic, create reader interest, and include your thesis statement at or near the end of the paragraph.

2. Develop support for your thesis statement in your middle paragraphs. As a general rule, develop each point in a separate paragraph, providing evidence to substantiate each claim. Begin paragraphs with a topic sentence expressing the main point of the paragraph. Towards the end of the middle paragraphs, introduce and counter one or two opposing arguments.

3. Conclude your paper in a manner that reinforces your thesis statement and makes your purpose clear, whether it be to move readers to action, to keep readers from acting, or to get them to rethink their viewpoint.

4. Keep your reading audience and purpose in mind as you write, and maintain the tone that will help accomplish your purpose.

Sample First Draft (Audience - local elementary school trustees)

Grade-School Testing

When I went to elementary school, I remember having fun and doing a lot of different things: working on art projects, putting on little plays, building an ant house and a dinosaur diorama, and doing a lot of singing. Of course there was a lot of reading, writing, spelling, and math, but the other things are what still stand out in my mind. When I look at elementary school today, especially through the eyes of my seven-year-old niece, I see a much different and much more somber place. Schools have taken the fun out of learning and replaced it with testing and more testing. The current testing program in our elementary district is taking the life out of school for many students, and it needs to be changed.

My niece is a happy-go-lucky, fun child who loves to do anything creative. However, her school experience is turning her into a worried, fretful little person. The happy, creative child is still in there, and sometimes it still comes out, but for the most part it has been replaced by someone who continually worries about her school work and the tests that are always looming on the horizon. Those tests, and the tremendous emphasis that the school and her teacher puts on them, create a lot of stress on young children, and it's not right. From everything that I have read, children learn best in a non-stressful, supportive environment where they are not afraid to make mistakes or try new things. That is the exact opposite from the learning environment that my niece and her classmates are in. Mistakes and wrong answers are the worst thing in the world, and the pressure they are feeling is bad for learning and I think bad for young children.

Since teachers feel they must "teach to the test" in order to improve children's test scores and improve their own job security, the majority of the time in class is spent on developing reading and math skills. Although such skills are important, the overemphasis on improving them, and improving them in ways that improve children's test-taking abilities, takes away from other important areas. Teachers say over and over that there isn't enough time in the day to do everything, and that "everything" that often gets left out includes art, music, history, and science. Instead of using such subjects to help teach reading and math, they are often ignored as large blocks of time are taken up for reading, math, and test-related activities. What kind of education are students getting when they are missing out on subjects that every child should be exposed to regularly? What are we doing to children when we frustrate their creative potential by ignoring the subjects that help to bring it out?

Speaking of creativity, the greatest minds in any field usually belong to the most creative thinkers, whether they be famous scientists, musicians, teachers, architects, or even politicians. Creative people know how to "think outside the box," and are able to go beyond what other people have done in their field or to look at things in different ways. How does testing and teaching to the test develop children's creative side? And for some children, like my niece, their creativity is their greatest strength, yet with all the emphasis on testing, they are not able to use it or allowed to let it expand. It is like the schools have decided that children should only use one half of their brain - the right side that fosters logical thinking, organization, and memory - and let the left side die - the part that fosters creativity, problem solving, and original thought. Schools seem determined to stunt the educational growth of children, and it is a sad and unacceptable situation.

In today's schools, children also equate education with testing. They get a warped impression of what education should be like, and knowing nothing different, believe that education should all be wrapped up in preparing for endless testing. They become little test-taking automatons, believing that this is what education and school is all about. They learn how to follow directions, do what they're told, practice, practice, practice, get rewarded for doing well, and feel awful for not doing so well. This sounds like an educational system that belongs in a country like Communist China where children are told what to think and what not to think, and they are raised not to question anything: their government, their standard of living, their lives. This is not an educational system for a free, democratic country like the US, where children should learn to question, to explore, to challenge, and to think for themselves.

School districts like ours feel that things are going well because test scores are improving. How could they not improve when that is all that is emphasized in the district? What's surprising, or maybe not so surprising, is that the improvement is not that dramatic considering that the entire curriculum is geared towards testing success. When children learn in a sterile, test-oriented environment, all the fun and enjoyment is taken away from learning, and children don't learn as much or as fast as they could.

Beyond that, what do better test scores really mean? What do they say about a child's problem-solving ability, ability to work with other children, ability to come up with new ideas, or ability to draw or sing or dance or build? Testing mines such a narrow strip of a child's potential learning ability that it provides a distorted view of what a child is capable of doing, and it doesn't help make a child more capable in many important learning areas.

Of course, there is a need for some testing in schools, and if children are moved from grade to grade without learning how to read, write, or compute, something is wrong. So there is a place to evaluate the progress of every student, and testing is one method of doing that. However, it should not be the major focus of every child's education That focus should be on learning and on expanding a person's knowledge and on the creative processes and on learning by doing things and on making school a place where children discover the joy in reading and writing, not to do better on some test, but to make life-long readers and writers out of them.

Whenever I read an article about a particular teacher in the area receiving a "teacher of the year" award, those teachers usually have some things in common: they love teaching and children, they pass their enthusiasm on to their students, they are creative and make learning fun, and their kids learn well from them. Never do I read that these teachers do a great job of teaching to the test. Unfortunately, great teachers become just as stunted as the children when they are required to raise test scores and worry about little else. They lose their enthusiasm for teaching, and many of them drop out of the profession. Other stay in and fight for what they believe is important in education. Still others give in and do what they're told, even when they know it's not right.

Pretty soon, perhaps a generation from now, all new teachers will be the products of the test-taking educational system that they are teaching in, and they will teach like they were taught and never question the system. If that is where we are headed, education in our country, and in this school district, will be as dismal as in any country where they are taught that thinking for themselves is bad.

Revision Guidelines

After setting your draft aside for awhile, begin the revision process by applying the following guidelines to your draft. Make any changes you feel will improve the paper, and include them in your second draft.

1. Reread your paper and reevaluate your thesis and support. On careful analysis, have you taken a position on the issue that you feel is the most valid and defensible? At this point, you are not obligated to retain your current thesis if on reexamination and reflection, you are persuaded that a different or altered position is more valid or makes more sense. If that is the case, revise your thesis and support to reflect your change of mind.

2. Check your opening paragraph to make sure you have clearly introduced you topic, created some interest for readers, and included your thesis statement. Is there anything you can add or change to make your opening more effective?

3. Check your middle paragraphs to make sure that each paragraph relates to and supports your thesis statement in some manner. In addition, make sure that you have provided effective evidence to support each claim that you have made, and that you have included one or two opposing arguments to your thesis and countered them in some manner.

4. Check your concluding paragraph to make sure that it provides readers with a sense of completion, reinforces your thesis statement, adds something new for readers, and makes your purpose clear.

5. Read each paragraph to see if there is anything you can add - an example, a

reason in support of your thesis, a specific detail or description, an explanation, additional evidence for a claim - to make the paper more interesting, informative, or complete.

6. Check your use of transitional wording to tie sentences and paragraphs together. Add any transitions (e.g. first, second, also, in addition, finally, therefore, however, etc.) that will help readers understand your ideas and how they are related.

7. Check your paragraphing to make sure you have begun a new paragraph when you move to something new in your paper: a different part, a different reason, a new example, a different claim, new evidence. Divide overly long paragraphs, and combine very short paragraphs containing related material.

8. Check the organization of your paper to see whether you have presented your points in the most effective order, and reorder any paragraphs or sentences that would fit better in another location.

9. Check the wording of each sentence, and revise sentences to make them clearer, smoother, and more concise by eliminating unnecessary words or phrases, rewording awkward or unclear sentences, and replacing questionable word choices.

10. Read your paper to make sure that you have done everything you can to accomplish your purpose, including establishing the best tone to influence readers.

Sample Revised Draft (Audience - local elementary school trustees)

Grade-School Testing

When I went to elementary school, I remember having fun and ~~doing a lot of different things:~~ working on art projects, putting on ~~little~~ **small** plays, building an ant house and a dinosaur diorama, and doing a lot of singing. Of course there was ~~a lot of~~ reading, writing, spelling, and arithmetic, but the ~~other~~ things I did are what ~~still~~ stand out in my mind. When I look at elementary school today, especially through the eyes of my seven-year-old niece, I see a much different, ~~and much~~ more somber place. Schools have taken the fun out of learning and replaced it with testing and more testing. The current testing program in our elementary district is taking the life out of school for many students, and it needs to be changed.

My niece is a happy-go-lucky, fun child who loves to do anything creative: draw, paint, put on shows, build forts, or make up new games. However, her school experience is turning her into a worried, fretful little person. The happy, creative child is still in there, ~~and sometimes it still comes out,~~ but for the most part it has been replaced by ~~someone who continually~~ **a child who** worries about her school work and the constant testing ~~that are always looming on the horizon~~. Those tests, and the tremendous emphasis that the school and her teacher put on them, create a lot of stress on young children, and it's not right. From everything that I have read, children learn best in a non-stressful, supportive environment where they are not afraid to make mistakes or try new things. That is ~~the exact opposite from the~~ **not** the learning environment that my niece and her classmates are in. Mistakes and wrong answers are the worst thing in the world, and the pressure they are feeling ~~is bad for learning and I think bad for young children.~~ **can't be good for them**.

Since teachers feel they must "teach to the test" ~~in order~~ to improve children's test scores and ~~improve~~ their own job security, the majority of ~~the time in~~ class **time** is spent on developing reading and math skills. Although such skills are important, the overemphasis on improving them, ~~and improving them in ways that improve~~ **to increase** children's ~~test-taking abilities~~ **test scores** takes away from other important ~~areas~~ **subjects**. Teachers say over and over that there isn't enough time in the day to do everything, ~~and that "everything" that often gets left out includes~~ **which often means that** art, music, history, and science are largely ignored. Instead of using ~~such~~ **these** subjects to help teach reading and math, ~~they are often ignored as~~ **teachers devote** large blocks of time ~~are taken up for~~ to generic reading and math study, and to test-related activities. What kind of education are ~~students~~ **children** getting when they are missing out on subjects that every child should be exposed to ~~regularly~~? What are we doing to children when we frustrate their creative potential by ignoring ~~the~~ subjects like art, music, and science that help to ~~bring~~ **nurture it** ~~out~~?

Speaking of creativity, the greatest minds in any field ~~usually~~ **often** belong to the most creative thinkers, whether they be famous scientists, musicians, teachers, architects, or even politicians. Creative people ~~know how to~~ **can** "think outside the box," ~~and are able to~~ going beyond what other people have done ~~in their field~~ or to looking at things ~~in different ways~~ from different perspectives. How does ~~testing and~~ teaching ~~to the test~~ **based on testing** develop a ~~children's~~ **child's** creative side? And for some children, like my niece, their creativity is their greatest strength, yet with all the emphasis on testing, they are ~~not~~ **seldom** able to use it or ~~allowed to let it~~ expand their ability. ~~It is like the~~ **Have** schools ~~have~~ decided that children should only use one half of their brain - the ~~right~~ **left** side that fosters logical, ordered thinking ~~organization, and memory~~ - and let the ~~left~~ **right** side ~~die, the part that~~ which fosters **creative, intuitive thought, just die**? ~~creativity, problem solving, and original thought~~. Schools seem determined to stunt the educational growth of children, perhaps unintentionally, ~~and~~ **but** it is a ~~sad and unacceptable~~ **terrible** situation.

In today's schools, children also equate education with testing. They get a warped impression of what education ~~should be like~~ **is,** and knowing nothing different, believe that education ~~should all be wrapped up in preparing for~~ **means** endless testing and preparation. They become little test-taking automatons, ~~believing that this is what education and~~ **because that is what** their education is all about. They learn ~~how~~ to follow directions, do what they're told, practice ~~practice, practice~~ for the test, get rewarded for doing well, and feel awful ~~for not doing so well~~ **when they don't**. This sounds like an educational system that belongs in a country like Communist China, where children are told what to think ~~and what not to think~~, and ~~they~~ are raised not to question ~~anything:~~ their government, their education, ~~their standard of living, their lives,~~ or their future. This is not an educational system ~~that~~ **for** a free, democratic country like the US, where children should learn to question, ~~to~~ explore, ~~to~~ challenge, and ~~to~~ think for themselves.

School districts like ours feel that things are going well because student test scores are improving. How could they not improve when that is ~~all that is~~ **the only thing** emphasized in the district? What may be surprising, ~~or maybe not so surprising,~~ is that the improvement is not that dramatic. ~~considering that the entire curriculum is geared towards testing success.~~ When children learn in a sterile, test-oriented environment, ~~all the fun and enjoyment is taken away from~~ **they lose the joy for learning**, and ~~children~~ don't learn as much or as fast as they could. Beyond that, what do better test scores really mean? What do they say about ~~a child's~~ **children's** ~~problem-solving~~ ability to solve problems, ~~ability~~ to work with other children, ~~ability~~ to come up with ~~new~~ interesting or unique ideas, ~~ability~~ or to draw, ~~or~~ sing, ~~or~~ dance, or build? Testing ~~mines~~ **covers** such a narrow ~~strip~~ **range** of ~~a child's potential~~ **children's** learning ability that it ~~provides a distorted view of~~ **doesn't reflect** what ~~a child~~ **they** are capable of doing, ~~and it doesn't~~ or help them ~~make a child more capable in many important learning areas.~~ **develop skills and abilities that the tests don't measure.**

Of course, there is a need for some testing in schools, and if children are shuttled from grade to grade without learning how to read, write, or compute, something is wrong. ~~So~~ There is a place to evaluate the progress of every student, and testing is one method ~~of doing that~~. However, it should not be the major focus of every child's education. That focus should be on learning, ~~and~~ on expanding ~~a person's~~ **children's** knowledge, ~~and~~ on nurturing their ~~creative processes~~ **creativity**, ~~and on learning by doing things~~ and on ~~making school a place where~~ **having** children ~~discover the joy in~~ reading and writ~~ing~~, not to do better on some test, but to make life-long readers and writers out of them.

Whenever I read ~~an article~~ about ~~a particular~~ teachers ~~in the area~~ receiving a "teacher of the year" award, ~~those teachers~~ **they** usually have some things in common. They love teaching and children, they pass **on** their enthusiasm ~~on~~ to their students, they are creative and make learning fun, and their ~~kids~~ **students** learn ~~well~~ from them. Never do I read that these teachers do a great job of teaching to the test. Unfortunately, great teachers can become just as stunted as their ~~children~~ students when they are required to raise test scores and **ignore everything else.** ~~worry about little else.~~ They lose their enthusiasm for teaching, and many of them drop out ~~of the profession~~. Others stay ~~in~~ on and fight for what they believe is important in education, and still others give in and do what they're told, even when they know it's not right. ~~Pretty soon, perhaps a generation from now,~~

Before too many years, if nothing changes, ~~all~~ many new teachers will be the products of the test-taking ~~educational~~ system that they are teaching in, and, sadly, they will teach like they were taught ~~and never question the system~~. If that is where we are headed, ~~education~~ schools in our country~~, and in this school district,~~ will be ~~as~~ a dismal ~~as in any country where are taught that thinking for themselves is bad.~~ place for any child. This school district, and this board, have the power to bring greater meaning and purpose to education than the current test program provides. At stake is the education and well-being of every child in the district, and our children deserve much better than they are getting.

Editing Guidelines

Proofread your latest draft for errors by applying the following guidelines, and make the necessary corrections. Then write the final, error-free draft of your paper.

1. Check your sentences to make sure you haven't run any sentences together or put a comma between sentences instead of a period. Correct run-on or comma splice sentences by separating longer sentence with periods and combining shorter, related sentences with a joining word.

2. Check your draft for any sentence fragments: incomplete sentences with a period after them. To correct fragments, attach them to the sentence they belong with, or add words to make them complete.

3. Check your use of irregular verbs, making sure you have used the correct irregular forms and spelled them correctly.

4. Check your comma usage, making sure you have inserted commas into your sentences following the rules from Unit 2, and that you haven't inserted commas where aren't required.

5. Check the spelling of any word you are uncertain of, or run the spell check on your word processing program, to eliminate any spelling errors.

6. Check your verbs in each sentence to make sure that they agree with their subjects.

7. Check your pronouns in each sentence to make sure they agree with their antecedents, and that you are using the correct subject pronoun forms.

Readings

Global Weirding: Climate Change

by Thomas Friedman
(From *Hot, Flat, and Crowded*)

There have been many warning signs telling us that we have entered into a new era of climate change. Scientists point to substantial data - changes in global average temperature, rising sea levels, quickening glacial melt - indicating that man's activities are affecting the course of Mother Nature in unsettling ways. Among scientists, there is no question that global warming is a reality, that man is responsible, and that there could be dire world-wide consequences if we don't reduce the atmospheric emissions that are causing it.

The climate-change deniers come in three basic varieties: those paid by fossil fuel companies to deny that global warming is a serious human-caused problem; a small minority of scientists on the fringe who have looked at he data and concluded for different reasons that the rapid and extensive increase in greenhouse gas emissions is not a major threat to the planet's livability; and. finally, those American conservatives who simply refuse to accept the reality of climate change because they hate the solution: more government regulation and intervention. The net effect of all their writings, though, has been to throw into question the certainty that humans are causing dangerous climate change and to leave the impression that any assertion that human actions are changing the climate is merely a political opinion, not a scientific fact

Because Al Gore, a liberal politician, became the first most prominent voice for the threat of climate change, it was easy for the climate-change deniers and skeptics to insinuate that this was not a debate between science and politics, but between politics and politics. At the same time, some normally attentive environmentalists were slow to take up the climate-change issue in terms of its full potential global and human impact. In addition, the American media largely adopted the view of the climate-change deniers that climate change was a political issue, not a scientific reality, that it had two sides to it, and that, in effect, nothing about it was certain.

But this is not politics. That the climate changes naturally over time is settled science. That the climate is now changing in unusual ways against the backdrop of long-term natural variation is accepted by nearly everybody. There's a very strong understanding among knowledgeable scientists that humans are responsible through industrial activities for most of what's unusual about the current pattern of climate changes. Yet many in the media have treated climate change as if every point were still in doubt and the expert community were divided down the middle on it. As George Monbiot, a British environmental activist and writer noted, the climate deniers took full advantage of the media's instinct to give "balanced" coverage to any controversial issue and used it to put doubts in many people's minds. "They didn't have to win the argument to succeed," Monbiot said of the climate deniers, "only to cause as much confusion as possible."

So Al Gore stepped into this vortex, using his celebrity and political authority to draw global attention to the catastrophic potential of climate change. Because Gore, not some celebrity scientist, was the messenger, and because he presented his facts in an intentionally alarming way to get maximum attention, enormous time and energy have gone into debating about Al Gore rather than what is certain about changes in our climate system. That debate has diverted far too much public discussion from the current reality, which is that not only is the climate changing because of human activities, but that there is also mounting evidence that it is changing considerably faster than even the most worried climatologists were predicting three or four years ago, and that the change may unfold in an even more unmanageable and disruptive manner than they expected.

Consider just one of the assessments that came out in 2009 - a study released by MITs Joint Program on the Science and Policy of Global Change. It quietly updated its Integrated Global System Model, which tracks and predicts climate change from 1861 to 2100. "In our more recent global model simulations," the study explained, "the ocean heat-uptake is slower than previously estimated, the ocean uptake of carbon is weaker, feedbacks from the land system as temperature rises are stronger, cumulative emissions of greenhouse gases over the century are higher, and offsetting cooling from aerosol emissions is lower."

No one of these effects is very strong on its own, and even adding each separately together would not fully explain the higher temperatures. But rather than interacting additively, the study continues, "these different effects appear to interact multiplicatively, with feedbacks among the contributing factors, leading to the surprisingly large increase in the chance of much higher temperatures." There, wrapped in the sober language of a policy study, is an alarming fact: the climate is changing even more rapidly than the experts thought.

Alarming, but not surprising. After all, almost every day now there is a story in the newspaper that tells us of something unusual happening, something outside the normal variability of the climate. The heat wave in Europe in July-August 2003 - when it was consistently over 100 degrees Fahrenheit - killed 35,000 people, concluded John Holdren, the Harvard University climate expert who is now serving President Obama's science adviser. "That heat wave was estimated as one-in-a-hundred-year event," said Holdren. "Before we started fiddling with the climate, it was considered a one-in-250-year event. What the models now show is that by 2050 it will be a one-in-two-year event and by 2070 it will be an unusually cool summer in Europe."

A decade ago, people were thinking that at worst, the Arctic summer sea ice would be entirely gone by 2070, said Holdren. A few radical pessimists said 2040. And now people say it could all be gone in just a few years. No wonder: In the summer of 2007, warm temperatures melted so much Arctic sea ice that stretches of the Arctic Ocean that had never been fully navigable by ship were made so. The Northwest Passage was free for the first time in recorded history, enabling ships to pass through.

The Associated Press published the following story apropos of this unprecedented and unexpected event: "An already relentless melting of the Arctic greatly accelerated this summer, a warning sign that some scientists worry could mean global warming has passed an ominous tipping point. One even speculated that summer sea ice would be gone in five years. Greenland's ice sheet melted nearly 19 billion tons more than the previous high mark, and the volume of Arctic sea ice at summer's end was half what it was just four years earlier."

Despite the overwhelming evidence that man-created global warming is wreaking havoc on the environment, the climate-change deniers want us to believe that our business as usual could still lead to business as usual. They want us to believe that we are playing with dice that can come up only somewhere between two and twelve, with two being no climate change and twelve being the wild, crazy, outside possibility that something Al Gore said might come true.

Sorry, boys, but these are Mother Nature's dice. They are twenty-sided, thirty-sided, even sixty-sided dice. They might come up sixty, and there are some increasing indications they may. According to physicist and former assistant secretary in the Department of Energy under President Clinton, "The only important holes left in the science of climate change are whether climate change will be 'serious' or 'catastrophic,' and whether we will reach that point sooner or later."

When we were idealistic kids, some of us aspired to change the world when we grew up. Well guess what? We did. Now how do we change it back?

Questions for Discussion

1. What is the thesis of the essay?

2. What are the supporting points for the thesis, and how convincing are they? How does the author substantiate his claims?

3. What opposing arguments are presented, and how effectively are they refuted?

4. Based on the essay and your own knowledge, do you agree that man-made global warming is a reality and a serious problem?

5. If you accept the author's thesis, what, if anything, can individuals like ourselves do to help solve the problem?

Hip-Hop's Negative Impact on Kids

by Gary 'The G-Man' Toms

As a professional club DJ dating back to the infamous Studio 54 period, I have seen a number of groups come and go over the years. Many of the groups, like Tavares, KC and the Sunshine Band, The Village People, and The Rolling Stones are still selling out concerts to this day. Do you know why? It's because the music they made was fun, harmless and made you feel good. Sadly, the last 20 years has seen a negative shift in music, and some disturbing events have occurred as a result.

Hip-hop music became popular in the mid-to-late 70's because of DJ's like Afrika Bambata, Kool Herc and Grandmaster Flash. It was because of the enormous popularity of Run DMC that rap crossed over on the music charts and radio stations all over the world. The music was fun and harmless, but the 90's would change all of that with the introduction of gangster rap. DJ Jazzy Jeff and The Fresh Prince, UTFO, Curtis Blow and Biz Markie were no longer accepted in the rap game when the national anthem for hip-hop became Onyx's "Throw Ya Guns in the Air." The glorification of the thug, and all it encompassed, became the standard by which all rappers were judged, and many African-American communities, and eventually the suburbs, began to pay a heavy price.

Anyone who thinks there isn't a direct link between gangster rap, thug behavior and the problems that exist in inner city neighborhoods across this nation is misguided. You can take the position that many problems are the result of bad parenting, single-headed households or a lack of respect by today's youth, but the fact is we live in a visual era, and kids are affected by visual images more than anything else.

If kids see some big rap star on MTV or BET with expensive cars, gorgeous, half-naked women, expensive jewelry and living the thug lifestyle, they are going to want to be just like them. If it appears that anyone can make a billion dollars in the rap industry, as is so often projected, they are going to take a shot at it. Moreover, if their attempts to get a record deal never materialize, they may decide to take it to the next level and become a "true player for real" by getting into the drug game in order to live the "Big Willie Style" that is so often projected in music videos. What they don't realize is that today's rap star may very well be tomorrow's welfare recipient or prison inmate. It has happened to a number of hip-hop artists who were highly regarded at one time.

Too many kids are growing up without a decent education because they are dropping out to pursue a record deal, live a thug lifestyle, or become a drug kingpin in order to "get paid." Communities and generations of youth are suffering because of the negative visualizations, ignorant hip-hop stars and record company executives, producers, and urban contemporary mediums like BET and New York's HOT 97, who promote all the negative rap. How can they say they support positive images of African-Americans while playing songs like "Me and My Bitch" and videos that glorify thugs, drugs and humping on rugs. I have a real problem with six and seven-year-olds walking down the street calling each other "nigger" and cursing worse than a sailor on weekend leave. They do this because of the images they see and the music they have easy access to. "Keeping it real" should not come at the expense of our communities or our children.

If many of the influential artists like 50 Cent or The Game stressed the importance of education and kids working towards their diplomas or degrees, they would be less likely to leave school. The record company executives aren't interested in education, they're interested in sales and profit. Moral responsibility and community be damned as far as they're concerned. No one in the industry cares about the negative impact of rap music on kids.

The industry is also guilty of robbing the cradle. More and more emphasis is being placed on younger performers. Several years ago, I heard a rap group from Britain was being exported to the U.S., and the members were between seven and eight years of age! Before you know it, some label will have two infants on stage wearing Pampers laced with company logos lip synching some rap song.

I can understand the American message that anyone can have success in this country, but the problem is that you run the risk of having many inner-city kids casting off education to pursue entertainment gigs. Not that these careers are necessarily bad, but for each success story there are a thousand failures, not a good ratio.

Moreover, having dangerous, degrading rap images thrust into their faces twenty-four hours a day, many kids want to become that image. In the process, they lose all perspective of who they are, what they really need and want, and what they believe in. Some kids are educated enough to separate the two worlds, allowing them to pursue a positive course. Unfortunately, far too many minority kids are not making the distinction, and they are falling into traps and filling our jails to capacity.

I have worked with young talent as a producer. I had strict guidelines for my artists, and these same guidelines should be adopted by the industry. No artist should be signed until they have obtained a high school diploma, GED or some type of technical training degree, and they should be at least 18-years-old. There is an overflow of artists that are too young, too ignorant and too greedy to make clear, conscious and sound decisions regarding their careers. The people who manage them couldn't care less because all they are interested in is making money, and as soon as sales start to drop, the label drops them. Translation: if you don't have an education or a trade to back you up, you're screwed.

I am not trying to crush anyone's dream. I encourage you to pursue a career in the music industry if that is what you truly want to do. However, I suggest that you make sure to have the education credentials to equip yourself for whatever you may face in the business and that you don't add to the corrupting music that is flooding the country. The music industry is sending a dangerous message to our young people, and I believe it will only get worse. As a deejay, I only play old school hip-hop, disco, underground dance and house music. I refuse to spin anything that degrades my race or anyone in society. That should be the standard for the music industry and every rap artist.

Questions for Discussion

1. What is the thesis of the essay?

2. What evidence does the essay provide in support of its thesis, and how effective is it?

3. What opposing arguments are presented, and how effectively are they refuted?

4. Based on the essay and your own experience, do you agree with the author's thesis? What impact, if any, do you feel the type of hip-hop music the author objects to has on today's youth?

Unit 5
Problems and Solutions

One of the greatest contributions that writers make is addressing the myriad of problems that confront us and providing solutions to help solve those problems. On any day in the newspaper you might find an article on the dangers of global warming and how it can be combated, on the recent local drought and how residents can help by reducing water usage, on a solution to a marital problem posed by a reader to "Dear Abby," and on how local school districts facing a decline in student enrollment can survive the unexpected shortfall.

Since problems confront us all of the time - the loss of a job, not getting the classes we need, the unhealthy effects of increasing pollution, the rising cost of tuition, textbooks, gasoline, and housing - there is always something to write about. In addition, writing about problems helps to develop our problem-solving abilities, which we can apply at school, in the workplace, and in our personal relationships.

Writing about problems and solutions is a complex task which may involve determining exactly what the problem is, what caused the problem, what its affects are, who or what is affected, and what possible solution or solutions could eliminate or reduce the problem. Since most problems worth writing about don't have any simple, obvious solution, one of the greatest challenges is coming up with solutions that can work and that people are willing to try.

In this unit, you write about a particular problem and how it might be solved. You can write about any problem you want, from the personal to the universal. The purpose of this assignment is to engage you in a complex writing task which draws upon your evaluative, analytical, and creative thinking skills. In addition, writing about problems and solutions can often help the writer, who may find a new solution to a nagging problem, and the readers, who may have similar problems and benefit from the writer's ideas.

Prewriting

Since a problem/solution paper contains a number of different elements, each element requires some attention during the prewriting process. A prewriting activity introduced in this section helps writers analyze those elements: asking questions. The traditional journalistic questions of *who, what, where, when, and why* help writers probe a subject and generate material for a paper.

Selecting a Topic

Writers can usually find problems to write about since they are seldom in short supply. The decision to be made is which problem stands out as the best topic for your upcoming paper. To help you decide on a problem to write about, consider the following criteria.

1. Choose a problem that is affecting you in some way and that may affect others as well.

2. Choose a problem that is serious enough to engage readers' interest. For example, if the problem is that you can't find a dry cat food that your finicky cat will eat, readers may find the problem more amusing than engaging.

3. Choose a problem that doesn't have an obvious solution that you have discovered. One purpose of this paper is to try and find solutions to a problem where no simple solution is apparent. For example, if the problem is that your car has a flat tire, the solution - to get it fixed - is a bit too obvious.

4. Choose a problem that is nagging and persistent rather than passing. For example, if you are short on cash this month because your financial aid check is late, you have a temporary problem that will soon take care of itself.

5. You may choose any kind of problem: personal, family-related, school-related, work-related, or a particular local, state, national, or universal problem.

6. Since this is not a "research" paper, choose a topic that you are knowledgeable about.

Prewriting Activity 5.1

To generate possible topics for your paper, brainstorm some ideas, writing down any problems that come to mind without evaluating them. From this list, you may find your writing topic.

Sample Brainstorming Session

trouble with boyfriend	size of campus	smells from sewer plant
loneliness at new school	gaining weight	lack of jobs for students
making budget work	lack of school activities	required health fee
step-father problems	managing time better	unfair property tax law
probation for grades	violence where I live	treatment of athletes
no social life	lack of campus arena	lack of computer labs
living with roommate	cliques of local students	city pollution
torn up city streets	not having a car	sharing a computer

Prewriting Activity 5.2

Choose a topic for your upcoming problem/solution paper keeping in mind the criteria presented and your brainstormed list of problems.

Sample topic selection: lack of jobs for graduates

Analyzing the Problem

Now that you have selected a problem to write on, you can begin analyzing the problem with the goal of finding a workable solution. To help you analyze the problem, you answer questions that will help you probe its various elements.

Asking Questions

Asking and answering questions helps writers think more deeply about a topic and analyze its different parts. The following questions will help you dissect the problem you are writing about.

1.   What exactly is the problem? How would you describe it in one sentence?

2. When did the problem begin, and how did it get started?

3. What are the causes of the problem?

4. Who or what is affected by the problem?

5. What are the effects of the problem?

Prewriting Activity 5.3

To help you analyze the problem and generate some material for your upcoming paper, answer the five questions just presented. Take some time to consider each question since your answers may help lead you to a solution.

Sample Answers

Topic: lack of jobs for graduates

1. What exactly is the problem?

   The difficulty of finding a good job after college graduation

2. When did the problem begin, and how did it get started?

   It began some years back as America lost jobs to foreign countries through "outsourcing" and got worse when the recession hit.

3. What are the causes of the problem?

   Outsourcing is a big cause as corporations have shifted millions of jobs to foreign countries where labor is cheaper. The recession caused private and public job opportunities to shrink as employees were laid off and hiring freezes were implemented. Many businesses have permanently downsized their operations, meaning a lot of jobs won't be coming back in the future.

4. Who or what is affected by the problem?

   College graduates and current college students are affected as well as people who have lost their jobs due to outsourcing and the recession. Job opportunities are scarce and graduates find themselves competing with out-of-work employees for available jobs.

5.   What are the effects of the problem?

Many college graduates can't find jobs in their field and are forced to take whatever low-paying jobs they can find. Many can't begin paying off their college loan debt. Some return to school to work on a higher degree or to change majors. Many students currently in college face a bleak job market on graduation.

Finding Solutions

Solving difficult problems isn't easy. Sometimes unresolved problems between a brother and sister, a parent and child, an employee and supervisor, or even neighboring countries can go on for years, poisoning relationships and damaging lives. While some problems eventually work themselves out with time, others stubbornly persist despite the best efforts to solve them.

In seeking solutions to a problem, the following suggestions will help you consider different possibilities and evaluate their chances for success.

Solution Guidelines

1.   Exactly what does solving the problem mean? What do you hope to accomplish? For example, if there is a parking problem for students on campus, does solving the problem mean that every student would be able to find a parking place or that the problem would be alleviated enough to satisfy most students?

2.   How can the solution get to the roots of the problem, its underlying causes? If a solution doesn't address the causes of a problem, it seldom succeeds. For example, solutions to the Israeli-Palestinian conflict may have failed over the years because they haven't adequately addressed the underlying cause: both groups believing that they have the historical right to the same land.

3.   What are possible alternative solutions to the problem? Often with difficult problems, different solutions have to be tried before something works, or different combinations of solutions. For example, with the parking problem, a possible solution might include car pooling incentives for students, tram rides for students parking farthest from classes, and the creation of a new parking lot.

4.   Is compromise an important part of the solution? With problems involving individuals, groups, or even nations, there often has to be some give on both sides for a solution to work. If the solution is good for one party and not the other, it probably won't work. For example, any solution to the Israeli-Palestinian conflict will probably involve Israel giving up more land than they want and Palestinians

getting less land than they would like.

5. What is a realistic solution to the problem? Can the right solution completely eliminate the problem, or can it make a bad situation better? For example, with college enrollments increasing and parking areas being limited by space, parking problems may remain with a particular college for a long time, but that doesn't mean that solutions that reduce the problem and make the situation tolerable shouldn't be tried. On the other hand, it appears that there is no half-way solution to a problem like the Israeli-Palestinian conflict. Either Palestine will become a sovereign nation alongside Israel or the conflict will continue.

6. What do other people think? Often there are people to turn to when seeking solutions to thorny problems. That person may be an interior designer if your problem is too little living space and too much furniture, a college advisor if you can't seem to work your class schedule around your work schedule, a marriage counselor if your marriage is in trouble, or a time management expert if you never have enough time to do what you need. Sometimes part of the solution is seeking out someone who may help you find it.

Prewriting Activity 5.4

Based on the six suggestions presented, consider some possible solutions to your problem. Generate a number of solutions without evaluating their relative worth. At this point, you don't need to decide on a particular solution or solutions for your first draft. Get some ideas on paper to think about, and be open to discovering different solutions as you give the problem more thought.

Sample Alternative Solutions

Topic: lack of jobs for graduates

Solutions: Stop the outsourcing and bring jobs back to America.
            Government should stimulate the economy and help create jobs.
            Colleges must work with business community.
            Students must consider majors in fields with job availability.
            Colleges should let students know where the jobs are going to be.
            Students must be flexible in where they are willing to work.
            Colleges should help students find jobs.

First Drafts

Now that you have selected a problem to write about, analyzed the problem in some depth, and considered possible solutions to the problem, you are ready to write your first draft. Before you begin, consider the people you want to read this paper - your reading audience - and your reason for writing to them - your purpose.

Audience and Purpose

Since most writing is a form of communication, the people that will read your writing and your reasons for writing to them help shape the content of your paper. Your audience and purpose influence what you include in your paper, what you emphasize, the tone of your writing, the types of examples you provide, and how you open and conclude the paper. Writing for a reading audience with a purpose in mind brings meaning to your writing that writing as an exercise can never provide.

   In deciding on your audience and purpose for your paper, consider these suggestions.

1.   Whom would I like to read this paper?

2.   Who might benefit from reading the paper?

3.   By reading this paper, who might help in some way to solve the problem?

4.   What is my purpose in writing to this audience? What do I hope to accomplish?

5.   What is the best tone for this paper to help accomplish my purpose?

Drafting Activity 5.5

Decide on a reading audience and purpose for your paper, and a writing tone that will help you accomplish your purpose.

Sample audience/purpose/tone

Topic: lack of jobs for graduates

Audience: fellow students, most of whom will be affected by the problem, and college board and administration

Purpose: to make students aware of problem and what they can do to enhance future employment opportunities, and to get college to do more

Tone: serious, concerned

Drafting Guidelines

As you write your first draft, keep the follow considerations in mind.

1. Introduce the problem in your opening paragraph, its significance, and why readers should be aware of it.

2. In the middle paragraphs, incorporate material from your question-and-answer activity to help readers understand when and how the problem started, its causes, who is affected, and what the effects are.

3. Conclude the draft by suggesting a solution or combination of solutions to the problem which may eliminate it or reduce its impact.

4. Change paragraphs as you move to different aspects of the problem: its beginnings, its causes, its effects, possible solutions.

5. As you write, keep your reading audience in mind and your purpose: what you want to accomplish.

6. Give your draft a simple title that tells what it is about.

Drafting Activity 5.6

Write the first draft of the problem/solution paper following the guidelines presented.

Sample First Draft

Finding a Job

Joel Ortiz graduated a year ago with an electrical engineering degree and has yet to find a job in his field. Myrna Crosby has taught part-time three years at a community college and feels she is no closer to full-time employment than when she started. After getting his two-year degree in forestry services, Jonathan Briggs sought employment with the state Fish and Game Department only to find out that there was an indefinite hiring freeze in place.

These college graduates, like thousands of others nationwide, are discovering that the traditional belief that employment in one's major field awaits the college graduate no longer applies. In fact, graduates are finding it harder and harder to find a job in their field in today's economic climate, and the reality may be that there will fewer job opportunities for college graduates for years to come. A college degree is no longer a guarantee of a good-paying job, and college students need to look to their future with eyes wide open.

A variety of circumstances appears to have created a bleaker job market for college graduates. The Great Recession which began in 2008 is certainly a factor, with many businesses large and small not only not hiring but laying off employees, particularly in businesses associated with the housing and finance industries. Due largely to reduced revenues, Federal and state governments are running record deficits, and jobs that are often filled by college graduates at the city, state, or Federal level when employees retire are going unfilled.

In addition, the U.S. has lost hundreds of thousands of jobs over the past ten years due to companies outsourcing jobs to other countries where they can pay lower wages. Since these "multinational corporations" have no loyalty to American employees and will locate wherever they can find qualified employees and save money, the chances of these jobs returning to the U.S. are slim-to-none, and it is more likely that we will continue to lose additional jobs to outsourcing. Some companies, in fact, are advising college engineering and computer science majors to consider working abroad upon graduation since that is where the jobs will be, albeit at much smaller salaries.

The effects of the weak U.S. job market on college graduates are depressing. With many graduates having sizable college loans to pay off, their inability to find good paying jobs can put them in a great bind. Unable to find jobs in their field, many take whatever hourly wage job they can find, often working in retail sales, waiting tables, or scouring the "want ads" for any available employment. Many take on multiple part-time jobs since many industries, including colleges, hire part-time employees because they are cheaper to employ. Many who end up working outside of their field never return to it. Unable to find a decent job, many graduates re-enroll in college, seeking a degree in a more employable field or getting a higher degree or getting a teaching credential. Sometimes going back to college pays off in the long run; other times, it merely puts a person's wage-earning future on hold.

There are no simple solutions to the current disparity between the number of college graduates seeking employment and the number of jobs available. However, it is a problem that clearly needs to be tackled not only for the future of all college students but for the future of the country. As the lack of good-paying jobs decreases, the size of the middle class shrinks, as it has been doing for the past ten years. A large, robust middle class has been integral to the economic success of America. As the middle class erodes, the country erodes.

Colleges have a great obligation to justify the cost of education to students today. If there is little correlation between the two-year or four-year degrees that a college churns out and the percentage of graduates that find jobs in their field, colleges must take some of the blame. There is much that colleges can do to help, including providing students with job market trends in every educational field, steering students in the direction of fields with the greatest job availability, and partnering with private and public business to do everything possible to assure graduates of future employment. Colleges need to feel a strong obligation to do everything possible to help graduates find jobs, and they are just scratching the surface of what may be possible.

Clearly, the outsourcing of jobs to other countries needs to be addressed. What can the government do to get companies to keep jobs in the U.S. and to bring outsourced jobs back? Currently, it is doing nothing; in fact, corporations that outsource jobs get the same tax breaks as those that don't. The Federal government needs to form a commission to study the outsourcing problem and figure out a way to solve it. Otherwise, the time may come when the only decent jobs left in America are those that for logistical reasons can't be outsourced.

Finally, students need to take responsibility for their own futures. They need to arm themselves with all of the knowledge possible about the job market that they will soon be facing. They need to be realistic about what field to major in, balancing their interests with where the job are. When necessary, they also need to be willing to move to an area where they can find a job, whether it be a different part of the state or another state. While the ideal is often finding a job in an area where you want to live among friends and family, that doesn't always work out, and Americans have constantly migrated throughout history to other states or areas: from the country to the city, from the Midwest to the West, from the South to the North.

Given the shrinking job market for college graduates, some skeptics are wondering whether it is worth it to go to college at all and pay the high cost of tuition. The problem is, what are you going to do *without* a college degree? Sure, there are the computer geniuses and born salespeople who do great, but for the vast majority, the lack of a two-year or four-year degree closes most decent employment doors, leaving open the more easily attained, dead-end hourly jobs at a Wal-Mart, McDonald's, or your local mall.

A college education provides no guarantees, but it still provides by far the greatest employment opportunities and the greatest chance to live the American Dream: the house, the comfortable life, the good salary, the comfortable retirement. College is still the best choice to make, but students need to be aware more than ever of the pitfalls in the current economic landscape and do their best to avoid them.

Revisions

Now that you have written the first draft of your problem/solution paper, you are ready to revise it and make any changes you feel would improve its content, organization, or wording. As you reread your draft, you may find a better way to organize your middle paragraphs, better wording options for some of your sentences, and perhaps a new solution that you hadn't previously considered. As you revise, be open to new ideas that may come to you, and feel free to incorporate new material as you improve what you have already written.

Varying Sentence Structures

Writers sometimes get into ruts, relying too much on the same sentence structures and connecting words. In the following example, the writer has a tendency to overuse compound sentences joined by and or but.

> We flew into Los Angeles at night from New Orleans, and we noticed flames on the ground. The flames were on the far western side of the LA basin, and they appeared to cover a large stretch of area. I thought it might be a controlled weed burn in the foothills, but the flames appeared to stretch lower than that. I tried to determine the exact city where the fire might be burning, but we were too high to tell. I read the paper the next morning, and the fire was in the Malibu area. It covered over 10,000 acres, and hundreds of residents had to evacuate their homes. A number of people were treated in hospitals, but there were no fatalities. The fire was caused by an arsonist, and it spread due to powerful Santa Ana winds and extremely hot Southern California weather.

As you can see, the writer relies solely on one sentence structure, the compound sentence, and on two joining words: *and* and *but*. The following revised version of the paragraph provides some structural variety.

> Flying into Los Angeles at night from New Orleans, we noticed flames on the ground. The flames, which were on the far western side of the L.A. basin, appeared to cover a large stretch of area. I thought it might be a controlled weed burn in the foothills, but the flames appeared to stretch lower than that. Although I tried to determine the exact city where the fire might be burning, we were too high to tell. I read in the paper the next morning that the fire was in the Malibu area. It covered over 10,000 acres, and hundreds of residents had to evacuate their homes. A number of people were treated in hospitals; however, there were no fatalities. The fire was caused by an arsonist and spread by powerful Santa Ana winds and extremely hot Southern California weather.

As you can see, the revised paragraph contains a variety of sentence structures and is more interesting to read. When a writer relies too heavily on one or two structures and a limited number of joining words, the writing can become monotonous to read and detract from the writer's ideas.

Commonly Used Sentence Structures

Writers have a variety of sentence structures at their disposal, including the following.

1. Simple sentence - a sentence with one subject and one verb:

    <u>Joaquin</u> *hates* working out at a gym. (Subject underlined, verb
    italicized)

    Variations:

    Simple sentence with an introductory phrase:

    During the hot summer months, <u>Joaquin</u> *hates* working out at a gym.

    Simple sentence with a *compound subject* or *compound verb*:

    <u>Joaquin</u> *hates* working out at a gym but *enjoys* running on the campus track.
    <u>Joaquin</u> and <u>Angie</u> both *hate* working out at a gym.

2. Compound sentence - two complete sentences joined by *and, but, or, so, for, or yet:*

    <u>Alchemists</u> *believed* they could turn base metals into gold, but <u>they</u> never *succeeded*.
    <u>Isaac Newton</u> *was* a seventeenth century scientist, and <u>he</u> *was* also an alchemist.

3. Complex sentence - two sentences joined by subordinate conjunctions like *although, if, when, because, since, unless while, as, before, after, until,* or *whenever.* The conjunction may begin the first half or the second half of the sentence:

    Examples (subordinate conjunction in italics):

    While you were waiting at the E line subway, I was upstairs at the F line.
    I enjoy going boating on the ocean *although* I get seasick rather easily.
    Unless the weather clears up soon, we should scrap our plans to study outside.

4. Sentence with a *relative clause* - a sentence containing a group of words beginning with a *relative pronoun - who, which, whom, that, or whose -* that modifies the word or group of words it follows.

    Examples (*relative pronoun* in italics):

    The Brooklyn Bridge, *which* connects Manhattan with Brooklyn, is a walking and a driving bridge.
    Last semester my grade point average was above 3.0, *which* shocked my parents.
    The students *who* organized the canned food drive on campus did a great job.

5. Sentence containing a compound and complex sentence structure, two complex sentence structures, or two compound sentence structures.

    Examples:

    Although the weather report calls for rain, the sky has been clear all morning, and there are no clouds on the horizon. (Complex/compound combination)

    Lobotomies were an accepted operational procedure on mentally ill patients in the 1950's, and the barbaric practice continued into the '60's although the outcomes were often disastrous. (Compound/complex sentence)

    The recent fires in Southern California forced over 500,000 people to evacuate their homes, and they raged over 50,000 acres from San Diego to Santa Barbara, but fortunately, no one was killed as a direct result of the fires. (compound/compound sentence)

    If you are driving to the football game on Saturday, plan on coming at least an hour before game time because the parking lots will fill quickly. (complex/complex sentence)

6. Sentence beginning or ending with a *participial phrase* beginning with a *participle*: *walking* to the park, *waiting* beside the library, *sleeping* in the bough of the tree, *troubled* by her son's behavior, *thwarted* by the opponent's defense.

    Examples (*Participles* in italics):

    Walking to the park, Gretchen was drenched by a sudden downpour.
    Sleeping in the bough of the tree, the baby monkey was barely visible.

Troubled by her son's behavior, Gladys met with his 5th grade teacher.
Thwarted by the opponent's defense, the football team resorted to trick plays.

Revision Activity 5.7

Combine the following sentences to create the different sentence structures provided.

Example: complex sentence

I don't think I would like eating sushi. I might give it a try.

Although I don't think I would like eating sushi, I might give it a try.
(complex sentence beginning with subordinate conjunction *although*)

Compound sentences (joining words: *and, but, so, for, yet, or*)

1. A lot of alternative rock music today sounds the same. That could be said of rock music from any time period.

2. The new river walk on the east bank of the Thames is easily accessible. Tourists and locals take the walk from the London Eye ferris wheel to the new restaurants farther down river.

3. Disneyland in Los Angeles still attracts more visitors than Disney World in Orlando. It is located in a more heavily populated area.

Complex sentences (joining words: *although, if, when, because, since, unless, of, while, before, until, whenever, as*)

4. You may want to get a 4.0 GPA this semester. It will be difficult carrying twenty units.

5. For a few hours, the river actually reverses directions at its mouth. The ocean tide rises higher than the river that feeds it.

6. I have been traipsing all over the library looking for books on the Druids. You have been wisely researching the ancient religious sect on the Internet.

7. You want to get the best seats possible for the concert. Go on-line to Ticketron a month in advance.

Sentences with a relative clause (relative pronouns: *who, whose, whom, which,* or *that.* Delete or replace unnecessary words, and move words or phrases around if necessary.)

8. The Brooklyn Bridge connects Brooklyn with Manhattan. It is a walking bridge and a driving bridge.

9. St. Johns, New Brunswick was settled in 1781 by British loyalists. They had been living in the New England colonies before the Revolutionary War.

10. I'd suggest taking the Washington D.C. subway to Georgetown. That is the fastest way to get there.

11. The Dalai Lama has been hired as a professor at Emory University in Atlanta. He is an internationally famous former Tibetan monk.

Simple sentences with compound subjects and/or verbs

12. Freda is doing well in Dr. Taylor's calculus class. Matthew is also doing well. Their friend Felix is also doing well.

13. Samantha enjoys visiting her grandma on holidays. She also likes browsing yard sales on weekends. Finally, she relishes taking long walks in Central Park with her dog.

Compound/complex, complex/compound, compound/compound, or complex/complex sentences

14. Freeman likes doing experiments in his chemistry class. He gets bored sitting through lectures on chemistry. He prefers the active, hands-on learning which the experiments provide.

15. The destruction of the World Trade Center occurred over four years ago. Workers are still clearing the site. Construction on a replacement building won't begin for many months.

16. I'm going to register on-line for classes for the fall semester. It will be easier than going through on-campus registration. I will also have the best chance of getting the classes and times that I need.

17. I've been studying for tests earlier in the morning. I've gotten better grades. The material is fresh in my head.

18. The Chicago Cubs haven't won a World Series in over fifty years. Their record is improving almost every year. They may have a good chance in the next five years.

Sentences with a beginning or ending *participial phrase* (You may delete words or move them around.)

19. Joanna returned to work after a two-week vacation. She had over two-hundred e-mails awaiting her.

20. Malcolm didn't get to the subway station until after midnight. He hoped to catch the last train to the airport.

Revision Activity 5.8

The following paragraph contains a number of similarly structured sentences that could bother readers. Combine groups of related sentences into single sentences using a variety of sentence structures and joining words. Add, delete, and replace words and move them around to combine sentences most effectively.

Example:

My roommate and I set the thermostat in our apartment at eighty-two degrees in the summer. We set it there so that the air conditioner won't run all the time. In the winter we set the thermostat at sixty-eight degrees. We set it there to save on our heating bill. I go around the apartment in shorts and a t-shirt in the summer. It is always a little warm. I go around the apartment in sweats in the winter. It is always a little cool. It is difficult to adjust to a fourteen-degree change in temperature. That change occurs between summer and winter. It is necessary. We save a lot of money on utilities.

Revised:

My roommate and I set the thermostat in our apartment at eighty-two degrees in the summer so the air conditioner won't run all the time. In the winter, we set the thermostat at sixty-eight degrees to save on our heating bill. Since it is always a little warm, I go around the apartment in shorts and a t-shirt in the summer while in the winter, I wear sweats since it is always a little cool. It is difficult to adjust to the fourteen-degree change in temperature that occurs between summer and winter, but it is necessary because we save a lot of money on utilities.

My five year old nephew is in kindergarten, but he is already reading at 4th grade level. He also has a great memory. He has memorized all of the planets. He also knows all of the states and their capitals. He also knows the order in which they were admitted into the Union. He can also add and subtract two-column figures in his head. He can do basic multiplication and division. He won't have that in school for two years. Kindergarten is extremely easy for him. He already knows everything that they are doing, and that makes school boring at times. Kindergarten is where he belongs socially. He is an average five year old. He likes to play and have fun. He would be out of place in a higher grade. He could certainly do the work. There are no gifted programs for kindergarten students, so his teacher gives him extra work for home. That includes more challenging reading. It also includes more advanced math. His mother serves as his tutor at home. She is a high school teacher. Home is where he does most of his learning.

Revision Activity 5.9

Revise the first draft of your problem/solution paper by applying the following guidelines.

Revision Guidelines

1. From your opening, do readers clearly understand the problem you are writing about and its significance? Is there anything that you can add or change in your opening to engage the readers' interest further?

2. From your middle paragraphs, can readers clearly understand the causes of the problem? Do they see its effects and understand who is affected and how? What might you add or change to strengthen the paragraphs that deal with the problem's causes and its effects?

3. Read your draft to see whether your ideas are organized in the most effective way. Does one paragraph follow logically from the preceding one? Is there any paragraph or sentence that seems out of place and could be moved to a more effective location?

4. Read your conclusion to see whether you have presented your solution(s) clearly and effectively. Evaluate your solution one last time, making sure that it is the most sensible, workable solution to the problem, one that addresses its causes.

5. Read your sentences to see whether you have used a variety of structures to present your ideas most effectively. Revise sentences as you have done in the sentence variety activities to improve sentence variety and eliminate repetitive structures and joining words.

6. Read your sentences and eliminate unnecessary words or phrases, reword vague sentences, smooth out any awkward sentences, and replace questionable word choices.

7. Check your paragraphing to make sure that you have changed paragraphs as you move to new ideas in your paper. Divide overly long paragraphs and combine strings of short paragraphs that have related content.

8. Read your paper with your audience and purpose in mind. Make any changes that would make the draft more interesting, meaningful, or informative for readers, or that would help you accomplish your purpose.

Sample Revision (audience - college students, board and administration)

Finding A Job

Joel Ortiz graduated a year ago with an electrical engineering degree and has yet to find a job in his field. Myrna Crosby has taught part-time three years at a community college and feels she is no closer to full-time employment than when she started. After getting his two-year degree in forestry services, Jonathan Briggs sought employment with the state Fish and Game Department only to find out that there was an indefinite hiring freeze in place.

These college graduates, like thousands of others nationwide, are discovering that the traditional ~~belief~~ **assumption** that ~~employment in one's major field~~ **a good-paying job** awaits the college graduate no longer applies. In fact, graduates are finding it ~~harder and harder~~ **more difficult than ever** to find a job in their field in today's economic climate, and ~~the reality may be that there will~~ **there may be** fewer job opportunities for college graduates for years to come. A college degree is no longer a guarantee of **employment** ~~a good-paying job~~, and college students need to look to their future with eyes wide open.

A variety of circumstances ~~appears to~~ have created a bleaker job market for college graduates. The Great Recession which began in 2008 is certainly a factor, with many businesses ~~large and small~~ ~~not only not hiring but~~ laying off employees **and imposing hiring freezes.** ~~particularly in businesses associated with the housing and finance industries.~~ Due largely to reduced revenues, Federal, ~~and~~ state, **and local** governments are running record deficits, and **white-collar** jobs that are often filled by college graduates ~~at the city, state, or Federal level~~ when employees retire ~~are going unfilled~~ **remain vacant.**

In addition, the U.S. has lost hundreds of thousands of jobs over the past ten years ~~due to companies~~ **to corporate** outsourcing, **with** jobs ~~to other countries where they can pay~~ **shipped overseas where employees work for** lower wages. Since these "multinational corporations" have no loyalty to American employees and ~~will~~ **re**locate wherever they can ~~find qualified employees and~~ save money, the chances of these jobs returning to the U.S. are slim~~-to-none~~, and ~~it is~~ more likely that we will continue to lose ~~additional~~ jobs to outsourcing. Some companies, in fact, are advising college engineering and computer science majors to consider working abroad ~~upon graduation~~ since that is where the jobs will be, albeit at much smaller salaries.

The effects of the weak U.S. job market on college graduates are depressing. With many graduates having sizable college loans to pay off, their inability to find good paying jobs ~~can~~ puts them in a ~~great~~ bind. Unable to find jobs in their field, many take ~~whatever~~ **any** hourly wage job they can find, ~~often working~~ **whether** in retail sales, waiting tables, or scouring the "want ads" for any available employment. Many take on multiple part-time jobs since many ~~industries~~ **employers**, including colleges, hire part-time employees because they are cheaper. ~~to employ.~~ Many who end up working outside of their field never return to it. Unable to find a decent job, ~~many~~ **other** graduates re-enroll in college, seeking a degree in a more employable field **or** getting a higher degree or ~~getting~~ a teaching credential. Sometimes going back to college pays off ~~in the long run~~; other times, it merely puts a person's ~~wage-earning~~ future on hold.

There are no simple solutions to the ~~current~~ disparity between the number of college graduates ~~seeking employment~~ and the number of jobs available. However, it is a problem that ~~clearly needs to~~ **must** be ~~tackled~~ **addressed** not only for the future of ~~all~~ college students but for the future of the country. As the ~~lack~~ **number** of good-paying jobs decreases, the size of the middle class shrinks, as it has been doing for the past ten years. A large, robust middle class has been ~~integral~~ **key** to the economic success of America. As the middle class erodes, **so does** the country. ~~erodes.~~

Colleges have a great obligation to justify the **significant** cost of education to students ~~today~~. If there is little correlation between ~~the two-year or four-year~~ **the number** degrees that a college churns out and the percentage of graduates that find jobs in their field, colleges must take some of the blame. There is much that colleges can do ~~to help~~, including providing students with job market trends ~~in every educational field~~, steering students ~~in the direction of~~ **towards** fields with the greatest job availability, and partnering with private and public business to ~~do everything possible to assure~~ **help place** graduates **in jobs** ~~of future employment~~. Colleges **should** ~~need to~~ feel a strong obligation ~~to do everything possible~~ to ~~help~~ **assist** graduates **in** find**ing** jobs, and they ~~are just scratching the surface of what may be possible.~~ **can do much more than they are to help.**

Clearly, the outsourcing of jobs to other countries needs to be addressed. What can the government do ~~to get companies~~ to keep jobs in the U.S. and ~~to~~ bring outsourced jobs back? Currently, it is doing nothing; ~~and~~ in fact, corporations that outsource **jobs** get the same tax breaks **and subsidies** as those that don't. The Federal government **should** ~~needs to~~ form a commission to study the outsourcing problem and figure out a way to solve it. Otherwise, the time may come when the only decent jobs left in America are ~~those~~ **the few** that ~~for logistical reasons~~ can't be outsourced **for logistical reasons.**

Finally, students need to take responsibility for their own futures. They ~~need to arm themselves with all of the~~ **must become as** knowledge**able as** possible about the job market that **awaits them.** ~~they will soon be facing.~~ They need to be realistic about what field to major in, balancing their interests with where the job **opportunities lie** ~~are~~. When necessary, they ~~also need to~~ **must** be willing to move ~~to an area~~ **someplace** where they can find a job, whether ~~it be~~ **to** a different part of the state or another state. ~~While the ideal is often~~ **Unfortunately,** finding a job ~~in an area~~ where you ~~want to~~ live ~~among friends and family, that doesn't always work out~~ **isn't always possible**, and **throughout history,** Americans have ~~constantly~~ migrated ~~throughout history to states or areas~~ **towards opportunity:** from the country to the city, the Midwest to the West, the South to the North. **Today, for example, many applications for teaching jobs in New York come from out of state.**

Given the shrinking job market for college graduates, some skeptics are wondering whether it is worth ~~it to~~ go**ing** to college ~~at all~~ and pay**ing** the high cost of tuition. The problem is, what are you going to do *without* a college degree. ~~Sure,~~ There are the computer geniuses and born salespeople who do great **without it**, but for the vast majority, the lack of a two-year or four-year degree closes ~~most decent~~ **most** employment doors, leaving open the more easily attained, dead-end hourly jobs at a Wal-Mart, McDonald's, or your local mall.

A college education provides no guarantees, but it still provides ~~by far~~ the ~~greatest~~ **best** employment opportunities and the ~~greatest~~ chance to live the American Dream: **the good salaried job,** the house, the comfortable life, ~~the good salary, the comfortable~~ **the secure** retirement. College is still the best choice ~~to make~~, but students **must** ~~need to~~ be aware more than ever of the **employment** pitfalls ~~in the current economic landscape~~ **that lie ahead** and do their best to avoid them. **And the time to begin is now.**

Editing

The final phase of the writing process is to correct any errors in punctuation, spelling, or grammar usage in your paper before passing it on to readers. With all of the work you have put into writing and revising your paper, you owe it to yourself and your readers to produce an error-free final draft.

In this section you review the elements of punctuation and grammar usage covered in previous units. You are also introduced to new punctuation marks - colons, semicolons, and dashes - and to a new grammar consideration - comparative and superlative adjectives. The use of colons, semi-colons, and dashes gives you more options for expressing yourself most effectively, and using the correct comparative and superlative adjectives forms will help you make comparisons in your writing and avoid common usage errors.

Colons, Semi-Colons, and Dashes

While colons, semi-colons, and dashes are used somewhat sparingly by most writers, they nonetheless serve useful functions. Once you clearly understand how to use them, you will find ways to insert them into your writing naturally and effectively.

The following guidelines will help you use colons, semi-colons, and dashes effectively in your writing.

1. A colon (:) is used to set off a word or group of words that follows it and relates to the complete statement preceding the colon.

    Examples:

    There is one thing that most students look forward to: Christmas break.
    We will need several items for the camping trip: tents, sleeping bags, food, and flash lights.
    I usually get my best grades on one type of test: multiple choice.
    One misnomer leads to disappointment among many first-time stock market investors: unrealistic expectations about making fast money.
    One trait stands out among people who are successful in the sales business: perseverance.
    There are several things that trouble us about Theodore: his slovenly appearance, his poor hygiene, his sarcastic manner, and his habit of borrowing books and not returning them.

2. A semi-colon (;) joins two sentences that are closely related in meaning. A transitional word such as *however* or *therefore* often follows the semi-colon.

Examples:

I'm going to pull weeds in the front yard for a while; you can continue planting bulbs if you want.
The morning has been warm and mild; however, a powerful storm is coming in later this afternoon.
There is no way to study for Dr. Garcia's philosophy tests; therefore, you just have to relax and do the best that you can.
I don't really want to go to a movie this evening; I'd much rather stay and home and watch TV.
Sam got a speeding ticket in a 35 mile an hour zone; consequently, he has to go to traffic school.

(Note: For clarity, semi-colons can also be used in place of commas to separate series of long phrases or clauses. Example: The feeding frenzy created by the huge school of grunion included thousands of small seafaring birds that blackened the water; hundreds of pelicans dive bombing the surfing area; waves of seagulls launching their attacks from the beach; and numerous dolphins encircling their prey like sharks.

3. A dash (-) is used similarly to a colon, setting off information referred to in the statement preceding it, and can be used in place of a colon in more informal writing. More frequently, however, dashes are used in pairs, before and after the information referred to, and the sentence continues after the second dash.

    Examples:

    Most of the migratory birds on the lake - mallards, coots, geese, and mergansers - feed off of the thousands of minnows that populate the waters.
    Three are many ways to cook chicken - bake, fry, boil, grill, or roast - but my favorite is to barbecue.
    Everyone who attends plays on campus - students, townspeople, parents, and school officials - raves about the quality of the performances.
    The most frequent errors that writers make - running sentences together, misspelling words, omitting commas - are usually caught and corrected during the proofreading phase of the writing process.
    One thing that my history professor harped on - never waiting until the night before a test to study - finally sunk in before I took my mid-term exams.

The following paragraph provides example of how colons, semi-colons, and dashes can be incorporated into your writing.

Working full-time and going to college is really hard. I attend school in the morning and work from 1:00 p.m. until 8:00 p.m. at a fast-food restaurant. Most evenings follow the same routine: eat, study, and go to bed late. I'm always tired. I also work the same shift on Saturdays, so I have little time to spend with my friends. After I spend the money I make on necessities - college expenses, car payments, and insurance - I have little left for other things. However, without the job, I wouldn't be in college or have a car; that is the reason I work. While some students may look forward to going out partying, I look forward to something a little different: sleep.

Editing Activity 5.10

Punctuate the following sentences correctly using colons, semi-colons, or dashes.

Example: You will need the following ingredients to make tacos hamburger meat, taco flavoring mix, tomatoes, onions, cheese, lettuce, avocados, corn tortillas, and salsa.

Corrected: You will need the following ingredients to make tacos: hamburger meat, taco flavoring mix, tomatoes, onions, cheese, lettuce, avocados, corn tortillas, and salsa.

1.   To make tacos, put a pound of hamburger meat in a skillet then break up the meat with a fork.

2.   When the meat is browned, add one ingredient taco mix to flavor the hamburger meat.

3.   Next, cut up your vegetables tomatoes, onions, lettuce, and avocados and grate your cheese.

4.   Then put a thin layer of cooking oil in a second skillet cook your tortillas in the skillet one at a time.

5.   Next, take a tortilla and fill it with all of your ingredients hamburger meat, cheese, and vegetables and then add salsa on top.

6.   Make sure not to fill the tortilla too full of meat the bottom could fall out while you are eating it.

7.   You have now learned to make the best kind of meal delicious, easy to make, and inexpensive.

8.   If you get tired of hamburger meat, replace it with something else chicken, fish, or even shrimp to add variety to your tacos.

Editing Activity 5.11

Read the following paragraph and insert colons, semi-colons, or dashes where they are needed.

Example:

At the natural art museum, the side-by-side skeletons of a young gorilla and an eight-year old boy who lived 20,000 years ago are eerily similar the same skeletal frames with the exception of the gorilla's longer arms and bigger feet. The other difference is the size of the skull the boy's skull is larger and rounder, housing a larger, more advanced brain.

Corrected:

At the natural art museum, the side-by-side skeletons of a young gorilla and an eight-year old boy who lived 20,000 years ago are eerily similar: the same skeletal frames with the exception of the gorilla's longer arms and bigger feet. The other difference is the size of the skull; the boy's skull is larger and rounder, housing a larger, more advanced brain.

We have a large family living in a three-bedroom rental four kids and two parents. A few months ago, my aunt and uncle immigrated to the U.S. with their kids. They moved in with us until they could find a place to stay, and they are still here. Now there are ten people living the house. The obvious problems three kids to a bedroom, no privacy, constant noise will only be solved when they move out. They are nice people and we get along well, but with that many people in one small house, things are going to come up. My uncle is a smoker he keeps it out of the house, but he brings the smell in on his clothes. My aunt does a lot of the cooking, and she's not a very good cook. It's hard having my boyfriend over because wherever we go, my little nieces have to be there, giggling all the time. It's crazy around the house, and studying is impossible. There's one thing that I'd pay to have peace and quiet.

Editing Activity 5.12

For practice, write six original sentences: two with colons, two with semi-colons, and two with pairs of dashes.

Comparative and Superlative Adjectives

Writers frequently use adjectives to describe things in their papers: hungry children, ominous clouds, a talented pianist, a difficult test. They also use adjectives to compare things: the higher humidity in Atlanta than in Chicago, the more difficult problem of global warming compared to pollution, the lower price of gas in the U.S. compared to Europe, or the tallest mountain peak in the world compared to all others. Adjectives that compare have a number of different forms, depending on how many things are being compared and how many syllables the adjective has. Some basic grammatical rules govern the forms these adjectives take, and once you learn them, you will have little problem using the correct forms in your writing.

Comparative Adjectives

Comparative adjectives compare one thing to another. The following rules apply to comparative adjectives.

1. Add *er* to one-syllable adjectives.

    I am *shorter* than you are.
    Sam is *thinner* than Phil.
    Mercury lights are *brighter* than florescent lights.

2. Add *more* in front of adjectives with two or more syllables.

    I am *more* introverted than you are.
    Samantha is *more* graceful than Phyllis.
    Mercury lights are *more* effective than florescent lights.

    Exception: Add *er* to two-syllable words ending in *y* or *ow*.

    I am *lonelier* than you are.
    Margo is *sillier* than her brother.
    Mercury lights are *prettier* than fluorescent lights.
    The river is *shallower* along the banks than in the middle.

Superlative Adjectives

Superlative adjectives compare three or more things. The following rules apply to superlative adjectives.

1. Add *est* to one-syllable adjectives.

    I am the *tallest* person in my family.
    Sam is the *smartest* gorilla in the zoo.
    Mercury lights are the *brightest* lights for football fields.

2. Add *most* in front of adjectives with two or more syllables.

Felipe is the *most* dependable person in the family.
Sam is the *most* curious gorilla in the zoo.
Mercury lights are the *most* expensive lights for outdoor home lighting.

Exception: Add *est* to two-syllable words ending in *y* or *ow*.

I am the *rowdiest* person in my family.
Sam is the *heaviest* gorilla in the zoo.
Mercury lights give off the *loveliest* glow on dark nights.
The Dead Sea is the *shallowest* ocean in the world.

Editing Activity 5.13

Each of the following sentences compares two things. Fill in the correct comparative form of each adjective in parentheses. Determine the number of syllables the adjective has, and add *er* to one-syllable adjectives and two-syllable adjectives ending in *y* or *ow*, and add *more* in front of adjectives of two syllables or more.

Examples: (quick)   You are a *quicker* thinker than I am.

         (beautiful) The elm trees on campus are *more* beautiful in the spring
                      than in the summer.

1. (interesting)   The first week of school was _____ than I thought it would be.

2. (friendly)   The students were _____ than I imagined.

3. (fascinating)   The classes were _____ than my high school classes.

4. (short)   The classes were also _____ than usual, since it was the first
                    week.

5. (fast)   The whole day went by _____ than I expected.

6. (tedious)   I thought the school work would be _____ than it was.

7. (enthusiastic) Now I am _____ than ever about school.

8. (long)   However, next week's classes will be _____ than this week's.

9. (difficult)   The homework will get _____ as the semester progresses.

10. (typical)   The next weeks will be _____ of the rest of the semester.

Editing Activity 5.14

Each of the following sentences compares three or more things. Fill in the correct superlative form of each adjective in parentheses. Determine the number of syllables the adjective has; add *est* to one-syllable adjectives and two-syllable adjectives ending in *y* or *ow*, and add *most* in front of adjectives with two syllables or more.

Examples: (quick)   That was the quickest that Ricardo has ever completed a biology experiment.

        (unusual) The modern art display in the library is the most unusual display of the year.

1. (interesting)   The first week of school was one of the _____ weeks I've spent.

2. (unusual)   I met some of the _____ teachers I've had.

3. (fascinating)   The class subjects were the _____ I've been exposed to.

4. (long)   The classes were also the _____ I have ever attended.

5. (fast)   It was the _____ week of school I've been through.

6. (tedious)   I thought biology would be the _____ class of the semester.

7. (enthusiastic)   Now I am the _____ I've ever been about taking biology.

8. (hard)   Although the classes are the _____ I've had, I enjoy them.

9. (difficult)   Although the homework is the _____ I've done, I don't mind it.

10. (typical)   Students say that the fourth and fifth weeks of school are the _____ weeks to judge school by.

Editing Activity 5.15

Fill in each of the following blanks with an appropriate comparative or superlative adjective by following the rules presented. Include both one-syllable and two-or-more syllable adjectives.

Examples: In winter the evenings grow *shorter* while in summer they
grow *longer*.

That is the *most expensive* textbook I've ever bought.

1. The oboe is _____ to play than the clarinet.

2. The saxophone is the _____ woodwind
    instrument to play.

3. The alto saxophone has the _____ sound of any
    woodwind.

4. The French horn is _____ than the trumpet.

5. The tuba is the _____ brass instrument.

6. The band director appeared the _____every time the
    woodwind section took over the melody.

7. When a woodwind squeaks, it is one of the _____
    sounds there is.

8. A French horn can produce the _____ sound of
    any brass instrument.

9. Percussion instruments are often the _____ to play.

10. The snare drum is _____ to play than the timpani.

Editing Review

Throughout the text, you review elements of punctuation, spelling, and
grammar that give writers problems. The purpose of these review activities is
to give you more proofreading and editing practice and ultimately to eliminate
such problems in your writing. Even writers who make few mistakes find an
occasional error to correct during the editing process, and all writers can
profit from editing practice.

_____

Editing Activity 5.16

Proofread the following draft for errors involving run-on sentences or comma splices,
sentence fragments, irregular verbs, comma usage, subject-verb agreement, subject
pronouns, or pronoun-antecedent agreement, and make the necessary corrections.

Read the draft several times, looking for different types of errors each time. Example:

The stucco on the outside of my aunt's house is cracking, there is several long cracks running across the walls. The house is relatively new and the cracks occurred when the stucco on the walls were drying. The cracks on the front of the house is particularly noticeable, it runs long and deep from the sides to the front door. One of the cracks are jagged instead of straight and they are very noticeable. My aunt and me plastered over the biggest cracks and once the plaster on the walls are dry we will paint over them. We smoothed out the plaster so that it blends in smoothly with the stucco, once we paint over them the walls should look as good as new if you don't stand too close.

Corrected:

The stucco on the outside of my aunt's house is cracking. There are several long cracks running across the walls. The house is relatively new, and the cracks occurred when the stucco on the walls was drying. The cracks on the front of the house are particularly noticeable. They run long and deep from the sides to the front door. One of the cracks is jagged instead of straight, and it is very noticeable. My aunt and I plastered over the biggest cracks, and once the plaster on the walls is dry, we will paint over it. We smoothed out the plaster so that it blends in smoothly with the stucco, so once we paint over it, the walls should look as good as new if you don't stand too close.

Unique Campus

Our school campus is built on a hill. At the top of the hill is two small ponds which provides water for the water features on campus. Some of the water from the ponds run down several copper troughs which are located on each side of several stairways that runs from the top of the hill to the bottom across the campus. Water from the ponds also create several small waterfalls throughout the campus which feeds into small water basins. Water is pumped back up the hill from the basins and they are recycled into the ponds on top of the hill.

   With all the water features you can hear water running everywhere on campus, they create a relaxing sound. In addition the beauty of the waterfalls and the water running down the copper troughs makes the campus very special. Unlike any campus I've ever seen. With the ponds above the campus the water features throughout the campus the hilly environment and the pine and eucalyptus trees growing between the buildings our campus almost feel like a resort area, students enjoy just hanging out here after his or her classes.

Editing Activity 5.17

Proofread your paper for errors by applying the following guidelines, and make any necessary corrections. Read the draft several times, looking for different types of errors each time.

Editing Guidelines

1. Check your sentences to make sure you haven't run any sentences together or put a comma between sentences instead of a period. Correct run-on sentences or comma splices by separating longer sentence with periods and combining shorter, related sentences with a joining word.

2. Check your draft for any sentence fragments: incomplete sentences with a period after them. To correct fragments, attach them to the sentence they belong with, or add words to make them complete.

3. Check your use of irregular verbs, making sure you have used the correct irregular forms and spelled them correctly.

4. Check your comma usage, making sure you have inserted commas into your sentences correctly and not in places they aren't required.

5. Check the spelling of any word you are uncertain of, or run the spell check on your word processing program, to eliminate any spelling errors.

6. Check your verbs in each sentence to make sure that they agree with their subjects.

7. Check your pronouns in each sentence to make sure they agree with their antecedents, and make sure you are using the correct subject pronoun forms.

8. Check your use of colons, semi-colons, and dashes to see whether you are using them correctly and effectively. If you have used none, see whether there may be an occasional sentence that you might improve by revising it to require a colon, semi-colon, or dashes.

9. Check your use of comparative and superlative adjectives, and make sure that you have used the correct forms following the usage rules in this section.

Writing Summary

At the end of each unit, you write a second paper applying what you have learned without interruptions for instruction or activities. The purpose of this assignment is for you to work independently on your writing, to gain more experience writing problem/solution papers, and to continue improving your writing skills.

Prewriting

The following prewriting activities will help prepare you to write your first draft.

Topic Selection

To select a topic for this paper, follow these guidelines.

1. Choose a problem to write on that is very different from the topic of your first paper. If you wrote on a personal problem, choose a problem that affects many people. If you wrote on a more universal problem, choose a problem that affects you the most directly.

2. Choose a problem that is serious enough to engage readers' interest and concern.

3. Choose a problem that doesn't have an obvious solution that you have already discovered.

4. Choose a problem that is nagging and persistent, one that will not go away by itself.

5. Since this is not a "research" paper, choose a topic that you are knowledgeable about.

Sample Topic: the cost of college textbooks

Problem Analysis

Once you have selected a problem, answer the following questions to analyze the problem in some detail and to generate material for your first draft.

1. What exactly is the problem?

2. When did the problem begin, and how did it get started?

3. What are the causes of the problem?

4. Who or what is affected by the problem?

5. What are the effects of the problem?

Finding Solutions

Use the following questions to help you generate possible solutions to the problem.

1. Exactly what does solving the problem mean? What do you hope to accomplish?

2. How can the solution get to the roots of the problem, its underlying causes?

3. What are possible alternative solutions to the problem?

4. Is compromise an important part of the solution?

5. What is a realistic solution to the problem? Can the right solution completely eliminate the problem, or can it make a bad situation better?

6. What do other people think? Often there are knowledgeable people to turn to when seeking solutions to thorny problems.

Audience and Purpose

To determine the reading audience and purpose for your problem/solution paper, consider these suggestions.

1. Whom would I like to read this paper?

2. Who might benefit from reading the paper?

3. Who might help to solve the problem?

4. What is my purpose in writing to this audience? What do I hope to accomplish? How do I want readers to respond?

5. What is the best tone to take in this paper to help accomplish my purpose?

First Draft Guidelines

Write the first draft of your paper keeping the following in mind.

1. Introduce the problem in your opening paragraph, its significance, and why readers should be aware of it.

2. In the middle paragraphs, incorporate material from your activities to help readers understand the causes of the problem and its effects.

3. Conclude the draft by suggesting a solution or combination of solutions which address the causes of the problem and could eliminate it or reduce its impact.

4. Change paragraphs as you move to different aspects of the problem: its causes, its effects, possible solutions.

5. As you write, keep in mind your reading audience, your purpose, and the tone you want to maintain.

Sample First Draft

The Cost of Textbooks (audience: instructors, administration, trustees)

Last semester I spent over $400 on textbooks, and that was just for six books. One biology text cost over $100, and the six books averaged over $66 apiece. This was not an unusual semester for me either, and the cost was similar to what many students had to pay. You go to a regular bookstore like Barnes and Noble and its hard to find a book of any kind that costs over $50. In our bookstore, it's hard to find any textbook that costs less than $50. There is something seriously wrong, and the excessive cost of textbooks is a problem for many students.

Obviously textbook publishing companies don't care how much of a burden the price of textbooks is on students. They clearly are out to make the biggest profit they can, and they sell books for the highest prices they can. In addition, as more used copies of a particular book get into circulation, they come out with a new edition at a higher price. The new edition always has enough changes in it so that you can't buy a used copy of the previous edition. Many instructors often aren't even aware of the cost of a particular textbook before they decide to order it for their courses. In addition, the bookstore bumps the cost of the books up 30% in order to make its nice profit. And no one seems to see a serious problem here, at least no one who could perhaps help change the situation.

The high cost of textbooks is definitely a problem for students, at least for those who aren't rolling in money. After paying for tuition, which is always going up, many students can't afford $400 or $500 a semester for their textbooks. Most of us try to buy used books whenever we can, but there are never enough copies to go around, and with new editions of texts constantly coming out, and with instructors frequently changing the textbooks they use, you can't get around paying a lot of money. Some students resort to sharing texts, which is seldom a good situation, and others go as long into the semester as they can without purchasing a text, which often has the obvious effect on their grades that you would guess.

In addition, some students end up taking fewer classes than they want to in order to pay for both tuition and their textbooks. That has the effect of students having to go to school longer and in the long run paying even more, and sometimes it can even affect their financial aid if they go below the required minimum number of units to qualify. Finally, some students even resort to stealing other students' textbooks, and if you forget your books in the cafeteria or the library, you can kiss them goodby.

The high cost of textbooks is a problem that students are certainly aware of, but it doesn't seem to be a problem that has the attention of many instructors or the college in general. Most instructors require that students buy textbooks for their classes, and they don't seem to care too much how much the books cost. To help solve the problem, it is important that instructors are very aware of it and that they do their part in helping to keep the costs down. While textbooks will probably always be a part of most classes, at least teachers can be aware of the cost of the textbooks in their field and shop around for the least expensive books. They can also consider letting classmates share books, say two students to one book, which would cut the cost of books in half for students. Some teachers may say that sharing textbooks doesn't work well, but the only measure of that would be to give it a try and see how students perform.

Instructors could when possible replace textbooks with other kinds of learning materials such as printed hand-outs and restrict their courses to no more than one textbook. Some instructors have you buy two or three books for their class as if it is the only class that you are taking. Some instructors I'm sure could even develop their own learning materials, like some of my instructors have done, so that they don't need to have students purchase textbooks at all. There are a lot of things that instructors could do to help, but most importantly, they must recognize what a big problem the cost of textbooks is for students and acknowledge that the instructors are part of the problem so they need to be a big part of the solution.

The board of trustees also need to be aware of this problem and help find ways to reduce the cost of textbooks. The bookstore, for example, could have a policy of not making any money on used textbooks so that students can buy them at the lowest possible cost. They could also reduce their profit margin on new books so students would pay less. They are also in the best position to research the cost of competing textbooks and let instructors know what the most reasonably priced textbooks are. All of this would require changes in the bookstore's policy, and that would be where the trustees and other college decision-makers could play a role.

Finally, near a number of colleges are off-campus bookstores that sell new and used textbooks at a lower price than college bookstores. While getting one of these stores to locate in our town might not be good for our college bookstore, it would be good for students, and that should be what is most important. This could be one area where students could get involved and research the possibility of a store fromone of the bookstore chains opening a store near our campus.

As you can see, there are a number of ways that the high cost of textbooks for students could be reduced, but the only way any of this is going to happen is for the people who can help change the situation - instructors, trustees, administrators - to recognize the severity of the problem and put their heads together to see what can be done about it. I hear some people say, " That's just the way it goes. With inflation, everything is going up in cost, and textbooks go up like everything else." That is the kind of attitude that will result in nothing changing and in the situation growing worse every year. Where there is a will there is a way, and hopefully there will be the will to solve the problem once it gets everyone's attention.

Revision Guidelines

Set your first draft aside for a while, and then reread it and make the changes that you feel will improve its effectiveness. To help you revise your paper, apply the following guidelines.

1. From your opening, do readers clearly understand the problem you are writing about and its significance? Is there anything that you can add or change in your opening to get your readers' attention?

2. From your middle paragraphs, can readers clearly understand the causes of the problem? Do they see its effects and know exactly who is affected and how? What might you add or change to strengthen those sections dealing with causes and effects?

3. Reread your draft to see whether your ideas are organized in the most effective way. Does one paragraph follow logically from the preceding one? Is there any paragraph or sentence that seems out of place and that could be moved to a more effective location?

4. Reread your conclusion to see whether you have presented your solution(s) clearly. Evaluate your solution one last time, making sure that it is sensible and workable, one that addresses the causes of the problem.

5. Read your sentences to see whether you have used a variety of structures to present your ideas most effectively. Revise sentences as you have done in the sentence variety activities to improve your sentence variety and eliminate patterns of similar structures and word choices.

6. Read your sentences and eliminate unnecessary words or phrases, clarify the meaning of vague sentences, and smooth out awkwardly worded sentences.

7. Check your paragraphing to make sure that you have changed paragraphs as you move to new ideas in your paper. Divide overly long paragraphs and combine strings of short, related paragraphs.

8. Check your use of transitional wording to tie sentences and paragraphs

> together. Add any transitions that would help readers understand the relationship between ideas and move smoothly from one paragraph to the next.
>
> 9. Read your paper with your audience and purpose in mind, and make any changes that would make the draft more interesting, meaningful, or informative, or that would help you accomplish your purpose.

Sample Revisions

The Cost of Textbooks

Last semester I spent over $400 on textbooks, ~~and that was just~~ for **just** six books. One biology text cost over $100, and the six books averaged over $66 apiece. This was not an unusual semester ~~for me~~ either, and the cost was similar to what many students had to pay. **When** you go to a ~~regular~~ bookstore like Barnes and Noble, its hard to find ~~a~~ **any** book ~~of any kind~~ that costs over $50, **but** in our bookstore, it's hard to find any textbook that costs less than $50. ~~There~~ Something **is** seriously wrong, and the ~~excessive~~ high ~~cost~~ **price** of textbooks is a problem for many students.

~~Obviously~~ **Clearly**, textbook publishing companies don't care ~~how much of a~~ **about the** burden ~~the~~ **that** high priced ~~of~~ textbooks ~~is~~ **place** on students **or they wouldn't charge so much** . They ~~clearly~~ are out to make the biggest profit they can, and they sell books for the highest prices ~~they can~~. In addition, as more used copies of a particular book ~~get into~~ circulate~~ion~~, ~~they~~ **companies** come out with a new edition at a higher price. The new edition always has enough changes ~~in it so~~ that you can't buy a used copy of the previous edition. Many instructors ~~often~~ **also** aren't even aware of the cost of a particular textbook before they ~~decide to~~ order it ~~for their courses~~. In addition, the bookstore ~~bumps the cost of the book up~~ **adds another** 30% **to the cost** ~~in order to make its nice~~ **for** its profit. And no one - **the instructors, the bookstore manager, other college personnel** - ~~sees a serious problem here, at least no one who could perhaps help change the situation.~~ **seems to realize that all of this affects students**.

The high cost of textbooks is definitely a problem for **most** students~~, at least for those who aren't rolling in money~~. After paying for tuition~~, which is always going up,~~ many students can't afford an **additional** $400 or $500 a semester for their textbooks. Most of us try to buy used books whenever we can, but there are never enough copies to go around, and with new editions ~~of texts~~ constantly coming out, and with instructors frequently changing the textbooks ~~they use~~, you ~~can't get around~~ **end up** ~~paying~~ **spending** a lot of money. Some students resort to sharing texts, ~~which is~~ seldom a good situation, and others go as long ~~into the semester~~ as they can without purchasing a text, which often ~~has the obvious effect on~~ **hurts** their grades ~~that you would guess~~.

In addition, some students end up taking fewer classes than they ~~would like~~ **want** in order to pay for both tuition and **books** ~~their textbooks~~. ~~That has the effect of~~ **As a**

result, students ~~having to~~ go to school longer and ~~in the long run~~ paying even more, and sometimes it ~~can even~~ affects their financial aid if they ~~go~~ **fall** below the required number of ~~required~~ units ~~to qualify~~. Finally, some students even resort to stealing other students' textbooks, and if you forget your books in the cafeteria or the library, **you won't see them again** ~~you can kiss them goodby~~.

The high cost of textbooks is a problem that students are ~~certainly~~ aware of, but it doesn't ~~seem to be a problem that has~~ **have** the attention of many instructors ~~or the college in general~~. Most instructors require ~~that students buy~~ textbooks for their classes, and they don't seem to care ~~too much~~ how much the books cost. To help solve the problem, ~~it is important that~~ instructors ~~are very~~ **must be** aware of it and ~~that they~~ do their part ~~in helping~~ to keep the costs down. While textbooks ~~will probably~~ **may** always be ~~a part of most classes~~ **required**, at least teachers can be aware of their cost ~~of the textbooks in their field~~ and shop around for the least expensive books. They ~~can~~ **should** also consider letting **two** classmates share a book~~s, say two students to one book,~~ which would cut the cost of books in half ~~for students~~. ~~Some teachers may say that sharing textbooks doesn't work well, but the only measure of that would be to give it a try and see how students perform.~~ **If sharing books doesn't hurt students' performance, it could become a widespread practice.**

When possible, instructors could ~~when possible~~ replace textbooks with other kinds of learning materials such as ~~xeroxed~~ **printed** hand-outs ~~and~~ **or** restrict their courses to ~~no more than~~ one textbook~~. Some instructors have you buy~~ **rather than the** two or three books ~~for their class as if it is the only class that you are taking.~~ **that some courses require**. Some instructors ~~I'm sure~~ could even develop their own learning materials **to replace textbooks**, like ~~some of~~ **my** psychology instructors ~~have done~~ **did**. ~~so that they don't need to have students purchase textbooks at all.~~ There are a ~~lot of~~ **many** things that instructors could do to help, but most importantly, they must recognize ~~what a big~~ **the** problem ~~the cost of textbooks is for students and acknowledge that the instructors are part of the problem so they need to be~~ **and accept that they are** a big part of the solution.

The board of trustees also ~~need to~~ **must** be aware of this problem and help find ways to reduce the cost of textbooks. The bookstore, for example, could have a policy of not making any money on used textbooks so that students can buy them at the lowest ~~possible~~ cost. ~~They~~ **It** could also reduce ~~their~~ **its** profit margin on new books so students would pay less. ~~They~~ **The** bookstore personnel are also in the best position to research the cost of competing textbooks ~~and~~ **to** let instructors know what ~~the most reasonably priced~~ textbooks are most reasonably priced. ~~All of this would require~~ **All of these** changes in the bookstore's policy~~, and that~~ would ~~be where the~~ **require** trustees' **authorization** ~~and other college decision-makers could play a role.~~

Student leaders should also play a role in addressing the problem. If trustees and administrators aren't as aware of the problem and its effects as they should be, the student council should make them aware. If instructors are oblivious to the effects that their high-priced textbooks have on students, the council should educate them. One of the roles of student government is to address problems that students face, and the cost of textbooks is certainly one of them. If student

leaders show their passion and concern on the issue, others will do the same.

Finally, a number of colleges have off-campus retail bookstores that sell new and used textbooks at a ~~lower~~ **reduced** price ~~than college bookstores~~. While ~~getting one of these stores to locate in our town might not be good~~ **such a store would compete** ~~for~~ **with** our college bookstore, it would be good for students, ~~and that should be what~~ **which** is most important. ~~This could be one area where~~ Students could **also** get involved ~~and~~ **in** researching the possibility of a bookstore ~~from one of the bookstore chains~~ opening ~~a store~~ near our campus.

As you can see, the high cost of textbooks is a serious problem for students, ~~and~~ **but** there are a number of ways that the ~~high~~ cost ~~of textbooks for students~~ could be reduced. ~~but~~ The only way, however, ~~any of this is going to happen~~ **that anything will change** is for the **decision-makers** ~~people who can help change the situation~~ - instructors, trustees, administrators - to recognize the ~~severity of~~ the problem and ~~put their heads together to see what can be done about it.~~ help to solve it. ~~I h ar~~ Some people may say, " That's just the way it goes. With inflation, everything is going up in cost, ~~and~~ including textbooks ~~go up like everything else~~." ~~That is the kind of attitude that will result in~~ **Given that way of thinking**, nothing will change~~ing, and in~~ the situation will grow~~ing~~ worse ~~every year~~. ~~Where there is a will there is a way, and hopefully there will be the will to solve the problem once it gets everyone's attention~~. **However, this is a solvable problem if everyone works together. The time to start is now.**

Editing Guidelines

Proofread your latest draft for errors by applying the following guidelines, and make the necessary corrections. Then write the final, error-free draft of your paper.

1. Check your sentences to make sure you haven't run any sentences together or put a comma between sentences instead of a period, and make any necessary corrections.

2. Check your draft for any sentence fragments: incomplete sentences with a period after them. To correct fragments, attach them to the sentence they belong with, or add words to make them complete.

3. Check your use of irregular verbs, making sure you have used the correct irregular forms and spelled them correctly.

4. Check your comma usage, making sure you have inserted commas correctly into your sentences.

5. Check the spelling of any word you are uncertain of, or run the spell check on your word processing program, to eliminate any spelling errors.

6.   Check your verbs in each sentence to make sure they agree with their subject.

7.   Check your pronouns in each sentence to make sure they agree with their antecedents, and make sure you are using the correct subject pronoun forms.

8.   Check your use of colons, semi-colons, and dashes to see whether you are using them correctly and effectively. If you have used none, see whether there may be an occasional sentence that you might improve by revising it to require a colon, semi-colon, or dashes.

9.   Check your use of comparative and superlative adjectives, and make sure that you have used the correct forms.

Readings

Are You A Procrastinator?

By Julianne Kuroda

Are you a procrastinator? Sure you are, just like every other human being. We all put off doing something at one time or another, whether it be making the bed, studying for a test, or paying the bills. What varies from one person to another is the frequency with which we procrastinate, the kind of tasks we put off until tomorrow, and the extent that it affects our lives. Among individuals, procrastination ranges from an occasional random act to a habitual, chronic pattern. For people who fall towards the latter end of the spectrum, procrastination can be a serious problem.

Procrastination is familiar to us all. We know the car needs washing badly. We'll do it this morning but after we read the morning paper. Then there's something on TV to watch, so the car can wait a little longer. It's starting to get hot outside, and the car could spot badly if it isn't dried off quickly after rinsing. Tomorrow morning will be cooler, so it would be smarter to wash it tomorrow. Besides, there's a 10% chance of rain tonight, which could ruin the wash job. So tomorrow morning it is.

It is not difficult to understand why people procrastinate. We prefer avoiding things we don't particularly enjoy doing. For most of us, it is not great fun washing dishes, cleaning out the garage, beginning a research paper, or confronting someone we have a problem with. Instead of tackling the task, we put it off by substituting a more pleasurable activity: watching TV, taking a nap, or playing a video game.

Laziness is certainly a culprit in much of our procrastination. Lying around and relaxing sounds a lot better than beginning the thirty-page reading assignment for biology class. Fear of failure or rejection is another, like putting off a job interview or failing to call someone you're attracted to. Indecisiveness can also lead to procrastination, like letting a deadline pass for a college application. Anxiety is also responsible for our putting off certain tasks, so we reschedule the dentist appointment or feign illness on the night we are to have dinner with our boyfriend's parents. As you can see, a range of negative emotions often lie behind our procrastination, and to change the situation, we must at some point overcome them.

Is procrastination really a problem that we need to address? After all, if everyone procrastinates at one time or another, what's the big deal? For some people, procrastination isn't a problem. If you occasionally put off some everyday task but still get it done, your life probably isn't the worse for it. However, if you put tasks off until the kitchen sink is stacked high with dishes or loads of dirty clothes lie around for days or you have to cram two weeks of assigned reading into one night, procrastination is controlling your life in negative ways. And like most procrastinators, you probably carry around your share of guilt.

Procrastination can also have more devastating effects. For people who put off the more important things in life, the consequences can be severe: loss of a job, flunking out of school, divorce, lost job opportunities, a negative credit rating, a knock on the door by the IRS, a court date for outstanding parking tickets. For chronic procrastinators, life can be one long series of mishaps and failures resulting from their chronic pattern of putting things off. And all too often procrastinators don't think of the negative impact that their actions, or inactions, can have on those around them: husbands, wives, friends, roommates, or co-workers. Frequently other people end up doing for the procrastinators what they should have done themselves.

There are some people for whom procrastination is but a symptom of some deeper psychological or emotional problem, and such people need professional help. However, for most of us, procrastination is simply a bad habit that we've allowed ourselves to fall into and done little to escape. The fact is that procrastination is a choice we make, and we always have an option. As we choose to procrastinate, we can also choose not to.

To stop procrastinating, as the Nike commercial says, Just Do It! We all know when we procrastinate, so there is seldom a problem identifying the situation. We look out the window and see weeds growing taller than the shrubs in the flower bed. We walk across the bedroom and step over clothes and shoes that we stepped out of the night before. We see the pile of bills sitting on the kitchen table. We see the gas gauge needle on the car sitting near the big E. We know the mid-term geography test is scheduled for this Friday. We notice our computer printer is printing out faint gray letters and pinkish-purple pictures. We smell an odor of urine from our toddler's diapers. We know Mother's Day is tomorrow and we don't have a card or flowers.

When you see something that needs to be done and you are the person responsible to do it, jump right in. Getting started is the hardest part; if it wasn't, we wouldn't procrastinate. Frequently the task doesn't take long - loading the dishwasher, taking the garbage bins to the street for pick-up, doing the bills, filling the car with gas - so getting started is more than half the battle. If it's a bigger task, like filling out a lengthy job application, studying for a final exam, or cleaning the apartment, start with the idea of putting in at least twenty minutes before taking a break. More often than not, you will keep working longer than you planned, sometimes to the point of completing the task.

Of course, "just doing it" is easier said than done, particularly against a lifetime of "just doing it later." There are always those more pleasurable instant-gratification options that frequently win out, and they aren't going to go away. So try reversing the order of action. If there is something you really want to do - see a particular movie, go out with the guys or girls, watch a particular TV program, play some basketball, continue reading your romantic page-turner, play Wii Fitness - reward yourself by doing it after you complete what needs to be done. Give yourself some positive reward for doing the task, something to look forward to on its completion.

There is one way almost certainly to fail in your attempt to stop procrastinating, and that is to go to extremes. When you think about it, there is almost always something that could be classified as "needs to be done." You could go from room to room of your house or apartment and find things to do all the time. You could do the same with your studies, your job, your relationships. If you try to do too much at once, you will wear out quickly and fail utterly, lapsing in relief to your previous pattern of procrastination. Start by taking one thing that you previously would have put off and get it done. You will feel good about it and get a little more done the next day.

While it's probably impossible to end all procrastination, it is something that we can certainly bring under control so that it doesn't hurt our lives or those around us. We can replace our habit of procrastination with new habits: paying the bills within the first week of the month, keeping the bedroom picked up, getting a start on a school or work assignment the day it is assigned. People actually do these things, and so can we. The good news is we don't have to do away with any of the pleasurable things in our lives. We just have to put them off for an hour or two occasionally.

If you are a hardcore procrastinator with an absolute anathema about starting something you don't want to do, try this: give the task an immediate five minutes of your time. Five minutes is nothing out of a 1440-minute day. Stop after five minutes if you want to, and try it again the next day on a different task. Your greatest problem is not doing the work but getting started on it, and the five-minute approach is a start.

The upside of taking control of our procrastinating ways is significant: greater feelings of self-worth, greater chances of success, more things accomplished, improved work habits, decreased feelings of guilt, greater feeling of accomplishment, better relationships, more enjoyment of pleasurable activities. In short, less procrastination can change our lives for the better, sometimes dramatically, so isn't it worth a try? If you're thinking, "Well, maybe I'll think about changing and decide tomorrow," you know what's in control. Try deciding today.

Questions for Discussion

1. When, according to the author, is procrastination a problem? Do you agree?

2. What are the causes of procrastination? Which causes do you identify with?

3. What are the effects of procrastination? Which affects do you identify with?

4. What solutions does the author present? Does the essay compel you to try them?

Drinking-Age Revolt Gains Converts

By Elizabeth Hamilton

James F. Jones Jr., who is in his fifth year as president of Trinity College, knows he is incurring the wrath of Mothers Against Drunk Driving, and probably more than a few parents, by suggesting that the drinking age be lowered. But, frankly, he doesn't really care.

He's that fed up with the consequences of what he calls "the clandestine culture" of underage drinking among college students. It's a culture, Jones and other college administrators say, that has led to some very dangerous, and often tragic, behavior. "Who in the world is going to stand up against Mothers Against Drunk Driving? It would be like standing up against motherhood and apple pie," Jones said. "But the current drinking age is counterproductive because it simply fosters this counterculture of binge drinking, which is epidemic at colleges."

Jones is one of roughly 100 university administrators who have joined the Amethyst Initiative, calling on lawmakers to consider lowering the drinking age from 21 to 18. The movement, started by John McCardell, former president of Middlebury College in Vermont, has been gathering supporters across the United States for about a year.

Binge drinking has been a tragic problem at college campuses across the United States. One of the best known incidents occurred at Quinnipiac University in Hamden in 2001, when junior Matt Oliveri died of alcohol poisoning after a night of binge drinking. Such incidents have occurred across the country, and there is no indication that binge drinking among college students is waning.

Jones, like some of the other administrators who have signed on to the movement, has emotional, practical and philosophical reasons for wanting the issue debated again. First, the practical. "The fact that kids can't drink until they're 21 legally simply forces them to do it clandestinely, and when they do, you get irresponsible behavior," Jones said. "You get younger students getting older students to go to the liquor store for them, and you get the binge drinking in the dorm rooms and at parties."

Jones also has trouble with the disconnect in the message the government sends 18-year-olds, who can vote, serve on a jury, sign a contract and serve in the military, but not drink. "If we're going to send someone to fight in Iraq, I don't understand why that is an adult prerogative but buying a beer legally is not," Jones said, adding that students don't believe the drinking age limit should apply to them, in part, because of this disconnect.

Lee Peters, vice president for student affairs at the University of Hartford, agreed and said the scope of underage binge drinking problem is enormous. "I have hundreds of students, and I know every other college administrator has the same thing, who are sitting in their rooms throwing down multiple drinks so they can pre-load their bodies with alcohol before going out," Peters said. "It's a recipe for disaster."

Peters said he saw firsthand what happens when the illegality issue is removed from drinking when he helped lead a semester at sea in 2004 with 440 college students from around the country. Once the ship left shore and entered international waters, Peters said, there was no drinking age, which meant that the 18- to 22-year-old students on board could socialize - and drink - openly with the faculty on the trip. Because of that openness, Peters said, he and staff members could monitor what was happening, and there were fewer incidents of drunken behavior. "Before I went on that trip, I wasn't a big fan of this idea," Peters said. "I thought it was kind of a cop-out, to try to change the law rather than work within the law. But I learned you have much more influence on students by dealing with their behavior and not focusing on whether they broke the law."

Officials with both the national and state offices of MADD would say that lowering the drinking age is a cop-out, however, and will lead to more fatal car accidents. They also maintain that studies have clearly shown raising the drinking age has reduced drunken-driving deaths nationally - a claim backed up by the Centers for Disease Control and Prevention and others. In fact, according to a federal study of fatal drunken-driving accidents from 1982 to 1998, the state of Connecticut saw a decline of about 85 percent in accidents involving drivers age 16-20. "We're opening up the floodgates here," said Janice Heggie Margolis, executive director of the Connecticut chapter of MADD.

Margolis said that while the higher age limit has helped decrease the number of fatal accidents, she and other MADD officials are concerned that people have become complacent recently. She cited a national study showing Connecticut experienced an 11 percent increase in fatal drunken-driving accidents in 2006. "We know that we must continue to decrease access and availability of alcohol to young adults, and if we drop the 21-year-old drinking age, that's going to make it that much easier for young people to get alcohol," Margolis said.

College administrators, though, say that students are continually finding new ways to obtain alcohol illegally and that the law simply isn't stopping them. "There's an entire fake-ID industry," Jones said. State Rep. Michael Lawlor agreed. Lawlor, an East Haven Democrat who serves as both the chairman of the legislature's powerful judiciary committee and as an associate professor of criminal justice at the University of New Haven, said students are "very resourceful" when it comes to getting around the drinking age law. "You can get a fake driver's license for $60. They look very real and all the kids have them," Lawlor said.

Lawlor said he can't envision the state lowering its drinking age without a corresponding move by the federal government, though. That's because of the 1984 National Minimum Drinking Age Act, which imposes a 10 percent penalty on a state's federal highway grant if it lowers the drinking age below 21. But that doesn't mean it shouldn't be discussed, he said. "It's worth talking about," Lawlor said. "If in fact you can pass a law to stop the behavior, then it's a good idea to pass the law. But if you pass the law and it makes the situation worse, which is arguably what is happening, then you need to rethink it."

That's where Pamela Trotman Reid, president of St. Joseph College, comes down. Reid said a public discussion about the issue, and a closer, more informed look at the data, are imperative because the problem of underage drinking is so acute.

She said she's not convinced that raising the drinking age is the only factor contributing to a decrease in drunken-driving fatalities, and wonders if increased education, stiffer legal consequences and the introduction of the concept of designated drivers have played equal parts.

Like Jones, Reid wants the issue reopened because she has seen firsthand the tragic consequences when students shut themselves up in their rooms to drink, where no one can monitor them. "When I was at the University of Michigan, a female student fell out of her dorm window after a night of binge drinking and died," Reid said. "No one wants to be in that position, to have to face parents and tell them their child has died."

Questions for Discussion

1. What is the problem discussed in the essay, and how convincingly is the problem presented?

2. What causes of the problem are presented, and how valid are they? What effects are presented, and what impact do they make on readers?

3. What counter argument is presented against the solution, and how effectively is the argument addressed in the essay?

4. Do you agree with the essay's solution to the problem? What arguments for the solution, if any, do you find most compelling?

5. In your experience and observation, is binge drinking a problem at your school? If so, would the solution presented in the essay affect student behavior?

Unit 6
Discoveries

Before writing a particular essay or article, writers often need to learn more about their subject. Most of us, for example, would need to do some research on a subject such as global warming before we could write about it knowledgeably.

Many of the subjects that interest us as writers go beyond our personal experience and knowledge, so the first step in preparing to write on a particular subject may be to find out more about it. We may have read, for example, that the fighting in Iraq involves Sunni and Shiite Muslims, members of Al Quaida, foreign insurgents, Iraqi soldiers, and American soldiers. However, exactly who is fighting whom and for what reasons is a complex subject that would require considerable research.

As writers, we research a particular topic to learn more about it, to evaluate different viewpoints on the subject, to help formulate our own viewpoint, and to expand our knowledge of the world around us. A wide range of topics may require some research: comparing models of hybrid cars, evaluating the effects of sex education on students' behavior, or analyzing the impact of a political candidate's race on voters.

In this final unit, you write on a topic that will require you to do some research. The purpose of the assignment is for you to learn to research a topic effectively, to write a research-oriented paper, to express and support your viewpoint based on your research, and to apply everything you have learned to writing an effective paper. In addition, this assignment will help prepare you for future research writing.

In this unit, you are introduced to the basic elements of research writing: investigating several sources, incorporating research material into your paper, acknowledging the sources as you use them, quoting some sources and paraphrasing others, formulating a thesis statement that expresses your viewpoint and is supported by your research, and maintaining your writer's voice throughout the paper.

All of this may sound more daunting than it actually is. As you research your topic, you compile the information that forms the core of your paper. Once your research is completed, the remaining task is to incorporate the material into your paper in a way that distinguishes the research material from your own ideas and that supports your thesis. At this point in the course, you are up to the task.

Prewriting

The prewriting emphasis for a research-oriented paper is on the research: finding sources for your topic, reading the material, and taking notes on anything you may include in your paper. Once you have completed the research, you are ready to evaluate the information and formulate a viewpoint on the topic. Your first task, of course, is to select a topic to research.

Selecting A Topic

To select a topic for you research-oriented paper, follow these guidelines.

1. Select a topic that you are interested in and would like to know more about.

2. Select a topic that you can research in the library and on the Internet.

3. Select a topic that you believe some reading audience would like to know more about. Steer away from traditional topics - abortion, child abuse, legalization of marijuana - that students frequently write about.

4. Select a topic that is limited enough to cover in a three-five page paper. For example, while the general topic of "steroid use among athletes" could fill a book, the more limited topic of "steroid use among high school football players" could be a manageable subject for a paper.

5. Select a topic that other classmates aren't writing about.

The following sample topics show the range of writing possibilities.

Should there be college football playoffs?	High cost of a college education
Steroids in junior high school	Is No Child Left Behind working?
Is loud rock music harmful to hearing?	Private vs. public grade schools
Is America ready for a female president?	Does "Three Strikes" law work?
Electoral college: keep it or junk it?	Should minors be tried as adults?
The dangers of global warming	Bullying in the schools
The best hybrid car available	TV's effects on children
Can ethanol-run cars solve energy problem?	Different ways that children learn
Do children grow up too fast?	Pre-school: key to success?
Childhood obesity: a solvable problem	Socialism in S. America - a threat?
Is universal health care our best choice?	Global economy's affect on jobs
Are we winning the war against drugs?	Is there any diet that really works?

Prewriting Activity 6.1

Select a topic for your research paper following the guidelines presented. Consider a couple different topics in case you can't find adequate research sources for one or the other.

Sample Topic:

Gang violence is a big issue in our community. You read about gang-related killings and drive-by shootings in the newspaper frequently. The situation seems to getting worse everywhere, no matter how much police try to crack down. I think it's worth investigating and perhaps writing about.

Researching Your Topic

A good research paper is based on reliable information from credible sources. For example, if you wanted to know which car performed better, the Honda Accord or Toyota Camry, you wouldn't get the most objective information from an advertising brochure at a Honda or Toyota dealership. Instead, you would be better off reading consumer magazines that do road testing on comparable vehicles and analyze the results.

Using credible research sources is one of several considerations when researching a topic. The following suggestions will help you find the best sources and harvest the most relevant information.

Finding Sources

1. Your college librarian can be of great help. When in doubt, seek out a librarian, tell him or her the topic you are researching, and ask the best way to proceed.

2. Most colleges index their books by topic on computers. The computers have simple instructions for entering the name of your topic and finding what books are available.

3. Many colleges have computer programs that locate information on topics in periodicals or newspapers, with the articles found on line. Ask your librarians about programs such as Proquest, Lexis Nexus, SIRS, and GALE, and learn how to access them on the library computers to research your topic.

4. You may find information on your topic on the Internet by using a topic search engine such as Google or Yahoo. When you find information on line, print the articles so that you can read them at your leisure, highlight important parts, and take notes.

5. Use credible sources for your research: articles from respected periodicals or newspapers, books from experts, and studies from well-known journals.

Taking Research Notes

1. Make sure to write down the following information for each source that you use to reference in your paper.

    Book: name of author, title of book, publishing company, publishing location, date of publication.

    Periodical: author (if given), title of article, title of periodical, volume number, date of publication, page numbers of article.

    Newspaper: author (if given), title of article, title of newspaper, volume/edition number, date of publication, page number(s) of article.

    Interview: name of interviewee, title of interviewee (medical doctor, marine biologist, county health inspector), date of interview.

    Online   author (if given), title of article, title of periodical or
    article: newspaper, volume/edition number, date of publication, page numbers (if available), address: http://www.Newsweek.com.

    From a   author (if given), title of article, name of organization providing
    website: article (Cancer Foundation, Bureau of Statistics), name of website, date of publication, page numbers, address: http://www.CancerFoundation.com.

2. Take notes from each source that contains relevant information on your topic, including anything that you might use in your paper. Write down the exact words from the article or book so that you can quote from them in your paper. Keep information from different sources separate so that you can identify each source as you use it in your writing. Use lined note cards for your note-taking with the source identified at the top of each card.

3. Note the date of each article or book you find, and use the most recent information you can find. For example, statistics on teenage pregnancy from articles in the early 1990's compared to the 2000's may be quite different, and you want the most updated findings.

4. Since you are writing a limited research paper of three-five pages, you aren't expected to investigate dozens of sources. However, you should use information from at least four or five different sources in your paper. To find that many good

sources, you may have to research at least ten since they won't all contain relevant or current information.

5. As you read through various articles or books, consider what you want to include in your paper. For example, if your topic is later-life pregnancies, you may want to know exactly what "later life" means, the risks for the woman and for the baby, how the risks might be minimized, what doctors recommend regarding such pregnancies, and how common they are. You would look for information in those areas as you read through your research materials.

   If you are writing on gang violence, you may want to know how pervasive gang activity is, who comprises the gangs and where they live, what kinds of violence are associated with gangs, what the effects are, and how gang violence can be reduced. You would look for sources containing such information.

Prewriting Activity 6.2

Following the research suggestions provided, research your topic using library sources, the Internet, and experts on your subject, if available. Find at least five good sources containing information you can use in your paper. Make copies of articles and check out books.

As you read, take notes on any information that you might use in your paper, keeping material from each source separate, and compile enough information for a three-five page double-spaced paper. Keep in mind what you want to know about your topic, and try to find information on each aspect.

Student sample (notes from one of five sources)

Topic: Gang Violence

Things to find out:

   How big of a problem is gang violence in the country?
   Who joins gangs and why do they join?
   What kind of violent activity are gangs involved in?
   What are the effects of the violence, and who is affected?
   What can be done to reduce gang violence?

Research source #1:

Grabianowski, Ed. "How Street Gangs Work," HowStuffWorks, p. 1, http://people.howstuffworks.com/street-gang.htm

Research notes from "How Street Gangs Work:"

Gang violence is a problem in every major city in the United States and membership is on the rise. According to the Department of Justice's 2005 National Gang Threat Assessment, there are at least 21,500 gangs and more than 731,000 active gang members. While gangs are less prevalent in rural areas, in major cities, gang violence is responsible for roughly half of all homicides. Gangs are also becoming more savvy, using computers and other technology to commit crimes.

Thesis, Audience, and Purpose

As you read through your research material, you will undoubtedly form opinions about your topic that will help you decide on a thesis for your paper, the best reading audience, and a purpose for writing to them. Depending on your topic, you may form opinions on its seriousness or importance, its positive or negative effects, the people who most need to be aware of it, why they should be aware of it, and the research information that you most want to share with them.

To help you decide on a thesis, an audience, and a purpose for your paper, consider the following suggestions.

Thesis

Your thesis statement expresses the main conclusion that you have reached on your topic. This viewpoint will be supported by your research material as it is presented in your paper. It represents your opinion on the topic that you formed from reading and analyzing the research material, and it unifies your paper by giving you something definite to support throughout the essay.

The follow thesis statements express the conclusions that writers reached on a variety of topics based on their research findings.

1. Breast feeding is the preferred way to nourish your baby, but if you are unable to breast feed, bottle feeding your baby will have no harmful effects.

2. We will continue to lose American's "war on drugs" unless we greatly reduce the demand for drugs through education and drug prevention programs.

3. The positive results of liposuction surgery far outweigh the risks.

4. While most teenagers may be unaffected by violent video games, it takes just one troubled teenager exposed to video game violence to commit a Columbine-like massacre.

5. Based on results from other countries, the legalization of drugs is not the answer to America's drug problem

6. While AIDS in America is no longer a front page story, it is still a danger to anyone who takes sexual risks.

Audience

For your primary reading audience, consider who would benefit most from reading your paper: Teenagers? Parents with children? Older adults? Women? African-Americans or Asians? Educators? College students? The general population? Select a particular audience that would be most interested in your topic and most likely to benefit from reading about it.

The following are examples of primary reading audiences for different research papers.

Topic:	Effects of global warming on wildlife
Thesis:	Global warming is changing the environment of many animal species and endangering their existence.
Audience:	general population

Topic:	College football playoffs
Thesis:	It is time that football follows other collegiate sports and has a national championship playoff system.
Audience:	NCAA governing body that determines post-season play for football

Topic:	Loud rock music
Thesis:	Rock music played at high decibels can permanently damage the hearing of teenagers.
Audience:	Teenagers who listen to rock music

Topic:	Health insurance for children
Thesis:	Millions of American children have no health insurance and are dangerously at risk.
Audience:	general public

Purpose

Considering your thesis and your audience, what is the purpose of your paper? What do you want people to think or do as a result of reading it? The following purposes are for papers generated from the six thesis statements in the preceding "Thesis" section.

1. To educate women on the effects of breast feeding and bottle feeding, and to

help them make an informed choice when they have a baby.

2. To get readers to support more legislation and programs that educate people to the dangers of drugs, similar to the education programs that have reduced smoking in America.

3. To educate people on the benefits and risks of liposuction surgery, and recommend it as a viable alternative for chronically obese people.

4. To educate everyone on the effects of violent video games on troubled teenagers, and to get the government to regulate their sale and use in some way.

5. To reach anyone who thinks that drug legalization would be a positive step and convince them that it would do more harm than good.

6. To educate teens and young adults on the dangers of AIDS, the kinds of sexual activity that lead to infection, and what they can do to eliminate the risk.

Prewriting Activity 6.3

Based on your topic, your research findings, and the suggestions presented in the text, decide on a thesis statement, audience, and purpose for your paper.

Sample topic: Gang Violence

Thesis: Gang violence is a plague upon America that must be eliminated.

Audience: General public, local city council

Purpose: To get the public to understand the serious effects of gang violence and to get the city to do something about it.

First Drafts

Now that you have selected a topic, done considerable research, and decided on a thesis, audience, and purpose for your paper, you are ready to learn more about writing a research paper. The following sections on "Source Acknowledgment," "Paraphrasing, Quoting, and Responding," and "Works Cited" will prepare you to write your first draft.

Source Acknowledgment

When you incorporate information from a particular source into your paper, you need to let your readers know. In this way, they can distinguish the research information from your own ideas and opinions. Source acknowledgment or citing is accomplished by identifying the research source when you use information from it in your paper. To acknowledge your sources, do the following:

1. Introduce the source in some manner when you present the information:

    According to Dr. Joanne Thurgood,
    In the article "Smoker's Last Breath" in <u>Healthier Living</u>,
    In Marlowe Dickson's book <u>Cosmetic Blunders</u>,
    The most recent <u>Times</u> magazine reported that
    In an interview with microbiologist Dr. Kim Lee,

2. At the conclusion of the source information, include in parentheses the author's last name and the page number(s) where you found the information. If the author isn't identified, reference the title of the article or book. In addition, there may be no page number to reference if the material is from an online article.

    According to Dr. Joanne Thurgood, radical mastectomy surgery for breast cancer is not necessary in many situations (Thurgood 12).

    In the periodical <u>Healthier Living</u>, the author states, "Someone who stops smoking after twenty years can still add ten more years to their life," ("Smoker's Last Breath" 8).

    In Marlowe Dickson's book <u>Cosmetic Blunders</u>, she concludes that the majority of practicing cosmetic surgeons are not skilled enough to take a chance on (Dickson 113).

    A recent <u>Times</u> magazine article reported that many child abuse cases go unreported because neighbors seldom report suspicious activity ("Hidden Horror" 18).

    In an interview with microbiologist Dr. Kim Lee, he stated, "The time lapse between successful cancer treatment results in lab experiments and getting a treatment product on the market can be ten-to-fifteen years," (Interview, Dr. Kim Lee, 4 September 2002).

3. You do not always have to introduce the source of your researched material as long as you cite the source in parentheses at the end of the entry so that readers know where the material came from.

    While gangs were once found almost exclusively in urban areas, today we are also seeing escalating gang activity in rural areas ("How Gangs Are Changing" 3).

    In cities where local neighborhood residents are taking a stand against gang violence, the level of violence is decreasing (Cervantez 11).

    As a general rule, use source introductions to highlight prominent experts, studies, or books/periodicals/websites that would lend weight and credibility to the material presented. Otherwise, citing the source in parentheses at the end of the entry is acceptable.

4. For subsequent references to the same source later in the essay, you only need to provide a parenthetical reference at the end of the entry.

    If neighbors were more proactive in reporting child abuse, the incidents of abuse could be reduced significantly ("Hidden Horror" 20).

    When women considering plastic surgery take the time to research thoroughly the surgeons in their area, including talking to previous patients, they greatly enhance their chances for successful surgery (Dickson 118).

Drafting Activity 6.4

Read the draft of "Gang Violence" in Drafting Activity 6.8, noticing how the writer acknowledges the sources of his research material with source introductions and parenthetical citations. You can use this model to help incorporate your research material into your draft.

Paraphrasing, Quoting, and Responding

A research paper typically contains three kinds of writing: *paraphrased* material from the sources, quotations from the sources, and your own ideas and responses, which include most of the opening and concluding thoughts, the thesis statement, and your responses to the research material: opinions formed, conclusions drawn, and observations made. As your audience reads your paper, they should always know when you are paraphrasing, when you are quoting, and when you are commenting or responding.

The following guidelines will help you incorporate paraphrasing, quoting, and your own ideas effectively in your paper.

Paraphrasing

As you write your draft, you *paraphrase* – put into your own words – most of the research information that you use. For example, in a paper on breast implants, you could retain some key words in the original text – e.g. *breast implants, silicone and saline implants, post-surgical scarring* – since you can't use a synonym for every word in an article, but present most of the information in your own words. The purpose of paraphrasing is to include research material in your paper while maintaining your own voice by using your wording. You don't want your paper to sound like a compilation of writing from different authors.

The following paraphrased material shows the difference between the source material and the paraphrased version. Notice that certain key words are maintained and that the meaning of the original material is unchanged although the paraphrased wording is significantly different.

Source Material

> Verbal abuse can be as detrimental to a child as physical abuse. When a parent constantly berates a child, criticizes him for the slightest mistake, never compliments or praises him, and tells him that he is worthless or will amount to nothing, that child will not only have a low opinion of himself, he will often grow up sullen and unresponsive, unable to find any good in others or respond normally to positive comments or kind behavior.

> Wilson, Loretta. "What We Say to Children," <u>Psychology Digest</u>, Spring, 2000, 18.

Paraphrased

> According to psychologist Loretta Wilson, verbal abuse can harm a child just as much as physical abuse. When a parent always puts a child down, scolds him for the least error, never compliments him for anything, and says that he is no good and will never accomplish anything, when he grows up, he will often be silent and gloomy, unable to respond to people or see the goodness in others or react to praise or kindness (Wilson 18).

So that readers can always distinguish between paraphrasing and your own comments, make sure that you always provide a source reference for the paraphrased material.

Quotations

When you quote from a source, you use the exact words from the article or book and begin and end the quote with quotation marks (" "). You typically use a quotation instead of paraphrasing when you are capturing a particularly striking or critical piece of information, and the exact source wording would have the greatest impact. Include both a source introduction and a page reference at the end of all quotes.

Examples:

According to Dr. Peg McDermott, "Liposuction surgery is not so much for weight loss as it is for resculpturing your body," (McDermott 23).

"Our ocean waters are slowly rising," bemoans oceanographer Adam Clayton, "and long-term effects could include the flooding of coastal areas such as Manhattan," (Clayton 12).

Quotations from your source material should be used sparingly and effectively to make important points. Most of your source material should be paraphrased in your paper in order to maintain your own voice.

Responding

The majority of the paper should be in your own words by incorporating paraphrased research material and providing your own comments. When you are commenting yourself, of course, there are no source references, so readers will know when they are reading your own thoughts.

Include your own thoughts in the opening and conclusion so that readers will know that you not only have researched your paper but understood the material, analyzed it carefully, and formed your own judgments. In the middle paragraphs, where you introduce most of your research material, provide your own comments and responses to the material so that readers feel your presence throughout the paper and understand that you are using the research material for your own purposes.

Drafting Activity 6.5

For practice paraphrasing research material, paraphrase the following paragraph by putting it into your own words and maintaining the original meaning. Begin the paragraph with a source acknowledgment, and reference the source and page number in parentheses at the end of the paraphrase.

Source Material

Dieting fails most people because they don't actually change their eating habits. They take in less food for a period of weeks or months, so they generally lose some weight. However, typically, they soon revert to their old eating habits, and the weight reappears or sometimes even increases. Losing weight for good means changing your eating lifestyle permanently: what you eat, how much you eat, how you eat, and how often you eat. It requires tremendous will-power, perhaps equal to that of quitting smoking.

Nagata, Emily. <u>Why Dieting Fails</u>, Hammond, Massachusetts: Pembroke Publishing, 1999, 132.

Drafting Activity 6.6

Do three things with the following source paragraph: paraphrase the majority of the material, include a quote from the paragraph, and comment on the information. In addition, provide source introductions and ending source and page references in parentheses to indicate when you are paraphrasing, quoting, and commenting.

Example:

Source material

Significantly more deaths in the home are caused by gun-related accidents than by murdering intruders. One month last year in a single rural county, two boys were killed in gun accidents. One boy killed his friend, pointing his father's gun at the boy and pulling the trigger of an "unloaded" gun. Another younger boy killed himself while playing with his father's gun that he found in an open bedroom drawer. In both cases, fathers were ultimately responsible for the deaths of youngsters whom they were trying to "protect" against would-be intruders. Such fatalities are far from unusual, yet handgun proponents sweep them under the carpet like so much dust.

Elmore, Ellen. "Household Deaths," <u>Children's Journal</u>, 3 March 2002, 20-21

Source material paraphrased, quoted, and commented on

Apparently the hand guns in American homes are more cause for a family's concern than the gun of a possible intruder. According to Ellen Elmore in an article in <u>Children's Journal,</u> more fatalities are caused by home gun accidents than by intruders who kill (Elmore 20.) Two deadly accidents occurred in the same rural county in one month. In one, a boy killed his friend with his father's gun that he thought was unloaded, and in the other, a younger boy playing with his father's gun he found in a bedroom drawer shot himself to death. In trying to protect their families against violence, the fathers unwittingly were responsible for the deaths of the boys. Although such accidents occur too frequently, says Elmore, "Handgun proponents sweep them under the carpet like so much dust," (Elmore 21). While such accidents are certainly horrible, what goes unsaid are the number of potential violent acts that may never occur because intruders don't risk going into homes where there may be guns. Is removing the guns from homes the answer, or stricter gun safety laws and prosecution for people who leave guns where children may get to them?

Later-life Pregnancies

While many women today are waiting longer to have children, they need to consider the risks associated with later-life pregnancies. One of the greater risks for women waiting until their mid-to-late thirties is possible birth defects in the baby. Females are born with all of the reproductive eggs they will need in their lifetime to conceive children. However, the older a woman gets, the older her eggs become. The older eggs sometimes develop problems solely due to their age, and one of the problems is the possibility of a baby being born with Down's Syndrome, which results in a combination of mental retardation and physical abnormalities. While the risk of a twenty-five year-old woman having a baby with Down's Syndrome is 1 in 1,250, the risk for a thirty-five year old is 1 in 378, and for a forty-five year old, 1 in 30.

"Pregnancy Risks for Older Women," Women's Health, February 2000, 6.

Works Cited

At the end of your paper, you provide a Works Cited section that lists alphabetically all of the sources that you used in the paper: books, magazines, periodicals, journals, newspapers, or interviews. The purpose of the Works Cited section is for readers to see the sources that you used for your paper and the breadth of research that you did, and to be able to find the books, magazines, or newspapers if they want to read further on the topic.

For the Works Cited section, include the following information for each source in the order and form presented. Notice that a second line or third line is indented five spaces.

book: author, title, publishing location, publisher, date of publication

Hinds, Clarence. The Last Hour, Cambridge: Camden Press, 1999.

article (periodical or newspaper): author, title of article, name of magazine or newspaper, volume number, date, page numbers of article

Fleming, Nancy. "Blue Skies Behind Us," Harper's, Vol. XXIII, 4 August 2001, 12-13.

Article online: author (if provided), title of article, name of organization and site where article is found, location of organization, date, date site accessed, address

Dobbs, Dr. Stanley. "Treatments for Squamous Cell Cancer," International Cancer Foundation. New York, New York. Med.Web. 3 November 2001. May 2008 http://www.InternationalCancerFoundation.com.

Drafting Activity 6.7

Go to the "Works Cited" section at the end of the draft of "Gang Violence" on page 240 to see the writer's sources and how they are listed.

Drafting Activity 6.8

Write the first draft of your research-oriented paper with the following guidelines in mind. You may want to read the following sample draft before writing your draft.

Drafting Guidelines

1. Introduce your topic in the opening, create interest for readers, and include your thesis statement.

2. Present your research findings in the middle paragraphs in support of your thesis statement. Cover the main aspects of your topic in separate paragraphs, each beginning with a topic sentence expressing the main idea of the paragraph.

3. Conclude your paper in a manner that reinforces your thesis statement and emphasizes the purpose of the paper. Keep your readers in mind and leave them with something to consider.

4. Organize your middle paragraphs to present your research findings in the most effective order.

5. As the writer, respond to the research material as you write. Your comments throughout the paper – opinions, conclusions, thoughts, feelings - put you in control of the paper, and show that you are incorporating the research material for your own writing purposes. Your responses should also reinforce your thesis statement in some manner.

6. Remember to paraphrase most of the research information, use an occasional striking quote, and provide source acknowledgments for all research material.

> 7.   Conclude your paper with a "Works Cited" section listing alphabetically the sources that you used in your paper.

Sample Draft

Gang Violence

Gang violence brought tragedy in May of 2009. Police say that a group of gang members walked up behind unsuspecting 25 year-old C.J. Davis as he was on his way to the market, and opened fire on him with an assault rifle. While speeding away from the scene with police in pursuit, the Cadillac carrying the gang members slammed into another car at an intersection, killing the other driver instantly. The impact sent the vehicles spinning out of control, striking and killing a pedestrian as well. While three of the gang members have since been apprehended, a fourth is still at large ("How Gang Violence Affects Communities").

This senseless tragedy reveals how far-reaching the consequences of gang-related violence can be to a community, in this case leaving three families devastated. Not only are gang members and their families affected by violence, but also innocent bystanders, who are often the victims of drive-by shootings ("Street Gangs: A Dead End for Our Children"). Residents of thousands of neighborhoods across the country live in constant fear because of violent gang activity. Children grow up in territorial battle zones, often suffering from psychological trauma similar to children living in war-torn countries ("The Effects of Community Violence on Children and Adolescents"). Community members want to take their neighborhoods back and rid them of gang violence and their dire effects, but only a long-term, multi-pronged solution involving police, schools, community services, and neighborhood residents will provide a lasting effect.

Gang violence is a problem in every major city in the United States and membership is on the rise. Department of Justice statistics reveal that there are at least 21,500 gangs and 770,000 active gang members. According to gang expert Ed Grabianowski, "In major cities, gang violence is responsible for roughly half of all homicides and the majority of crimes against property," (Grabianowski, "How Street Gangs Work" 1). Gangs also are on the increase in rural and suburban areas of the country as gang members flee increasing law enforcement pressure in urban areas or seek more lucrative drug markets ("Background on Gang Violence").

According to Grabianowski, 47% of gang members are Hispanic and 37% black, almost all living in the lower socio-economic inner cities across the country. Poverty is a driving force behind gang membership, with many gang members viewing drug dealing and theft as the only ways of making money and escaping poverty. Peer pressure also drives youths into gangs, with older gang members recruiting younger teens. Neighborhood gangs also provide an outlet for bored teens who have nothing to do. Finally, gang members often come from troubled homes with parents who may be addicts, gang members themselves, or simply non-responsive. A neighborhood gang gives teens a sense of belonging and the only real "family" they may have

(Grabianowski 1).

According to the article "Background on Ground Violence," gang violence stems from a variety of causes. Gangs stake out their territory and shoot members from other gangs who stray onto it, resulting in retaliatory shootings. Large street gangs employ violence to control and expand drug distribution activities, targeting rival gangs and dealers who neglect or refuse to pay extortion fees. Members also use violence to ensure that members adhere to the gang's code of conduct or to prevent a member from leaving. Authorities throughout the country report that gangs are responsible for most of the violent crime in major U.S. cities. Gangs engage in an array of criminal activities including assault, drive-by shooting, extortion, homicide, identification fraud, money laundering, prostitution operations, robbery, and weapons trafficking ("Background on Gang Violence"). The capability for violence is increasing because gangs are able to pay for more expensive weapons, including military-grade automatic weapons such as AK-47 rifles ("Drugs and Latin Gangs").

The effects of gang violence on individuals, neighborhoods, and communities is devastating. In gang-infested neighborhoods, adults and children live in daily fear, never knowing if the next gun shot might smash through their living room window or hit a friend or relative down the street. Families alter normal living patterns by staying off the streets at night and staying in their houses most of the time that they are home. Practically everyone in the neighborhood knows of a friend, acquaintance, or relative who has been killed in a gang-related shooting. Attending tearful funerals of teenage boys and girls is a common occurrence.

Gang membership extracts a terrible toll from the lives of all who come in contact with the members. Parents and relatives of gang members live in double fear, one for their family's safety and that of their gang-related child, who is 60 times more likely to be killed than a non-gang member ("Street Gangs: A Dead End for Our Children"). Tragically, the inevitable way that many gang members eventually leave a gang is in a body bag (Grabionowski 1).

According to Dr. Carole Goguen, Director of the Traumatic Stress Treatment Center, "Many children and adolescents living in violence-riddled neighborhoods suffer from PTSD, Posttraumatic Stress Disorder," (Goguen, "The Effects of Community Violence on Children and Adolescents"). Children with PTSD display disorganized or agitated behavior and have nightmares that may include monsters. They may become withdrawn, fearful, or aggressive, and they may have difficulty paying attention. They may regress to earlier behaviors such as sucking their thumbs and bed-wetting, and they may develop separation anxiety. They may also engage in play that compulsively reenacts the violence (Goguen)

Adolescents with PTSD also experience nightmares and intrusive thoughts about the trauma. They can become depressed, angry, distrustful, fearful, and alienated, and they may feel betrayed. Many do not feel they have a future and believe that they will not reach adulthood. This is especially common among adolescents who are chronically exposed to neighborhood violence. Other trauma-related reactions can include impaired self-esteem, learning difficulties, and acting out or risk taking behaviors such as running away, drug or alcohol use, suicide attempts, and inappropriate sexual activities (Goguen). In short, exposure to a violence-riddled environment can have severe long-term effects on children and adolescents that children in non-violent environments never experience.

Clearly, the disastrous effects of gang violence on millions of America's children and adults cry out for a solution to rid communities of such violence and free people to live normal, healthy lives. Of course, this is much easier said than done as witnessed by the lack of success that cities have had in curbing the problem. Police crackdowns involving sweeps of gang-infested areas to confiscate weapons and arrest wanted gang members results in a short-term reduction in violence. However, such crackdowns don't get at the root problems of gang violence: poverty, lack of positive outlets for youth, the demand for illicit drugs.

While police presence is vital in keeping neighborhoods safer, a more successful long-term approach requires multiple tactics that all boil down to one thing: give people something to live for other than a gang. This can include helping at-risk youth or current gang members find decent jobs or obtain an education. Block clubs and community centers bring the non-gang members, the majority of people, together to clean and maintain their streets, get rid of graffiti and otherwise show pride in where they live. Community events such as dances, football games and game nights give youth something to do other than hang out on porches with gang members. If held outdoors, they make those areas less attractive for gang activity because of all the non-gang members around (Grabianowski 4).

A preferred method of gang suppression today is the Department of Justice's "Weed and Seed" program. This combines police enforcement (**weeding** out the worst gang members) with community activism and economic opportunities (**seeding** the neighborhood with the means to overcome negative conditions). More than 3,000 Weed and Seed programs are active in the United States. Each site can receive up to $1 million to help fund law enforcement, community policing, prevention, intervention, and treatment, and neighborhood restoration (Grabianowski 4).

One of the most influential areas of a child or young adult's life is at schools. According to the article "Gang Violence as a Social Problem," "Providing more funding for schools specifically for anti-gang programs and including anti-gang messages in the curriculum is essential in creating a non-violent atmosphere." Funding for anti-gang violence is not the only way to promote it in schools. Strict rules of on-campus activity and truancy prevention will create an educational culture that will hopefully leak into students' lives outside school. These same messages and programs should also be reinforced in the communities outside of school. Developing after school youth programs gives children alternative options to gang affiliation ("Gang Violence as a Social Problem").

Preventing the recruitment of new gang members is a solution for the future, but other measures must be taken to curb the violence now. Legislation is the voice that is the most used when we talk about attempts to solve gang violence. We look to legislation and to government officials that have the authority to help protect us from gang violence. Establishing new laws that increase the severity of punishments for gang related violence is essential. Any act of criminality related to gangs should automatically have an increased sentence. Additionally, the recruitment of new members to gangs should have a harsh penalty. Recruiting anybody should be punishable by imprisonment, and recruiting a minor should have an increase in the sentencing ("Gang Violence as a Social Problem").

Clearly, any long-term solution to eradicating gang violence includes police enforcement, education, jobs, activity centers, and neighborhood involvement. However, resources must be available to the communities and schools to build programs and create jobs effectively, which takes money. Unfortunately, in cashed-strapped cities, ending gang violence is not the highest priority since the poor minorities most affected by such violence have the weakest voice among constituents.

The impact of gang violence on many of America's poorest citizens should be a priority from the city to the state to the Federal level, with funding support for anti-gang education programs, community activity centers, and jobs creation coming from all levels. Until we recognize and treat gang violence as the most destructive force on the health, welfare, and future success of millions of American children, the problem will continue to destroy lives. The solutions are available. The public resolve must also be.

Works Cited

"Background on Drug Violence," Do Something.org. July 2011 http://www.dosomething.org/tipsandtools/background-gangs-violence.

"Drugs and Latin Gangs," Duke University, 9 December 2006. May 2011 http://www.duke.edu/pgg2/history/Drugs.html.

"Gang Violence as a Social Problem," Soc3: Social Problems, wikispaces. May 2011 http://socialproblemsucd.wikispaces.com/Gangs+Violence.

Goguen, Dr. Carole. "The Effects of Community Violence on Children and Adolescents,"Traumatic Stress Treatment Center. June 2001 http://www.traumatic-stress-treatment.com/artcommunityviolence.html.

Grabionowski, Ed. "How Street Gangs Work," How Stuff Works. May 2001 http://people.howstuffworks.com/street-gangs.htm.

"How Gang Violence Can Affect Your Community," Family, Community, Kids, and Teens, AMW Safety Center. 5 November 2009. April 2011 http://safety.amw.com/family/how-gang-violence-can-affect-your-community.

"Street Gangs: A Dead End for Our Children," Lawton Police Department, May 2011. http://www.lawatonpd.com/cmprv/gangs.htm.

Revision

The revision process for a research-oriented draft is similar to that of other papers with a few added considerations. One of the most important considerations is making sure that readers clearly understand when you are incorporating research material in your paper and when you are providing your own comments. The following drafting guidelines will help you keep that distinction clear.

Revision Guidelines

Consider the following suggestions in evaluating your first draft.

1. Overview. Read the entire draft once to get a general idea of what you have done well and what areas may need some work. As you revise your paper, keep your reading audience in mind and how you would like them to respond.

2. Introduction. Does the opening introduce the topic clearly, create interest for readers, and include the thesis statement for the paper? How might the introduction be revised to make it more interesting or informative, or to highlight the significance of the topic?

3. Middle paragraphs. Is the research material incorporated effectively into the middle paragraphs? Can readers tell from source introductions and page references when you are using resource materials and when you are expressing your own thoughts? Is most of the resource information paraphrased in your own words? Are quotations used sparingly and effectively? Do most paragraphs begin with topic sentences that express the main idea of the paragraph?

4. Thesis support. Read the middle paragraphs to see how well they support your thesis statement. You formulated your thesis statement based on what you learned from the research, so the research material presented in the middle paragraphs should show readers why you reached the conclusion that you did. Revise your middle paragraphs to support your thesis statement most convincingly.

5. Organization. Are the middle paragraphs organized so that the main aspects of the topic are presented in the most effective order? Does the information in one paragraph follow logically and smoothly from the previous paragraph? Are there any sentences or paragraphs that would fit better in a different location? How might the organization of the middle paragraphs be improved?

6. Writer's input. Do you inject your thoughts into the paper – commenting, drawing conclusions, providing opinions, reacting to the research material – so that readers know you are in control of the paper and clearly understand the

research material? In addition, do your comments support the thesis statement in some manner?

7. Conclusion. Does the conclusion reinforce the thesis statement? Does it help you accomplish your purpose? How might the conclusion be improved to make a greater impact on readers?

8. Wording. Reread each sentence to see if it can be made smoother, clearer, more concise, or better worded. In addition, check to see whether you are using a variety of sentence structures and joining words, and whether there are transitions such as however, therefore, first, second, for example, on the other hand, as you can see, finally in key places to tie sentences and paragraphs together.

9. Works Cited. Check the "Works Cited" section at the end of the paper to make sure that you have included all sources, that the information is presented in the correct format, and that the sources are alphabetized.

Sample Revised Paper

Gang Violence

Gang violence brought tragedy to three California families in 2009. Police say May of that a group of gang members walked up behind unsuspecting 25 year-old C.J. Davis as he was on his way to the market, and opened fire on him with an assault rifle. While speeding away from the scene with police in pursuit, the Cadillac carrying the gang members slammed into another car at an intersection, killing the other driver instantly. The impact sent the vehicles spinning out of control, striking and killing a pedestrian as well. While three of the gang members have since been apprehended, a fourth is still at large ("How Gang Violence Affects Communities").

This senseless tragedy reveals how far-reaching the consequences of gang-related violence can be to a community, in this case leaving three families devastated. Not only are gang members and their families affected by violence, but also innocent bystanders, who are often the victims of drive-by shootings ("Street Gangs: A Dead End for Our Children"). Residents of ~~thousands of~~ **gang-infested** neighborhoods across the country live in constant fear because of ~~violent gang activity~~ **gang-related violence.** Children grow up in territorial battle zones, often suffering from psychological trauma similar to children living in war-torn countries ("The Effects of Community Violence on Children and Adolescents"). Community members want to take their neighborhoods back, ~~and~~ rid**ding** them of gang violence and their dire effects, but only a long-term, multi-pronged solution involving police, schools, community services, and neighborhood residents will ~~provide~~ **make** a lasting **impact** ~~effect~~.

Gang violence is a problem in every major city in the United States, and **gang** membership is on the rise. Department of Justice statistics reveal that there are at least 21,500 gangs and 770,000 active gang members. According to gang expert Ed

Grabianowski, "In major cities, gang violence is responsible for roughly half of all homicides and the majority of crimes against property (Grabianowski, "How Street Gangs Work" 1). Gangs ~~also~~ are **also** on the increase in rural and suburban areas ~~of the country~~ as gang members flee increasing law enforcement pressure in urban areas or seek more lucrative drug markets ("Background on Gang Violence").

According to Grabianowski, 47% of gang members are Hispanic and 37% black, almost all living in ~~the~~ lower socio-economic ~~inner cities~~ **urban centers** across the country. Poverty is a driving force behind gang membership, with many gang members viewing drug dealing and theft as the only ways of making money and escaping poverty. Peer pressure also drives youths into gangs, with older gang members **often** recruiting younger teens. Neighborhood gangs also provide an outlet for bored teens who have nothing to do. Finally, gang members ~~often~~ **frequently** come from troubled homes with parents who may be addicts, gang members themselves, or simply non-responsive. A neighborhood gang gives teens a sense of belonging and the only real "family" they may have (Grabianowski 1).

According to the article "Background on Gang Violence," gang violence stems from a variety of causes. Gangs stake out their **home** territory and shoot members from other gangs who stray onto it, **usually** resulting in retaliatory shootings. Large street gangs employ violence to control and expand drug distribution activities, targeting rival gangs and dealers who neglect or refuse to pay extortion fees. Members also use violence to ensure that members adhere to the gang's code of conduct or to prevent a member from leaving. Authorities throughout the country report that gangs are responsible for most of the violent crime in major U.S. cities. Gangs engage in an array of criminal activities including assault, drive-by shooting, extortion, homicide, identification fraud, money laundering, prostitution operations, robbery, and weapons trafficking ("Background on Gang Violence"). The capability for violence is **also** increasing because gangs are able to pay for more expensive weapons, including military-grade automatic weapons such as AK-47 rifles ("Drugs and Latin Gangs").

The effects of gang violence on individuals, neighborhoods, and communities is devastating. In gang-infested neighborhoods, ~~adults and children~~ **residents** live in daily fear, never knowing if the next gun shot might smash through their ~~living room~~ window or hit a friend or relative down the street. Families alter normal living patterns by staying off the streets at night and staying in**side** their houses most of the time ~~that they are home~~. ~~Practically~~ **Almost** everyone in the neighborhood knows of a friend~~, acquaintance,~~ or relative who has been killed in a gang-related shooting. **Neighborhood residents routinely** ~~attending~~ tearful funerals of teenage boys and girls. ~~is a common occurrence.~~

Gang membership extracts a terrible toll from the lives of all who come in contact with the members. Parents and relatives of gang members live in double fear, one for their family's safety and **for** that of their **gang-member** child, who is 60 times more likely to be killed than a non-gang member ("Street Gangs: A Dead End for Our Children"). Tragically, the inevitable way that many gang members eventually leave a gang is in a body bag (Grabianowski 1).

According to Carole Goguen, Director of the Traumatic Stress Treatment Center,

"Many children and adolescents living in violence-riddled neighborhoods suffer from PTSD, Posttraumatic Stress Disorder," (Goguen, "The Effects of Community Violence on Children"). Children with PTSD display disorganized or agitated behavior and have nightmares that may include monsters. They may become withdrawn, fearful, or aggressive, and ~~they may~~ have difficulty paying attention. They may regress to earlier behaviors such as sucking their thumbs and bed-wetting and ~~they may~~ develop separation anxiety. They may also engage in play that compulsively reenacts the violence (Goguen).

Adolescents with PTSD also experience nightmares and intrusive thoughts about the trauma. They can become depressed, angry, distrustful, fearful, and alienated, and they may feel betrayed. Many do not feel they have a future and believe that they will not reach adulthood. This is especially common among adolescents who are chronically exposed to neighborhood violence. Other trauma-related reactions can include impaired self-esteem, learning difficulties, and acting out or risk-taking behaviors such as running away, drug or alcohol use, suicide attempts, and inappropriate sexual activities (Goguen). In short, **children exposed** ~~exposure~~ to a violence-riddled environment can ~~have~~ **experience** severe, long-term **psychological** effects ~~on children and adolescents~~ that **other** children ~~in non-violent environments never experience~~. **don't experience.**

Clearly, the disastrous effects of gang violence on ~~millions of America's children and adults~~ **urban residents** cry out for a solution to rid communities of such violence and ~~free~~ **allow** people to live normal, healthy lives. Of course, this is ~~much~~ easier said than done, as witnessed by the lack of success that cities have had in curbing the problem. Police crackdowns ~~involving sweeps of~~ **in** gang-infested areas to confiscate **illegal** weapons and arrest wanted gang members results in a short-term reduction in violence. However, such crackdowns don't get at the root problems of gang violence: poverty, lack of positive outlets for youth, and the demand for illicit drugs.

While police presence is vital in keeping neighborhoods safer, a ~~more~~ successful long-term approach requires multiple tactics that ~~all boil down to~~ **result in** one thing: giving people something to live for other than a gang. This ~~can~~ **should** include helping at-risk youth or current gang members find decent jobs or obtain an education. Block clubs and community centers **can** bring ~~the~~ non-gang members, the majority of people, together to clean and maintain their streets, get rid of graffiti and otherwise show pride in where they live. Community events such as dances, football games and game nights make those areas less attractive for gang activity because of all the non-gang members around give youth something to do other than hang out on porches with gang members. If held outdoors, they make those areas less attractive for gang activity because of all the non-gang members around (Grabianowski 4)

A ~~preferred~~ **promising** method of gang suppression today is the Department of Justice's "Weed and Seed" program. This combines police enforcement (*weeding* out the worst gang members) with community activism and economic opportunities (*seeding* the neighborhood with the means to overcome negative conditions). More than 3,000 Weed and Seed programs are active in the United States. Each site can receive up to $1 million to help fund law enforcement, community policing, prevention, intervention, treatment, and neighborhood restoration (Grabianowski 4).

One of the most influential ~~areas~~ **places in** ~~of~~ a child or young adult's life is ~~in~~ **his or her** school. According to the article, "Gang Violence as a Social Problem," "Providing more funding for schools specifically for anti-gang programs and including anti-gang messages in the curriculum is essential in creating a non-violent atmosphere." ~~Funding for anti-gang violence is not the only way to promote it in schools.~~ **In addition,** strict rules ~~of~~ **for** on-campus **behavior** ~~activity~~ and truancy prevention ~~will~~ **can help** create an educational culture that will hopefully leak into students' lives outside **of** school. Th~~ese~~ same messages and programs should also be reinforced in the communities outside of school. Developing after school youth programs **in the community** gives children ~~alternative~~ **positive** options to gang affiliation ("Gang Violence as a Social Problem").

Preventing the recruitment of new gang members is a solution for the future, but other measures must be taken to curb the violence now. Legislation is ~~the voice that is the most used when we talk about~~ **a key in any** attempt to ~~solve~~ **reduce** gang violence. ~~We look to Legislation~~ **Legislators** and ~~to~~ government officials ~~that~~ have the authority to help protect us from gang violence. ~~Establishing~~ New laws ~~that~~ **must** increase the severity of punishment for gang related violence. ~~is essential.~~ Any ~~act of~~ **gang-related** criminal~~ity~~ **act** ~~related to gangs~~ should ~~automatically have an increased~~ **draw a longer** sentence. Additionally, ~~the recruitment of~~ **recruiting** new members to gangs should be a crime ~~have a harsh penalty~~. Recruiting anybody should be punishable by imprisonment, and recruiting a minor should ~~have~~ **draw** an increased ~~in the~~ sentence ("Gang Violence as a Social Problem").

~~Clearly~~ **Obviously**, any long-term solution to eradicating gang violence includes police enforcement, education, jobs, activity centers, and neighborhood involvement. However, resources must be **made** available to ~~the communities and schools~~ schools and communities to build programs and **help** create jobs ~~effectively~~, which **means** ~~take~~ money. Unfortunately, in cashed-strapped cities, ending gang violence is ~~not~~ **seldom** the highest priority since the poor minorities most affected by such violence have the weakest voice among constituents.

~~The impact of~~ **Eradicating** gang violence ~~on~~ **that affects** ~~many~~ **millions** of America's poorest citizens should be a priority ~~from the city to the state to the Federal government level~~, **at all levels of government,** with funding ~~support~~ for anti-gang education programs, community activity centers, and jobs creation coming from ~~all~~ city, county, state, and Federal levels. Until we recognize and treat gang violence as the most destructive force on the health, welfare, and future ~~success~~ of millions of American children, the problem will continue to destroy lives. The solutions are available, **but where is** the public resolve? ~~must also be.~~

Works Cited

"Background on Drug Violence," Do Something.org. July 2011
    http://www.dosomething.org/tipsandtools/background-gangs-violence.

"Drugs and Latin Gangs," Duke University, 9 December 2006. May 2011 http://www.duke.edu/pgg2/history/Drugs.html.

"Gang Violence as a Social Problem," Soc3: Social Problems, wikispaces. May 2011
http://socialproblemsucd.wikispaces.com/Gangs+Violence.

Goguen, Dr. Carole. "The Effects of Community Violence on Children and
Adolescents," Traumatic Stress Treatment Center. June 2001
http://www.traumatic-stress-treatment.com/artcommunityviolence.html.

Grabionowski, Ed. "How Street Gangs Work," How Stuff Works. May 2001
http://people.howstuffworks.com/street-gangs.htm.

"How Gang Violence Can Affect Your Community," Family, Community, Kids, and
Teens, AMW Safety Center. 5 November 2009. April 2011
http://safety.amw.com/family/how-gang-violence-can-affect-your-community.

"Street Gangs: A Dead End for Our Children," Lawton Police Department, May 2011.
http://www.lawtonpd.com/cmprv/gangs.htm.

Revision Activity 6.9

Revise the first draft of your paper following the revision guidelines presented. Then
exchange drafts with a classmate. Indicate any place in the draft where it is unclear
whether the information is from a research source or the writer, or where the paper
doesn't appear to support its thesis statement. Make any necessary changes, and write
the second draft of your paper.

Editing

This final editing section reviews what you have learned in previous units about avoiding errors and introduces some new punctuation marks and spelling concerns.

Punctuating Quotations

Since you may have used quotations from different sources in your research paper, it is important to punctuate them correctly so that readers know exactly what is being quoted. The following rules will help you punctuate quotations correctly.

1. Put quotation marks (" ") around the exact words from the source that you incorporate into your paper, placing the ending quotation mark outside the period:

    According to climate expert Max Shurer, "The warmer air temperatures of the last twenty years do not follow any natural cyclical pattern that we have seen in the past."

2. Always acknowledge the source of the quote along with the quotation, and separate the two with a comma.

    "Standing water of any kind provides a breeding ground for mosquitoes in warm weather," warned public health official Nancy McGowen.

    According to recent Gallop Poll results, "Women are more likely to vote for a woman candidate for President than men are."

3. Punctuate the following quotation situations in the manner shown.

    a. Quoted sentence divided by the source acknowledgment:

        "The best time to catch large-mouth bass on Hawthorne Lake," according to professional bass fisherman Brock Adams, "is at dawn or at sunset." (commas before and after source introduction, quotations marks before and after both halves of the quoted sentence)

    b. Two quoted sentences with source acknowledgment between sentences:

        "You can catch the most fish by fishing four-to-six feet deep," said Adams. "The bigger fish, however, are in the deeper waters." (period after source introduction, quotation marks before and after each quoted sentence)

c.   Source acknowledgment followed by two-sentence quote:
According to Adams, "Fishing successfully at Hawthorne Lake requires a lot of experience and skill. It is such a big lake that you have to know where to fish at different times of the year."
(no quotation mark before second sentence of the quote)

d.   Rather than quoting an entire sentence, the quote begins at mid-sentence:

Dr. Abrams believes that most alleged cures for arthritis are "worthless shams that cost desperate people millions of dollars a year."
(small letter begins mid-sentence quote, no comma after source introduction)

4.   Do not put quotation marks around an indirect quotation, which states what someone said rather than quoting his or her exact words:

Indirect quotation: Dr. Hall said that he did not believe in prescribing horse liniments for arthritis sufferers.

Direct quotation: Dr. Hall said, "I don't believe in prescribing horse liniments for arthritis sufferers."

Editing Activity 6.10

Punctuate the following quotations according to the rules presented by inserting quotation marks, commas, and capital letters where they are needed. Do not put quotation marks around indirect quotations.

Example:

Stock market expert Ivan Crookside said there is not enough good news related to the economy to sustain any kind of upward momentum in stocks over the short haul.

Punctuated:

Stock market expert Ivan Crookside said, "There is not enough good news related to the economy to sustain any kind of upward momentum in stocks over the short haul."

1.   Anti-war demonstrations have been planned in major US cities for October 28, according to demonstration organizer Lucy Planter.

2.   The demonstrations according to Planter will show the government that US

citizens don't support the continuing war in Iraq.

3.   In particular, the demonstrations will protest against any renewed funding for the war efforts said Planter we are wasting billions of dollars that could be going to education and health care.

4.   Planter said she believes that upwards of a million people will protest in ten cities.

5.   She said if the government doesn't get the message sent by a million Americans, it is no longer representing the people who elected it.

6.   Planter said that she felt Americans were more than frustrated by a war that was unnecessary and harmful. We should have never gone into Iraq in the first place said Planter Every day that we stay just amplifies the problem.

7.   News coverage of the upcoming demonstrations has been spotty at best said Planter and there appears to be a pro-war bias among conservative newspaper chains. They are reluctant to publicize the demonstrations at all.

8.   The people will be heard said Planter in summation. We are not going away.

Possessives

A final punctuation mark that gives some writers problems is the apostrophe in possessive words. Sometimes writers omit the apostrophe, sometimes they insert it in the wrong place, and sometimes they insert it in a plural rather than possessive word. The following rules will help you punctuate possessive words correctly.

1.   A possessive word shows ownership: something belongs to someone (e.g. father's watch, dog's bone, minister's sermon, tomorrow's weather forecast, orchid's color.).

2.   An apostrophe + s ('s) or s + apostrophe (s') indicates a possessive word. Two rules indicate where to insert the apostrophe:

   a.   If the possessive word is singular, add apostrophe + s ('s): cat's paws, a stone's weight, the cloud's lining, Mildred's boyfriend.

   b.   If the possessive word is plural, add an apostrophe after the s: civilians' rights, bushes' leaves, candles' glow, several soldiers' canteens.

      Exception: If the plural possessive forms its plural without adding s, add a apostrophe + s ('s) as if it were singular: people's will, men's sport coats, children's toys, geese's feathers.

3. Sometimes the possessive word is separated in a sentence from the word it possesses: That car in the alley is John's. (John's car)

4. Don't use an apostrophe in a plural word that isn't possessive: dogs in the alley, donuts and other pastries, girls hiding in the shrubs.

5. Don't use an apostrophe with possessive pronouns: *their, theirs, his, her, hers, our, ours, your, yours, its, my.* However, use apostrophes with possessive *indefinite* pronouns: *someone's* watch, *anyone's* chances, *everybody's* rights.

Editing Activity 6.11

In the following paragraph, add apostrophes to possessive words following the rules provided.

Example: The contestants response to the difficult question was correct.

Corrected: The contestant's response to the difficult question was correct.

The banks hours change in the summer. It opens at 10:00 a.m. and closes at 7:00 p.m. All of the loan officials offices are open until 6:00 p.m., but the tellers stations are all open until 7:00. The bank stays open longer in the summer because of its customers schedules. Many of them work later in the summer due to the longer days, so they often can't get to the bank by 5:30 or 6:00 p.m. One customers typical summer work hours, for example, are from 10:00 a.m. to 6:30 p.m., so she can't get to the bank before 6:45. Customers appreciate the banks longer summer schedule, and a number of its summer customers come from other banks who maintain traditional hours.

Similar Sounding Words

Spelling errors often occur when writers use a word that sounds similar to the word they should have used. Computer spell checks often don't pick up the errors because the words are correctly spelled. Such mistakes are frequently caused by mental lapses, such as writing a word without thinking about its spelling, and are easily correctable.

Confusing Duos and Trios

Writers often confuse the following pairs or trios of words, resulting in misspellings.

accept/except

accept: to receive willingly

I *accept* your resignation from the car rental company.
Growing older is hard for some people to *accept*.

except: not including; with the exception of

Everyone is going to the movies *except* Brad.
I did well on all my mid-term exams *except* for calculus.

advise/advice

advise: to recommend (verb)

I would *advise* you to take an umbrella to London.
Travel guides *advise* tourists not to carry large amounts of cash.

advice: recommendation (noun)

If you take my *advice*, you'll wear sun screen to the ball park.
Advice is often easier to give than to take.

affect/effect

affect: to produce an outcome or impression (verb)

Your decision to attend college will *affect* you for the rest of your life.
How Jonathan performs on the stress test will *affect* how the doctor is going to treat him.

effect: an outcome or impression (noun)

The *effect* of your attending college will be very positive.
What *effect* does air have on the speed of a falling object?

its, it's

its: possessive pronoun

The barn lost *its* roof in the hurricane.
The house received *its* final coat of paint yesterday.

it's: contraction for *it is*

It's really cold this morning.
I don't believe that *it's* going to rain this weekend.

new/knew

new: not previously used, owned, or in existence

There is very little *new* in the newspaper this week.
That *new* watch you are wearing is very attractive.

knew: past tense of the verb *to know*

I *knew* better than to wear tennis shoes in the snow.
She never *knew* her twin sister until they were reunited years later.

there/their/they're

there: introductory word or location

There are many ways to cook chicken.
You'll find the ladder over *there* behind the barn.

their: possessive; belonging to *them*

Their wallets were stolen.
I don't believe *their* downtown parking pass is valid on weekends.

they're: contraction for *they are*

They're going to be late for the concert.
Did you know that *they're* going with us to the swap meet?

were/we're/where

were: past tense of the verb *to be*

There *were* several geese on the pond last night.
Were you bothered by the sound of police sirens last night?

we're: contraction for *we are*

We're coming into town on the 3:00 p.m. train.
Megan and I are going to Central Park this morning, and then *we're* going

to the Natural History Museum this afternoon.

where: to what place or in what direction

Where are you going to put the decorative indoor fountain?
Do you know *where* your roommate is spending the holidays?

your/you're

your: possessive form of *you*

Your coat is behind the door on the peg.
I would like *your* opinion on the dismal showing of the stock market
lately.

you're: contraction for *you are*

You're one of the most optimistic people I know.
It doesn't seem that *you're* any less involved in charity work than last year.

Editing Activity 6.12

Fill in the blanks with the appropriate words from the list of "Confusing Duos and Trios."

Example:

You <u>were</u> expected to take heavy doses of Vitamin C on <u>your</u> doctor's advice.

_____ niece Nan's birthday party that you planned at the amusement park was a great success. I'm sure that _____ very happy with the results. All of the children had a great time, and I know that _____ telling all _____ friends about it. _____ the first time many of the children played miniature golf, and they _____ little about the game. All of them had fun, however, _____ for Jason, who knocked all of his balls in the water. The park is also reasonably priced, and I'm glad that Nan's mother took _____
Writings from Life 256
_____ and held it _____. By the end of the party, the _____ of the long day was evident in all the children, and I'm sure it _____ed the parents
similarly. However, I think everyone was willing to _____ a little weariness for a great day. Now _____ thinking of having our next family birthday party _____. I don't know _____ we could have more fun. Would you

_____ us to rent a room by the arcade for eating lunch and opening presents?

Editing Review Activity 6.13

To review what you learned in previous units, proofread the following paragraphs and eliminate errors in the following areas: run-on sentences or comma splices, sentence fragments, comma usage, subject-verb agreement, pronoun-antecedent agreement, subject pronouns, irregular verb forms, colons, semi-colons, and dashes.

Example

The school orchestras concert schedule is the more ambitious ever. They are playing four concerts this school year which is two more than usual. The reason for the increase according to the orchestra instructor are the crowds at last year's concerts which was sold out. The school believes that there is enough interest to attract good crowds to four concerts this year and they will use the added revenue to fund the orchestras summer concert performances in Europe.

Corrected

The school orchestra's concert schedule is the ~~more~~ most ambitious ever. They are playing four concerts this school year, which is two more than usual. The reason for the increase, according to the orchestra instructor, ~~are~~ is the crowds at last year's concerts, which ~~was~~ were sold out. The school believes that there is enough interest to attract good crowds to four concerts this year, and ~~they~~ it will use the added revenue to fund the orchestra's summer concert performances in Europe.

One of the amber trees alongside the apartments are shorter than the others. It also loses its leaves more early in the fall. And start to blossom more late in the spring. The tree is definitely the runt of the ambers, it isn't sickly but it's small. The apartment manager has tried giving it extra water and fertilizer but nothing seem to help. The soil is no different where the smaller amber is planted than for the rest of the trees so it is getting the same amount of nutrients from the ground. Apparently some trees are just inherently more small than others it doesn't mean it is less healthy or won't live as long. Some animals of course falls into the same category the runt of the litter. Nature has their runts among all species of plants and animals.

Editing Activity 6.14

Proofread your draft for errors by applying the following guidelines and make the necessary corrections. Then type the final draft of your paper.

Editing Guidelines

1.   Check your sentences to make sure you haven't run any sentences together or put a comma between sentences instead of a period, and make any necessary corrections.

2.   Check your draft for any sentence fragments: incomplete sentences with a period after them. To correct fragments, attach them to the sentence they belong with, or add words to make them complete.

3.   Check your use of irregular verbs, making sure you have used the correct irregular forms and spelled them correctly.

4.   Check your comma usage, making sure you have inserted commas correctly into your sentences.

5.   Check the spelling of any word you are uncertain of, or run the spell check on your word processing program, to eliminate any spelling errors. Also check any word from the list of "Confusing Duos and Trios" to make sure you have used the correct word.

6.   Check your verbs in each sentence to make sure that they agree with their subjects.

7.   Check your pronouns in each sentence to make sure they agree with their antecedents, and make sure you are using the correct subject pronoun forms.

8.   Check your use of colons, semi-colons, and dashes to see whether you are using them correctly and effectively.

9.   Check your use of comparative and superlative adjectives, and make sure that you have used the correct forms.

10.   Check your quotations in the paper, making sure that you have inserted quotation marks around direct quotations, separated quotations and source introductions with commas, and capitalized the first word of any quoted sentence.

11.   Check your possessive words to make sure you have inserted apostrophes in the correct places.

Readings

STDs: The Silent Epidemic

by Marianne Crowley

Julia Carter never imagined that she would ever contract a sexually transmitted disease. She had only slept with two men, one who was her current boyfriend, and both men practiced safe sex. Well, almost always. But one day Julia started getting sores in her genital area and went to her doctor immediately. She was diagnosed with genital herpes, a sexually transmitted disease with no cure. Julia will probably spend the rest of her life living with herpes and outbreaks of genital sores, a terrible price to pay for a few moments of indiscretion.

According to a State of the Nation report, sexually transmitted diseases (STDs) affect men and women of all backgrounds and economic levels ("Challenges Facing STD Prevention"). In the United States, the overall incidence of STDs has increased dramatically in recent years. The government's Center for Disease Control and Prevention (CDC) estimates that 19 million new infections occur each year, almost half of them among young people ages 15 to 24 (Weinstock, et al. 7). Despite the fact that STDs are extremely widespread and add an estimated 13 billion dollars to the nation's healthcare costs (Chesson, et al.), most people in the United States remain unaware of the risk and consequences of all but the most prominent STD - HIV, the virus that causes AIDS. STDs are not a common topic of conversation among young people, and those that contract a disease, often filled with guilt, shame, and embarrassment, seldom want anyone to know.

Sexually transmitted diseases are infections you can get by having sex with someone who has an infection ("STDs: Common Symptoms"). These infections are usually passed by having vaginal intercourse, but they can also be passed through anal sex, oral sex or skin-to-skin contact. STDs can be caused by either viruses or bacteria. STDs caused by viruses include hepatitis B, herpes, HIV and the human papilloma virus (HPV). STDs caused by bacteria include chlamydia, gonorrhea and syphilis ("STD: Common Symptoms"). Anyone who has had sexual relations may be at risk for having an STD. The risk is higher for those who have had many sex partners, who have had sex with someone who has had many partners, or who have had sex without using condoms.

Sexually Transmitted Diseases

Chlamydia is the most frequently reported bacterial STD in the United States. An estimated 2.8 million Americans are infected with chlamydia each year ("STDs Today"). However, under-reporting is substantial because most people with chlamydia are not aware of their infections and do not seek testing. The highest rates of chlamydial infection are in 15- to 19-year-old adolescents, regardless of demographics or location ("Sexually Transmitted Diseases").

Chlamydia can be transmitted during vaginal, oral, or anal sexual contact with an infected partner. A pregnant woman may pass the infection to her newborn during delivery, with subsequent neonatal eye infection or pneumonia. Even though symptoms of chlamydia are usually mild or absent, it can damage a woman's reproductive organs and cause serious complications. Irreversible damage, including infertility, can occur "silently" before a woman ever recognizes a problem ("STDs Today"). Chlamydia also can cause discharge from the penis of an infected man, although complications among men are rare. Although chlamydia can be easily treated and cured with antibiotics, the damage it may cause to a woman or her newborn are irreversible.

Genital herpes is a contagious viral infection caused by the herpes simplex virus (HSV) which has affected an astonishing one out of five (or 45 million) Americans ("STDs Today"). There are two types of HSV, and both can cause genital herpes. Genital HSV-2 infection is more common in women (approximately one out of four women) than in men (almost one out of five). Doctors estimate that as many as 500,000 new cases may occur each year. HSV type 1 most commonly causes sores on the lips (known as fever blisters or cold sores), but it can cause genital infections through oral-genital or genital-genital contact. HSV type 2 most often causes genital sores, but it also can infect the mouth.Both HSV 1 and 2 can produce sores in and around the vaginal area, on the penis, around the anal opening, and on the buttocks or thighs. Occasionally, sores also appear on other parts of the body where broken skin has come into contact with HSV. The virus remains in certain nerve cells of the body for life, causing periodic symptoms in some people ("STDs Today").

Genital herpes infection usually is acquired by sexual contact with someone who unknowingly is having an asymptomatic outbreak of herpes sores in the genital area. People with oral herpes can transmit the infection to the genital area of a partner during oral-genital sex. Herpes infections also can be transmitted by a person who is infected with HSV who has noticeable symptoms. The virus is spread only rarely, if at all, by contact with objects such as a toilet seat or hot tub ("STD's Today").

There is no treatment that can cure herpes, but antiviral medications can shorten and prevent outbreaks during the period of time the person takes the medication. Affecting one out of five Americans, genital herpes is a silent epidemic. It has been replaced in the public consciousness by the more life-threatening AIDS virus, but it remains nonetheless a terrible genital disease to live out one's life with, not to mention the effect it has on a person's partner or his or her future relationships.

Gonorrhea is caused by Neisseria Gonorrhoeae, a bacterium that can grow and multiply easily in the warm, moist areas of the reproductive tract. CDC estimates that more than 700,000 persons in the U.S. get new gonorrheal infections each year ("STDs Today"). The most common symptoms of infection are a discharge from the vagina or penis and painful or difficult urination. The most common and serious complications occur in women and, as with chalamydial infection, these complications include pelvic inflammatory disease (PID) ectopic (tubal) pregnancy, and infertility.

Gonorrhea can grow in the cervix, uterus, and fallopian tubes in women, and in the urethra in women and men. The bacterium can also grow in the mouth, throat, eyes, and anus. If it spreads to the blood or joints it can be life-threatening. In addition, people with gonorrhea can more easily contract HIV, the virus that causes AIDS. HIV-infected people with gonorrhea are also more likely to transmit HIV to someone else ("STDs Today"). Several antibiotics can successfully cure gonorrhea in adolescents and adults. However, drug-resistant strains of gonorrhea are increasing in many areas of the world, including the United States, and successful treatment of gonorrhea is becoming more difficult. New antibiotics or combinations of drugs must be used to treats these resistant strains.

Syphilis is caused by the bacterium Treponema Pallidum. The incidence of syphilis has increased and decreased dramatically in recent years, and in the United States, health officials reported over 32,000 cases of syphilis in 2002. Between 2001 and 2002, the number of reported primary and secondary syphilis cases increased 12.4 percent. Rates in women continued to decrease, and overall, the rate in men was 3.5 times that in women. This, in conjunction with reports of syphilis outbreaks in men who have sex with men (MSM), suggests that rates of syphilis in MSM are increasing ("STDs Today").

Syphilis is passed from person to person through direct contact with a syphilis sore. The first symptoms of syphilis infection may go undetected because they are very mild and disappear spontaneously. The initial symptom is a chancre (genital sore); it is usually a painless open sore that most often appears on the penis or around the vagina. It can also occur near the mouth, anus, or on the hands. Transmission of the organism occurs during vaginal, anal, or oral sex. Pregnant women with the disease can pass it to the babies they are carrying. If untreated, syphilis may go on to more advanced stages, including a transient rash and eventually, can cause serious involvement of the brain, nerves, eyes, heart, blood vessels, liver, bones, and joints. Chancres caused by syphilis make it easier to transmit HIV infection sexually. There is an estimated 2-5 fold risk of acquiring HIV infection when syphilis is present ("STDs Today"). The full course of the disease can take years. Penicillin remains the most effective drug to treat people with syphilis.

Trichomoniasis is caused by the single-celled protozoan parasite, Trichomonas vaginalis. It is the most common curable STD in young, sexually active women, and it affects men as well although symptoms are most common in women. An estimated 7.4 million new cases occur each year ("STDs Today").

The vagina is the most common site of infection in women, and the urethra (urine canal) is the most common site of infection in men. The parasite is sexually transmitted through penis-to-vagina intercourse or vulva-to-vulva (the genital area outside the vagina) contact with an infected partner. Women can acquire the disease from infected men or women, but men usually contract it only from infected women.

Most men with trichomoniasis do not have signs or symptoms; however, some men may temporarily have an irritation inside the penis, mild discharge, or slight burning after urination or ejaculation. Some women have signs or symptoms of infection which include a frothy, yellow-green vaginal discharge with a strong odor. The infection also may cause discomfort during intercourse and urination, as well as irritation and itching of the female genital area. Trichomoniasis can usually be cured with the prescription drug metronidazole, given by mouth in a single dose ("STDs Today").

AIDS (acquired immunodeficiency syndrome) was first reported in the United States in 1981. Since the beginning of the epidemic, an estimated 944,306 people have developed AIDS in the United States ("HIV/AIDS Surveillance Report"). AIDS is caused by the human immunodeficiency virus (HIV), a virus that destroys the body's ability to fight off infection.

People who have AIDS are susceptible to many life-threatening diseases, and to certain forms of cancer. Transmission of the virus primarily occurs during unprotected sexual activity and by sharing needles used to inject intravenous drugs.

Prevention

With the prevalence of sexually transmitted diseases in adolescents and young adults in the United States, the devastating long-term damage STDs can cause their victims, and the ease with which people who have STDs can pass them on to others, it is imperative that all Americans become knowledgeable on sexually transmitted diseases and how they can be prevented. Not one adolescent or young adult should have to live with an STD, and no one has to. To dramatically decrease the chances of ever contracting an STD, the following practices should be embraced ("Sexually Transmitted Diseases Overview").

Don't have sex. The best way to prevent any STD is to practice abstinence, or not have vaginal, oral, or anal sex. While this may not be feasible advice for all young adults, it certainly is the best possible advice for adolescents.

Be faithful. Have a sexual relationship with one partner who has been tested for STDs and is not infected is another way to reduce your chances of getting infected. Having sex with a number of partners greatly increases a person's chances of contracting an STD, as does having sex with a person who has had a number of partners.

Use condoms. Protect yourself with a condom every time you have vaginal, anal, or oral sex. Condoms should be used for any type of sex with every partner. For vaginal sex, use a latex male condom or a female polyurethane condom. For anal sex, use a latex male condom. For oral sex, use a dental dam, a rubbery material that can be placed over the anus or the vagina before sexual contact. Condoms are by far the best way to prevent STDs, and it only takes one lapse to become infected.

Know that some methods of birth control, like birth control pills, shots, implants, or diaphragms, will not protect you from STDs. If you use one of these methods, be sure to also use a latex condom or dental dam (used for oral sex) correctly every time you have sex.

Talk with your sex partner(s) about STDs, their sexual history, and using condoms. It's up to each individual to make sure he or she is protected. Do not have sex with anyone who refuses to wear a condom.

Talk frankly with your doctor or nurse and your sex partner(s) about any STDs you or your partner have or had. Not only do you have a moral obligation to let your partner know if you have been infected with an STD, you may also have a legal obligation, as people who have been infected by an STD carrier who remained silent are testing their legal options, including filing lawsuits or criminal charges.

Have regular pelvic exams. Women should talk with their doctor about how often they need an exam. Many tests for STDs can be done during an exam. Women should ask their doctor to test them for STDs. The sooner an STD is found, the easier it is to treat ("Sexually Transmitted Diseases Overview").

Treatment

Any persons who have been sexually exposed to a person with an STD or who have symptoms that they feel may derive from an STD should have a medical examination immediately. Seeing a doctor as soon as possible after exposure to an STD is important; these infections can easily spread to others and can have serious complications. Go to a hospital's emergency facility if an STD problem worsens, if a fever develops with other symptoms, or if it will be a few days before an appointment with a doctor can be scheduled ("Sexually Transmitted Diseases").

If a person is diagnosed with an STD, he or she should seek treatment immediately to stop the spread of the disease. It is important that all prescribed medicine is taken as directed. Sometimes follow-up tests are important, and future doctor's appointments need to be scheduled. In addition, it is important to avoid sexual contact while being treated for an STD. Finally, any person or persons that the infected person has had sexual contact with should be notified and urged to have a check-up ("Sexually Transmitted Diseases").

Sexually transmitted diseases will continue to infect million of adolescents and young adults every year, and if people remain ignorant to the risk of contracting an STD and the terrible consequences, including passing it on to a newborn child, the number of infections will continue to rise. That the chances of contracting genital herpes, a highly infectious disease with no cure, are one in five should strike enough fear in all young adults that they would do everything possible to avoid being infected.

However, it is up to our schools, the medical profession, and parents to educate all of our youth to the dangers of STDs and how to prevent them. This is not a problem without a solution, but as long as the spread of STDs among young people remains essentially a silent epidemic, millions of young lives will continue to be devastated by the effects.

Works Cited

"Challenges Facing STD Prevention in Youth," State of the Nation Report 2005. American Social Health Association. 2005. 6 August 2008 Http://www.ashastd.org/pdfs/ASHA_05.final.pdf.

Chesson H.W., Blandford J,M., Gift T.L., Tao G., Irwin K.L.. "The Estimated Direct Medical Cost of STDs Among American Youth, 2000," Abstract P075. National STD Prevention Conference. Philadelphia, PA. March 8-11, 2004.

"HIV/AIDS Surveillance Report 2004," Vol. 16. US Department of Health and Human Services, Center for Disease Control and Prevention. Atlanta GA. 2005.

"Sexually Transmitted Diseases," Sexual Health Center, WebMD. 2008. 10 Nov. 2008 http://www.webmd.com/sex/sexually-transmitted-diseases.

"Sexually Transmitted Diseases: Overview," WomensHealth.Gov. May 2005. 8 August 2008 http://www.4woman.gov/faq/stdsgen.htm.

"STDs Today," National Prevention Education Network. 13 May 2008 http://www.cdcnpin.org.

Weinstock H., Berman S., Cates W., "Sexually Transmitted Diseases Among American Youth," Perspective on Sexual and Reproductive Health. 2004. 36 (1): 6-10.

Questions for Discussion

1.   What is the thesis of the essay: the main point that the author is conveying to readers? In what ways does she get this point across?

2.   From the essay, what do adolescents and young adults need to know in order to avoid an STD infection?

3.   What did you learn about STDs from the essay that you weren't aware of?

4.   What do you think must be done to solve the problem of STD infection among young adults, and how do you think individuals can help?

Index